D1127971

DICTIONNAIRE DES MOTS CROISÉS

LES USUELS

DICTIONNAIRES LE ROBERT 27 RUE DE LA GLACIÈRE 75013 PARIS

direction éditoriale : société DICTIONNAIRES LE ROBERT
représentée par Pierre VARROD
directeur général

ÉDITION (conception éditoriale et
traitements de l'information) : LAURENT CATACH

RÉDACTION (assistance rédactionnelle
pour la sélection des noms propres) : CARL ADERHOLD

COUVERTURE : CAUMON

MAQUETTE (conception technique
et graphique) : GONZAGUE RAYNAUD

female-headed households contained less than ten members, almost 4 percent of them consisted of seven to nine members. Only nine families listed household heads born in California.[52]

Labor and African American Women

African American female wage earners in Los Angeles worked similar jobs as African American women in other parts of the country. Their work status, however, did not confine them to working class lives. A close examination of the United States Federal Censuses of 1850 and 1860 reveal very little in terms of women's work. Reasons for this lack of information is fourfold: first, females were very small in number; second, many only did occasional or temporary work, sometimes performing several jobs at different times during the year, but nothing that was substantial enough to be counted in a census report; third, the federal census eliminated certain categories of paid domestic work as employment that should be recorded; and fourth, some purposefully hid various aspects of their lives, including their work because they could never be certain what the consequences of full disclosure would be given their vulnerable status.

Most were likely domestics, while the remainder may have worked outside of their home, taking in boarders, or running small businesses such as catering or laundering within their home. Those who appear in the census as residents in white households undoubtedly were servants of some sort, typically maids, childcare providers, and cooks.[53] White women of this era also do not appear in census records as gainfully employed outside of their homes. Over time, African American women increasingly joined the work force.[54]

By 1870, the census instruction became much more detailed, cautioning enumerators against generalizing people's occupations, particularly "women's work." It began to differentiate, for example, between *housekeepers* and those who *keep house* for a living. Housekeepers were defined as women who earned a "distinct wage or salary for their service"; "women keeping house for their own families or themselves" were simply identified as keeping house.[55] Grown daughters who assisted their mothers were considered without an occupation; but working children who earned a wage could be described as such.[56] These changes brought much more clarity to the employment status of black women. While a number were labeled only as "keeps house," others worked as cooks, servants, and hairdressers.[57]

Domestic labor in Los Angeles, which in the mid-nineteenth century was claimed by Chinese men who worked as cooks and laundrymen, became the domain of black women after Chinese Exclusion (1882) eliminated much of their competition. Many Chinese men also worked as gardeners. Very few Chinese women were recorded in the Los Angeles census during these years, but a survey of local newspapers reveals that many did live in the city, most likely; several of them were sex workers.[58] Black men represent more occupational diversity than Chinese men, ranging from day laborers to professionals. Working class black women actually provided more job competition for Chinese men than their male counterparts.[59] Table 3.12 illustrates the various occupations black Angelenos held in 1880.

Ten (20% of the total of those who listed professions) worked as porters, while others served as hostlers, horseshoers, cooks, and janitors.

Figure 3.4 William and Winnie Spencer, ca. 1916. William Spencer owned his home free and clear on North Commonwealth. He worked as a letter carrier for the post office. His wife did not work. Both were literate. By 1916, they had four children—Roy, Lorenzo, Cecilia, and Mabelle. Los Angeles Public Library. Shades of L.A. Collection.

Many were also self-employed. Charles Owens's two children, Robert and Henry, both young adults, worked as teamsters, while his wife Ellen "kept house." Both Robert and Henry would go on to inherit the family business and the fortune amassed by their grandparents, Robert Owens and Biddy Mason. Similarly, Ann Pepper, who "kept house" in 1870, noted ten years later that she washed clothes in order to support her household. Unlike her friend Ellen Owens, Ann did not have the luxury to stay home. She would continue working to supplement her household income. Two of her sons, Manuel and Louis, worked with horses while her youngest son, Henry, worked for a blacksmith.[60]

While the black community in 1880 was only slightly larger than in 1870, there were more occupations represented. A very small part of this

Table 3.12 African American occupational trends, 1880

	Female	*Male*	*Total*
At school	4	7	11
Barber	0	5	5
Car Porter	0	1	1
Cook	2	3	5
Hairdresser	2	0	2
Horseshoer	0	2	2
Hostler	0	2	2
House Servant	4	1	5
Janitor	0	3	3
Keeping House	14	0	14
Laborer	4	0	4
Laundrywoman	1	0	1
Lodger	2	2	4
Midwife	1	0	1
Musician	0	1	1
Nurse	1	0	1
Porter	0	10	10
Servant	4	2	6
Tailor	0	1	1
Teamster	0	2	2
Waiter	0	1	1
Washing	1	0	1
Wood Yard	0	1	1
Work in Blacksmith shop	0	1	1
none/ unknown	12	3	15
Totals	**52**	**48**	**100**

Source: 1880 U.S. Federal Census

is due to two families having white household heads, Mourize Kromes (57), who was a tax collector. His wife, Matilda (42) was listed as "mulatto," and their her daughter lived in the household with Ann Daniels mentioned above. Frank Joel, a 42-year-old horseshoer was also married to a woman listed as "mulatto," Mary Ann, who was a 35-year-old immigrant from Ireland, just as her husband. Kromes was also an immigrant, but from France. The main jobs black men held in 1880 included barber (5), cook (3), janitor (3), laborer (4), and porter (8) there was also one blacksmith, car porter, house servant, musician, railroad porter, store

Table 3.13a Occupational trends—African American women ages 18 and over, 1900

At school	2	Lodging house keeper	5
Boardinghouse	2	None	1
Cook	30	None stated	396
Day laborer	7	Nurse	2
Domestic	3	Roomer	1
Dressmaker	10	Seamstress	5
Express man (woman)	1	Servant	39
Hairdresser	1	Server	1
Helps husband - printer	1	Sick nurse	1
House cleaning	2	Tailor	1
House maid	3	Teaches music	2
House servant	3	Trouser laundry	1
House worker	1	Type writer	1
House keeper	7	Unknown	6
Housewife	10	Waitress	4
Housework	13	Washwoman	26
Janitress	2		
Laundress	43		
Total			**633**

Source: 1900 U.S. Federal Census

porter, tailor, waiter, and one man who worked in the wood yard. There were two men for each of the following occupations: horseshoer, hostler, servant, and teamster. Forty-one men reported occupations, while thirty-three women did, including house servants (4), servants (3), cooks (2), and hairdressers (2). There was one black woman employed in each of the following jobs: washing, nurse, midwife, and laundry. Five black women age eighteen and older did not list any occupation, while fourteen reported, "keeps house" as theirs. There was also one black man who reported no occupation, eleven children in school, and an additional seventeen children, ages seventeen and under who were not listed in school.[61]

By 1900, Los Angeles was booming. More people migrated to the city, which in turn created a significant local economy, available to everyone. African Americans still faced limited opportunities, but managed to open businesses. Some moved into the more professional sector of the city. The number of African Americans in domestic positions also increased, but

Table 3.13b Occupational trends—African American men ages 18 and over, 1900

Actor	1	Hotel waiter	1
At school	8	House labor	1
Baggage	1	House painter	2
Bar tender	2	Ironer	2
Barber	17	Janitor	57
Bell boy	2	Junk dealer	9
Blacksmith	5	Junky - country jail	1
Boarding House Keeper	1	Laborer	42
Bookkeeper	2	Laundry	6
Bookstore	1	Leather Carver	2
Bootblack	14	Lodging House Keeper	2
Brick laborer	1	Machinist	2
Bricklayer	5	Messenger	1
Brick maker	1	Miner	1
Brick mason	6	Minister	4
Brickman	1	Musician	5
Broom maker	1	None stated	50
Butcher	3	Nurse	1
Butler	1	Office boy	1
Capitalist	1	Painter	1
Car cleaner	2	Paper hanger	2
Car repair	1	Patient	2
Carpenter	19	Physician	1
Carpet cleaner	1	Pickle factory worker	1
Carpet layer	1	Plasterer	3
Carriage blacksmith	1	Plumber	1
Caterer	3	Policeman	1
Cement maker	1	Porter	45
Cigar dealer	1	Preacher	2
Cigar maker	1	Publisher - printer	1
Clerk	3	Pullman porter	1
Coachman	9	Restaurant	1
Coal - wood yard	1	Salesman	1
Collector	1	Salesman in grocery	1
Construction	1	Saloon	1
Contractor	2	Secondhand store	1
Cook	22	Servant	9
Dairyman	1	Ship clerk	1
Day laborer	101	Shoemaker	3

Table 3.13b (continued)

Deputy District Attorney	1	Shoe shiner	1
Deputy - city pound	1	Stable	3
Driver	9	Stenographer	1
Express man	17	Storage	1
Farmer	1	Store clerk	1
Farm labor	2	Surgeon	1
Flagman	1	Tailor	4
Gardener	10	Teamster	23
Hauls brick	1	Tinner	1
Head bellman	1	Tunnel labor	1
Hod carrier	1	Unknown	18
Holster	2	Waiter	21
Horse shoer	2	White washer	2
Hotel carrier	1	Wood Carver	1
Total			**644**

Source: 1900 U.S. Federal Census

so did the number of artisans (tables 3.13a and 3.13b). While African Americans largely represented the domestic sector of society, many worked jobs that required some form of education or other training. Day laborers (mostly male) represented the largest group of workers, while domestic servants (including those who reported their occupations as maids, house servants, house workers, servants, and domestics) made up the second. Yet, the 1900 census shows a greatly increased diversity of available employment, and indicates several components of a thriving black community.[62]

First, there were four African Americans ministers and two preachers. As noted above, the church played a crucial role in the functioning of the black Angeleno community.[63] Second, 13 percent of the population included school-aged children. Most African American children, by 1900, attended public schools. A third observation is that African Americans had access to entertainment through music, acting, and even saloons, allowing a certain degree of socializing to occur outside of work, school, or church. A large number of men took jobs that helped build the city. Often, they worked for the parks, maintained streets, and manned construction sites for building homes.[64]

African Americans who arrived around 1910 found a thriving black labor force, even though many African Americans worked in the

Table 3.14 Occupational trends—African
American women ages 18 and over, 1910

Book Keeper	3
Catering	15
Chambermaid	25
Cook	158
Day Laborer (servant/domestic)	30
Domestic Servant	24
Dressmaker	57
General Housework	25
Hairdresser	29
Housekeeper (servant/maid)	112
Ironer	20
Janitor/Janitress (School/Office)	10
Keeper (rooming/lodging house)	26
Labor—Private Family	10
Maid	33
Matron	7
Milliner	5
Minister	1
Missionaries	6
Musician	4
None	1320
Nurse/Trained Nurse	25
Other	114
Own Income	12
Seamstress	26
Servant	220
Teacher	14
Waitress	23
Washing/Laundry	416
Unknown	11
Total	**2781**

Source: 1910 U.S. Federal Census

domestic and personal sector. Black Angelenos worked in significant numbers as artisans as well as other professions. Women, as usual, tended to dominate the domestic sphere, working as cooks, servants, housekeepers, and laundresses, while men had more diverse occupations, as table 3.14 shows.

Most black women worked either as laundresses, a job that they could do in their own homes while taking care of children who often assisted them, or as servants in someone else's home. Of the 2,747 women over the age of eighteen who were surveyed, just over 50 percent (1,400) of them reported no occupation to the census takers. It is unclear as to whether the economic position of the family allowed women to stay home, if they were temporarily out of work, or if they simply refused to state their occupations.

Some girls under the age of eighteen also worked as domestics for private families (26), hairdressers (2), laundresses (3), or nurses for private families (5).[65] Lillie May Cox worked as a checker at a grocery store when she was seventeen. Fifteen-year-old Dora Brown was a music teacher, while Eloise Marsalles taught piano. Vivian Campbell and Clara Green were employed as hairdressers at seventeen, and 12-year-old Florence Reed was employed as a nurse for a private family. The majority of girls fifteen to seventeen, however, did not work, or at least did not earn wages. Younger girls aged twelve and thirteen usually worked as domestics for private families. Out of 963 girls under the age of eighteen, 854 did not report an occupation for which they earned wages consistently, and forty-six attended school at the time the census was taken in 1910.[66]

Men's work was much more diverse. Men worked in a variety of occupations with an increase in both skilled labor and professional sectors, indicated in table 3.15. Far fewer men than women over eighteen reported no employment (64), and in turn, fewer boys reported that they attended school (42). Forty-seven men operated their own businesses including hotels, junk and second-hand stores, tailor and barber shops, or reported they had their own income. Three black men were doctors and one was a dentist. There were also twenty-six ministers, one preacher, and one missionary listed in the 1910 census. A small number of men also joined the civil service sector of the community, working as firefighters, police officers, railroad inspectors, and even real estate agents. As in the previous decade, men were employed in jobs that built and expanded the city. Of the 2,634 men surveyed, the largest single group was laborers (487,

Table 3.15 Occupational trends—African American men ages 18 and older, 1910

Agent	4	Merchant	4
Apprentice	2	Messenger	11
Assistant	2	Miner	4
Bar Keeper	1	Minister	26
Bar Tender	10	Missionary	1
Barber	49	Musician	6
Bell Boy	4	None	64
Bootblack	22	Odd Jobs	5
Bricklayer	36	operator	41
Brickmaker	8	Own Income	5
Brick Mason	39	Painter	16
Butler	7	Pastor	1
Carpenter	60	Peddler	5
Caterer	5	Physician	3
Cement Work	7	Plasterer	31
Chauffer	43	Plumbing	5
Chef	5	Police	4
Chiropodist	2	Porter	285
Cigar Worker	6	Preacher	3
Clerk	14	Proprietor	19
Contractor	24	Pullman	3
Cook	139	Railroad	2
Cooper	6	Real Estate	6
Dentist	1	Rubbish	7
Driver	39	Salesman	9
Engineer	11	Saloon	1
Express	28	Servant	34
Farmer	9	Sewer	5
Fireman	8	Shingler	2
Fisherman	1	Shipping Clerk	3
Foreman	7	Shoemaker	10
Garbage	2	Stableman	4
Gardener	50	Stage Coach - Mail	1
Headwaiter	4	Steward	3
Helper	10	Street Cleaner	6
Hod Carrier	51	Tailor	15
Housework	9	Teacher	2
Janitor	192	Teamster	172
Junk Dealer	3	Undertaker	3
Keeper	7	Wagon Driver	40

Table 3.15 (continued)

Laborer	487	Waiter	127
Laundry	3	Watchman	6
Lumberman	2	Wood Carrier	3
Machinist	12	Unknown/ Not Stated	12
Mail Carrier	9	Other	185
Manager	5		
Total			**2,645**

Source: 1910 U.S. Federal Census

or 18 percent), which included day workers. Teamsters, janitors, and porters made up 25 percent; and drivers, cooks, brick laborers and masons, carpenters, waiters, and gardeners represented 22 percent of black male workers. Eleven men worked in or kept bars and saloons. Collectively, African American men in Los Angeles contributed to the building of the community as a whole, representing all sectors, professional and otherwise of the city.[67]

Between 1850 and 1900, African Americans in Los Angeles built a distinct community of their own, equipped with churches, social organizations, hotels, and other businesses. This institution building benefitted from the skills and monetary support of working men and women. Cooks and laborers were the two major occupations African Americans held during the fifty years before 1900. Most women whose work was recognized in the census were laundresses.[68] Women who stated no employment outside the home, however, may have been day workers, or temporarily out of work. Some may have been prostitutes, just like women from all racial and ethnic backgrounds.

Although it was a profession that indeed existed throughout California, one cannot assume that the majority of women with no occupation were sex workers. In her investigation of black women in California, Willi Coleman notes that there were few accounts of African American prostitutes during the earliest period of black settlement, and few in Los Angeles through the turn of the twentieth century—as opposed to the several accounts of African American female prostitutes in Oakland and San Francisco. Coleman concludes that prostitution was not a "widespread pursuit" for African American women, and that the black middle class worked hard to combat the stereotyping of African American women as prostitutes.[69] After the turn of the century and Los Angeles became much more urban

Figure 3.5 Jerry and Henrietta and their three children, Jerry Jr., Grace, and Sterling, ca. 1910. Los Angeles Public Library. Security Pacific National Bank Collection.

and industrialized, women increasingly joined the workforce. Those who did work were typically employed in domestic and personal service, as servants, laundresses, or cooks. Whatever their true occupational status, many of them had the financial wherewithal to acquire property—many owned their own homes.[70]

The sharp increase in African American immigrants to Los Angeles, coupled with job competition in the railroad industry, heightened white fear and anxiety and fueled new racist and discriminatory policies toward the migrants. Between 1870 and 1917, European immigration also created competition for African Americans for housing and employment. The Ku Klux Klan became active around Los Angeles, particularly after the release of "The Birth of a Nation." The Klan left their initials all over town, and in the early 1920s led a campaign to force people out of their homes and neighborhoods.[71] White property owners refused to rent to newcomers. Like other cities across the country, by 1915 legal restrictions were adopted to prevent black people, as well as other groups including Mexicans, Jews, and Asians, from purchasing property in certain neighborhoods.

Figure 3.6 Los Angeles, 1909. This map shows how quickly Los Angeles grew, marking the rapid pace of industry in the city.

These restrictive covenants would remain in place through 1948 when the Supreme Court declared them unconstitutional in *Shelly v. Kramer*. Local black leaders found that African Americans received lower wages and worked in worse conditions compared to their white counterparts. This prompted a political and social reform movement focused predominantly on the African American community.[72]

Higher Education and the Black Professional and Business Class

Some African Americans living in Los Angeles established their own schools, not unlike their white counterparts. Some of the African American churches such as FAME assisted in securing qualified schools and teachers for black students.[73] All teachers, including those of African descent, in California, were required to have no less than one rigorous year of education at the State Normal School, whose Los Angeles branch was founded in 1882 and became the University of California, Los Angeles (UCLA), in 1919. Expectations for students were high, and admissions were strict. Each applicant was required to have a high school diploma and a letter of recommendation from the City Superintendent. They were required to, "pass an exam in Spelling, Reading, Geography, Math, and Grammar" in order to be accepted.[74] They were also required to have a letter of support signed by the County Superintendent or two school trustees. If they were unavailable to write, the applicants had to get letters from two permanent residents of the school district where the applicant lived.

Students had to be at least eighteen years old in order to graduate and, "must have passed creditably in all the studies of the prescribed course, and must have shown, by actual and continued teaching in the Practice School, an ability and fitness for governing and teaching well."[75] The Los Angeles Public School had four grades in the Practice School, and the full-time teachers supervised student teachers. No one was allowed to graduate until they proved that they were good teachers, so their careers depended on their performance at the Practice School. Tuition and books were free, but students were required to purchase lab materials when necessary, and had to pay their own room and board that cost between $16 and $20 per month in houses of private families who were handpicked by the faculty.[76]

In addition to attending the State Normal School in Los Angeles, some African Americans enrolled in schools in northern California such as the University of California at Berkeley (Cal) and Stanford University. A large portion of African Americans also stayed in Los Angeles, and attended schools such as the University of Southern California (USC), which was founded in 1880. Several graduates joined the professional class and became lawyers and doctors. Paul Revere Williams who was one of the city's most prominent architects, for example, attended USC. Vada Somerville and her husband John also went to USC and became dentists. An elite couple, the Somervilles also used their connections to fight for social and political equality by becoming active members of the NAACP, and remained in close contact with W. E. B. Du Bois after his visit in 1913.[77]

On 13 May 1913 a small group of black elites had organized a dinner in his honor. The event committee included John and Vada Somerville, Louis Blodgett, Dr. Thomas J. Nelson, and Dr. Alva C. Garrott among others. Thirty-five families were represented, including Robert and Ellen Owens, and Colonel Allen Allensworth.[78] The event must have impressed Du Bois because he gushed about the black elite throughout his "Colored California" essay in the *Crisis Magazine*. He was so impressed by their success, he featured their homes along with several others of the black elite to exemplify their many accomplishments, and to highlight the opportunities for other African Americans. He also maintained several correspondences with a few, such as the Somervilles, Williams, and Ralph J. Bunche. John Somerville was nominated for a position in the national branch of the NAACP. Vada Somerville was responsible for many of Du Bois's arrangements when he returned to the city in 1925.[79]

The African American business elite in Los Angeles were part of a wide network of black-owned businesses that offered many different services, not only for their community, but for the city as a whole. Black Angelenos owned tailor shops, second-hand furniture stores, hotels, and clothing stores, mostly in the busy downtown area. Robert Curry Owens, for example, owned a two-story brick building that housed an African American tailor shop, furniture store, and other businesses. Most people who traveled to Los Angeles passed through it. The railroads intersected this section of the city, allowing passengers to stop in the area. Downtown also served as the final destination for many immigrants and migrants, becoming the major port of entry for a great majority of early twentieth century settlers in the city.[80]

By the end of the nineteenth century and into the early twentieth, African Americans in Los Angeles had made a heavy contribution to the overall economy of the city, while creating a wealth base within their own community. B. W. Brown and his wife, for example, opened the first store offering dinnerware in the city, at 627 San Fernando Street. The couple later moved the business to Central Avenue, an area that became the center of the African American community after racially restrictive covenants were enacted in the 1910s and African Americans were forced out of the downtown area.[81]

On a seven-dollar investment, Hilliard Strickland opened a butcher shop by 1900, which grew into a multifaceted business block. By 1910, Strickland had become a successful real estate agent. According to Charlotta Bass, his business returned over $200,000 in value. The Strickland business block housed many stores, homes, and real estate. Hilliard and his wife, Sarah, owned a home at 2025 Santa Fe Street in Los Angeles, and created a comfortable standard of living for their five children, Leola, Jessie, Claude, Susie, and Dewey.

Many African American business owners and service providers joined Strickland at a successful, competitive level in Los Angeles, spurred in large part by the increase in migration to the region.[82] African American professionals often worked with (not for) whites, who served as part of the clientele. Alva C. Garrott, for example, became the first African American dentist in the city. Dr. Garrott attended Howard University, earning a graduate degree in Pharmaceuticals in 1892, and Dentistry in 1899. In 1901, he began practicing in Los Angeles, and soon opened offices on the Wilson block at the corners of First and Spring Streets. Garrott's patients included whites and black people, as well as much of the city's middle class residents. Garrott was extremely respected throughout the city, moved within the middle class sectors of both the black and the white communities, and maintained a certain degree of high-brow culture. He truly exemplified the kinds of opportunities African Americans created for themselves, in addition to the role they played within Los Angeles as a whole.[83] In 1909, Dr. Garrott published an essay in the *LA Times* celebrating black male achievement, noting that amongst the black professional men were five physicians, two dentists, five lawyers, one pharmacist, three newsmen, and one veterinarian who's combine wealth totaled $165,000. He also noted that the majority of them had little or no assistance in achieving their goals.[84]

Ralph J. Bunche: The First of the Central Avenue Corridor

Ralph J. Bunche was born in 1903 in Detroit. His family moved to Albuquerque when he was ten. Soon, his father left to find work, but never returned. His mother Olive died within a year, leaving Ralph and his sister Grace with his maternal grandmother, Lucy Taylor Johnson. In 1916, Mrs. Johnson moved her family to Los Angeles, where she had relatives that could help her raise Ralph and Grace. The family resided in the Central Avenue corridor of the city, a predominantly white neighborhood, in a home at 1221 East 37th Street. The home was a small, two-bedroom craftsman style house located at the middle of the block. A nice porch adorned the front of the house, and a large living room, a sitting room, and a good-sized kitchen completed the floor plan. Behind the home was a large yard with a few trees that offered shade.

Lucy Johnson strategically located her family in this neighborhood.[85] It had everything the family needed, including Jefferson High School, which Ralph attended before going on to UCLA. One of the oldest African American churches, Second Baptist, was only a few blocks away. Most importantly, the neighborhood had opportunity, especially for middle class families. The Johnson family had grown accustomed to a middle class lifestyle, both in Detroit and later in Albuquerque. Central Avenue resembled the Detroit neighborhood that the Bunches had once lived in. The Johnsons were the first African Americans to purchase a home in their neighborhood.[86] They could do so because no one knew that they were black. They essentially *passed* in order to get their home.[87]

The Johnsons did not pretend that they were white, or deny their own blackness. They simply never bothered to tell their neighbors. Their light skin and straight hair probably indicated to neighbors a different ethnicity, but not a completely different racial heritage. The family never challenged this perception. Yet, they never hid who they were. They attended a predominantly black church on Sundays, where they were extremely active members. They simply used their neighbors' lack of curiosity to their advantage. Once they purchased their home and become fixtures in the neighborhood, the Johnsons boasted to the neighbors that they were indeed African American.[88]

Ralph Bunche earned a degree in political science in 1927 and was valedictorian of his class at UCLA. As an adult, he became very active in politics. On 11 May 1927, just as Ralph was finishing his undergraduate work at UCLA, he wrote to Du Bois to ask for a job so he could support himself on his way to graduate school. He explained to Du Bois, "I have long felt the need of coming in closer contact with the leaders of our Race, so that I may better learn their methods of approach, their psychology, and benefit in my own development by their influence."[89] He hoped either to work at the *Crisis Magazine*, or teach. Unfortunately, Du Bois had no openings at the time, but Bunche still pushed onward with his education. He attended graduate school at Harvard University, where he became the first African American to earn a PhD in Political Science in 1934. Afterward, he taught at Howard University and then joined the State Department, where he was assigned to help plan the new United Nations during the closing months of World War II. Bunche was awarded a Nobel Peace Prize in 1950 for mediating the signing of the 1949 Armistice between Israel, Palestine, and four other Arab nations.[90] He was also present at the 1963 March on Washington and the 1965 Selma march.

Conclusion

Between 1870 and 1917, African Americans in Los Angeles created and maintained a firm middle class. In 1913, W. E. B. Du Bois concluded that

African Americans in Los Angeles were as cultured and successful as any group of African Americans he had ever met. By the beginning of the First World War, many owned property and businesses. They maintained their own forms of media, printing their own newspapers such as the *California Eagle*, and transmitting local politics and cultural events to their own community. The black middle class in Los Angeles, although numerically small, therefore made a firm impact on the city as a whole. They also created a space for new black migrants to receive economic and political assistance, and they established religious and social institutions that served the entire African American community.[91]

Yet even as the local black middle class and elite enjoyed their successes, black Los Angeles also had an underclass, whose experience was quite different than the one Du Bois boasted about. The poor and working class neighborhood in Los Angeles was referred to as *Calle de los Negros*, or Nigger Alley (an odd nickname, as it was actually a multiracial, multiethnic street, which would soon become the hub of Chinatown). The racial and economic barriers that the black middle class seemed to have overcome would ensnare others, both African Americans and other people of color. Under the surface of a relatively integrated and progressive Los Angeles lay a racial hierarchy, designed to keep whites dominant and people of color subordinate.

4
The Development of the Underclass

Los Angeles in the nineteenth century was a dangerous place, having the highest homicide rate in the country between 1830 and 1880. The late historian Eric Monkkonen noted homicide in Los Angeles remained high through the turn of the twentieth century. In spite of people's efforts to attain a safe, almost euphoric community, Los Angeles was still a frontier, and people behaved as such, engaging in several forms of violence such as murder and attempted murder, assault to commit either: injury, murder, rape, robbery, sodomy or crimes against nature, assault and battery, or highway robbery.[1] The invention of the revolver in conjunction with an already violent backdrop contributed to the high homicide rates. Los Angeles was easily more violent than San Francisco, Chicago, and St. Louis even while it was relatively small.[2] And as the city grew, so did the violence. White Angelenos, seeking to promote the city and transform its identity, turned their attention to controlling people of color and the working class by turning them into targets of propaganda.

The Los Angeles *Daily Times*, the most popular of the city's newspapers, led the media campaign against lower class Angelenos, constantly printing stories of illegal activities in their neighborhoods. As social stratification became more apparent, the *Daily Times* printed articles about criminal behavior in the most impoverished neighborhood of the city, commonly referred to as Nigger Alley, in what would later become Chinatown. These stories were actually used to promote the city, and encourage migration. They assured white elites and European immigrants of the city's no-tolerance attitude about criminal behavior, especially by people of color, thereby making Los Angeles a safe city for (white) people to live. The newspaper created an environment of heightened animosity, suspicion, and discrimination in housing, jobs, and education that would have severe lasting effects.[3]

Although African Americans established a community of their own, they also lived in multicultural, multiracial neighborhoods well into the beginning of the twentieth century, comprised of Mexican, Chinese, and African American families. One such neighborhood was Nigger Alley,

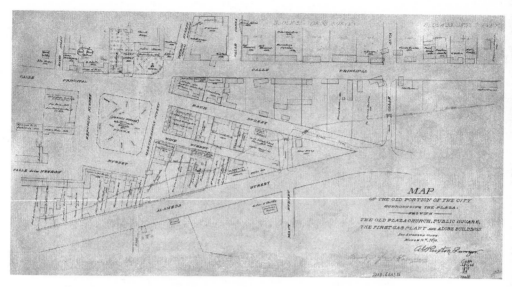

Figure 4.1 Map of Los Angeles, 1873. Includes Calle de Los Negros, or "Nigger Alley." Library of Congress.

located downtown near the Plaza and the center of the early Los Angeles working class. Many of its residents were laborers, and a large number of them did not have steady work, but took jobs as they came. The neighborhood originally consisted of adobes that lined one side of the street, which initially belonged to Mexican rancheros.[4]

By 1870, Chinese people increasingly immigrated to Los Angeles, establishing themselves within the city's social and economic sectors. Of the 203 Chinese people living in Los Angeles, thirty-two of them were women living in any of the thirty-two family units. Most reported no occupation, which was consistent with black and white women. Chinese men worked predominantly as launderers, laborers, and cooks, but the community had two physicians and two shoemakers. By 1880, the number of Chinese residents increased to 516 with 71 households. Of those, 44 were women who either kept house or were at home. Chinese men worked as launderers, cooks, laborers, and gardeners—many of whom maintained their own vegetable gardens. There were also several men who worked in skilled and professional occupations such as barbers, brick makers, shoemakers, grocers, tailors, and store workers. The Chinese community also had one priest, and 6 doctors.[5]

The area quickly became their home, and Nigger Alley became a racially fluid community consisting predominantly of people of color.

Many considered it the less desirable segment of town, plagued with violence and other forms of criminal activity. The area contained much of the city's saloons and gambling houses, which many believed, contributed to much of the city's problems. People allegedly ventured into the neighborhood to indulge in alcohol, drugs, and prostitution. The *Times* constantly published articles showing their contempt of such activity both inside and outside of the community.[6]

While black Angelenos welcomed new black migrants, offering them a variety of social programs and opportunities, whites met black people and immigrants of color with discrimination. This resulted in the formation of important interracial bonds among the non-white inhabitants of Los Angeles. African Americans lived in the same neighborhoods as Chinese and Mexicans, often working similar jobs and frequenting many of the same social institutions in the city. Thus they lived parallel lives, shared similar experiences, and found a sense of extended community. In this way, the culture of Los Angeles profoundly shaped its race relations during its frontier years. Angelenos of color were able to redefine their own relationships with whites as well as with one another, creating a multiracial, multiethnic bond that often defied traditional ideas about race and race relations.

While the white middle class developed reform programs for society as a whole, they also used them as a tool for controlling and judging the actions of people of other racial backgrounds. The emerging underclass found itself at odds with the law. Although relatively small in number, this "criminal element" often was the basis of the public's awareness of the larger African American community. The local newspapers fed this perception, and the state responded.

California adopted a strict policy against crime from its inception. The original legislature designed a series of laws reflecting the state's overall attitude about crime and violence that excluded the rights of African Americans and other people of color. The 1849 State Constitution defined the rights of citizens of California. On the surface, this constitution appeared nondiscriminatory, offering equal rights as well as equal protection to the state's non-white citizens.[7]

In defining the rights of California citizens, the legislature determined that all men were free and independent, and in similar ways as the United States Constitution, asserted the right to life, liberty, and the pursuit of happiness. The legislature also established the right of trial by jury for all. In terms of court procedures, the Constitution made clear that no person would incur excessive fines or bail for their crimes, nor would they receive cruel or unusual punishments. All people were eligible for bail, excluding those accused of capital offenses, and only with a sufficient amount of evidence. The legislature also established basic court procedure.[8]

Anyone accused of committing a criminal act was permitted a trial and legal representation. This applied to any trial in any of the courts in the state and available for most people. The court admitted newspaper accounts of certain criminal activity as factual evidence. The legislature authorized juries appointed by the courts to determine whether the accounts were indeed accurate, published with good intentions, and created with pure motives. This concession provided juries with a great deal of power in determining the fate of many citizens. The rule qualified jurors to make judgments about information in local newspapers, regardless of the degree of sensationalism of those stories. The state Constitution also provided ways of punishing and disenfranchising those convicted of crimes.[9]

Racial inequality was installed in early California in other ways as well. The second article of the Constitution of the State of California made all white male citizens of the United States age 21 or older eligible to vote (as well as those white male citizens of Mexico who elected to become U.S. citizens and lived in the state at least six months). It denied African Americans and women the right to vote, however, African Americans would not be enfranchised until the ratification of the Fifteenth Amendment in 1870; women did not gain the right to vote until a 1911 state referendum.[10]

While white men retained the power to elect officials for the state, they also were able to travel out of the state for extended periods without losing their status or voting rights. A person who engaged in any behavior deemed socially unacceptable or immoral automatically forfeited his right to vote. Article 2, Section 5 for example, stated that an insane person or a person convicted of an infamous crime would lose his right to vote. While these laws overwhelmingly privileged white males, they also created a racial hierarchy, which affected African Americans and other groups of people of color.[11]

The State Constitution denied African Americans and other people of color those basic rights afforded to whites, thereby placing them at the bottom of the hierarchy. Court proceedings, for example, prohibited them from testifying. In many of the early cases, such as that of

Archy Lee, Biddy Mason and Hannah Embers, African Americans were forced to rely on white attorneys, juries, and judges to make decisions that would affect their lives. This reliance, however, did not always prove successful.[12]

Early *Alcalde*: Using the Law to Establish a Racial Hierarchy

A survey of the *Alcalde* Court for the County of Los Angeles records indicates not only the racial hierarchy of the county in the nineteenth century, but also its violent characteristic. The Los Angeles court system tried various cases involving crimes allegedly committed by people of color. As demonstrated in the records, the outcomes of these cases—including sentencing and fines—depended upon the ethnicity of the accused and the severity of the crime. The *Alcalde* Court for the County of Los Angeles kept strict records of its cases. From 1830 to 1863, many people of color, and sometimes women, faced county judges. These cases offer a clear understanding of the attitudes that more elite members of society held toward people of the lower echelon.[13] Whether people acted violently or took items as a means for survival, these cases underscore the difficult terrain of Los Angeles. The criminal branch of the *Alcalde* Court considered cases of various offenses, from petty theft to murder, on a daily basis.[14]

Relatively minor crimes were common. On 5 August 1850, for example, an African American man named Henry B. F. Brogden was accused of assaulting and battering another African American man known only as George. This case was later dismissed.[15] Earlier that summer on 29 June a 16-year-old boy named José Ambrisio and a 19-year-old boy, Juan José Villeros, were accused of assault and battery after a street fight.[16] In July, Feliciano Primoneas was convicted and imprisoned for stealing a pistol from a local store.[17] In an unrelated case two days earlier, authorities arrested Chico Lopez for stealing a pair of pants from a store, but he escaped from jail.[18] These cases illustrate minor crimes and some of the typical sentences. Los Angeles was not, however, without its share of more violent and dangerous crimes.[19]

Violence characterized the frontier-like essence of Los Angeles during the mid-nineteenth century. William Sanchez, for example, was convicted of assault with intent to kill a man named Charles Burrows. He received a fine of $10.00 in addition to court and attorney's fees.[20] The court convicted Rafel Duarte for assaulting Sheriff T. Burrill on

22 August 1850. He was sentenced to five months in jail and fined $100.00.[21] On 6 September 1850, Merced Contreas was convicted of killing a Native American man named Romaldo, who apparently was randomly victimized.[22] Women were not exempt from these forms of violence and crime.[23]

Sometimes, court cases included female criminals. But more often than not, women were the victims of various crimes, including spousal abuse. On 14 August 1850, Juan Rivera assaulted and battered his wife, Luz Figueroa. He was fined 6 ¼ cents.[24] The next day, Martin Duarte appeared in court for assault and battery. He allegedly beat his wife on 2 July 1850. His conviction resulted in a fine of $10.00.[25] Not every form of violence committed by men toward women occurred within the institution of marriage. There were several cases of female victims of violence. Often, male brutality against women was also interracial.[26]

Native American women were often targets of violent white male aggression. On 3 September 1850, Matilda, an Indian accused George Herod of assault and battery. He was held to answer the charge.[27] On 10 September Juan de dios Garcia faced assault and battery charges. Garcia's victim, in this case, was also an Indian woman named Josefa. The two argued about whether or not she would go away with him. When she refused, he beat her with a club. Garcia was fined $1.00. Historian John Mack Faragher estimated one-fifth of the cases in the *Alcalde* courts concerned female victims.[28] The Superior Court contained far more cases, spanning a longer period of time, and female victims accounted for 7 percent of the criminal cases.[29]

In 1872 lawmakers began regulating improper treatment and abuse of women. The Court defined rape as sexual intercourse outside of the covenant of marriage by a perpetrator. Punishments often included a five-year prison term. Men who forced women to become prostitutes also received heavier sentences. Any man who forced girls under eighteen years of age into prostitution could receive up to five years in state prison, a fine of up to $1,000, or both. This law was amended in 1873, 1874, and again in 1905. The 1905 law stipulated that the fine for bringing Chinese or Japanese women into the state for prostitution varied from $1,000 to $5,000, or a county jail term of 6–12 months. California designed laws to control and to protect women's bodies.[30]

It was a felony to force unmarried women to live with any man, and another felony to pay women for sex. All of the following circumstances were used to define rape: females under the age of sixteen; women incapable of giving consent; women who resisted and were violently forced into having sex; women physically threatened by their assailant; unconscious women; or women who submitted because they believed the perpetrator was their husband. The court also deemed slight penetration a criminal act.[31] The early court in Los Angeles also recognized the level of violence women faced.

Women were often easy targets for men to take out their daily frustrations. The courts handled all of these cases in various ways, affording stiffer fines and sentences for violent acts committed on men than women. This contributed to the establishment of the city's overall attitude about social deviance. The city's mainstream easily isolated those marginalized groups of people by deeming them as criminal while highlighting their unlawful activities and violent behavior.[32]

By the mid-nineteenth century Los Angeles established a form of law and order to combat criminal behavior. Many acts of violence, reminiscent of a stereotypical western town, plagued the city. By 1854, one murder occurred each day. In 1855 a group named the Los Angeles Rangers organized with the express purpose of fighting "Mexican bandits." This "lynch mob" sought out particular groups of men, lynched them, and then returned to their daily lives. Stephen G. Foster, the city mayor, took a leave of absence to join the mob, and then returned after a lynching.[33] This brand of law and order continued for the next couple of decades. It culminated in 1871 with the brutal murder of 18 Chinese immigrants.

Los Angeles and Crime

California, by 1872, established the death penalty, which consisted of hanging a defendant by the neck until confirmation of death. The hanging needed to take place within the confines of a state prison, and executed by the warden. A physician and attorney general, in addition to twelve "reputable" witnesses were to be present at the time of the execution. The defendant was allowed two clergymen and up to five relatives and friends with the exception of children. The state amended the law in 1905.[34]

Angelenos took a firm stance against drinking, gambling, violence, and even prostitution. By 1872, there were at least sixteen laws regarding prostitution. Angelenos explicitly publicized the city's anti-alcohol policy. The local temperance movement exemplified attitudes towards alcohol abuse and town drunks. City authorities arrested anyone who violated local temperance laws. In January 1882 city officials began arresting saloonkeepers who violated a law prohibiting Sunday drinking.[35]

While white Angelenos believed that they were steering the city toward continued progress, they aimed to depict a virtually crime-free environment and sweep all mention of riots and vigilantism under the rug. By December 1881, the *Daily Times* was noting that "the present condition of our city is a matter of pride and satisfaction to everybody."[36] The story boasted of booming businesses, flourishing accommodations, a vast amount of dwelling places, and high revenue. In addition, the article noted that the city was "singularly free of tramps, pests, and petty criminals."[37] Thus, Angelenos portrayed themselves as a safe, booming community with limitless opportunity for those wanting to visit or even settle in the region.[38]

In keeping with the same attitude toward criminals, the court handed down strict punishments. Penalties for drunkenness varied from small fines to jail time, or even a stint on the city's chain gang. J. T. Riley, for instance, received a twelve-day sentence after three arrests for drunkenness. Henry Raymond received a serious punishment of twelve days on the city's chain gang for drunkenness.[39]

Alcohol consumption rose to the forefront of the city's political issues during the 1888 mayoral election. The incumbent, William H. Workman, insisted that the city should take a firmer stance on issuing liquor licenses, by increasing the license fee from $50 to $60.[40] The Mayor also implemented a midnight curfew for saloon goers, while confronting illegal drug abuse, especially opium use. The presence of late-night saloons and opium dens contradicted the city's reputation for being a pleasant and safe locale for anyone wanting to settle in the area. Since Chinatown contained the majority of the city's saloons and gambling houses, and because the majority of working class people of color resided there, the neighborhood and its predominantly non-white immigrants became the target of mainstream angst.[41]

Controlling the Chinese

While the Chinese population in Los Angeles was small in 1870, increased animosity and xenophobia coupled with vigilantism led to a violent attack on the community in 1871. Initially, two rival Chinese syndicates were fighting over a woman named Ya Hit. It is unclear whether she was kidnapped by one of the gangs, or had run a way from her "owner" who petitioned the court to have her arrested for larceny. Her owner accused her of stealing jewelry. Once she was arrested, Sam Yeun, of the rival gang, claimed her and posted her bond. Her owner, Yo Hing was ordered to return her, but refused.[42]

Yo Hing was a very successful merchant and extremely influential in the Chinese community. He had a reputation for circumventing the law on occasion in order to get what he wanted. Somehow, he convinced Ya Hit to marry him, so that he could be her legal owner and get her back. Since she agreed, his rivals placed a $1000 reward for Yo Hing's scalp. People in the community began to search for this marked man.[43]

On 23 October 1871, Yo Hing was walking down Nigger Alley when he was fired upon from one of the nearby stores owned by a Chinese merchant. He reported the incident to the local police, accusing Ya Hit's brother, Ah Choy and another man named Lee Tak. In return, the men filed charges against Yo Hing. All of the men posted their bonds, and re-tuned to Chinatown. They immediately began arming themselves.[44]

By 5:30 that evening, neighbors heard several shots fired in Chinatown. When people gathered around to see what was happening, Ah Choy began firing at the crowd. In 1894, C. P. Darland wrote about the incident. He said, "One old man when told to get inside the house pulled his pistol and emptied the contents at the crowd indiscriminately."[45] Officer Bilderain was shot in the shoulder along with one civilian, Robert Thompson, who was trying to help the police. Another man and a young boy were both injured in this melee.[46] As the violence increased, people ran for cover.

Several Chinese people took shelter in nearby buildings and shops and barricaded themselves behind doors and windows. As white vigilantes heard about the fight, people began gathering. One of the buildings rumored to be hiding Ah Choy was surrounded. One Chinese man escaped from the building and was shot. Another tried escaping and was captured and hanged.[47]

By 9:00 that night, the vigilantes breeched the building doors and swarmed. Several Chinese men who had been hiding inside were dragged out into the streets. All of them were assassinated. They tied a rope around one man's neck and dragged him through the street. Three men were hanged after being brutally beaten. Another two men and two young boys were hanged. A half hour later, Sherriff Burns found ten more men hanging on nearby Los Angeles Street, and four men on Nigger Alley who had been shot. Two of them survived and were taken to the county jail. Darland noted, "Five days after the riot, the coroner's jury reported that 19 persons had come to their deaths by the hands of a mob on the night of October 24, 1871."[48] In the wake of the riot, businesses were damaged, several fathers, sons and brothers killed, and there was increased tension between the Chinese and white communities in Los Angeles.

In November that year, a grand jury presented their conclusions to Judge Sepulveda about the riot. First, they found the Chinese at fault for the violence. In a classic case of victim blaming, the grand jury said that the Chinese created the panic, "which opened the way for evildoers, and in the excitement that followed, the worst elements of society not only disgraced civilization by their acts, but in their savage treatment of unoffending human beings, their eagerness for pillage and bloodthirstiness exceeded the most barbarous races of men."[49] Finally, the jury found the police derelict in duty which made the city look bad in addition to costing the city vital resources. Had they performed their jobs properly, the grand jury concluded, they would have avoided the riot altogether.[50]

While the grand jury found the Chinese at fault, they did recognize that none of those who were murdered was involved in the shooting that initially sparked the violence with the exception of Ah Choy. When the fighting began, Yo Hing and his gang fled out of the country, leaving the rest of the neighborhood victim of collateral damage in lives and money. One merchant claimed a loss of $4000, while others reported several hundred dollars in damages. Some estimated their losses at thousands of dollars. In all, between $30,000 and $70,000 worth of damages were reported.[51] For the next decade, the Chinese became targets of racial attacks, culminating in the national laws to stifle Chinese immigration. City lawmakers made several attempts to close Chinatown, primarily by upending Nigger Alley, the neighborhood's main street. The *Los Angeles Times*, for the next two decades, portrayed the community as a den of iniquity, attracting drunkards, gamblers, opium addicts, and various other criminals.

Social problems constantly challenged Los Angeles's reputation. Cases concerning the arrests of people like J. M. Trotman, a man deemed insane, for disturbing the peace, petty larceny, and vagrancy were often detailed in the local paper.[52] Most often, perpetrators who allegedly committed these kinds of crimes were white. Yet there was a great deal of public attention to crime—petty and serious—that centered on African

Americans as well as other people of color. The Chinese were part of a fierce smear campaign during the years of exclusion, particularly at the beginning in the 1880s. The initial number of African Americans, however, living in Los Angeles remained low, under a couple of hundred residents, which helped to downplay some of their illegal activities.

Notice of intra and interracial violence increased as more people of color flocked to the city. On 18 April 1906, the *Times* printed an article about interracial violence involving three African American men accused of attacking a group of Italian immigrants. The story titled, "Bullets Kill and Wound," did not detail the event, but stated that an African American trio attacked the Italians. That same year, the *Los Angeles Times* investigated illegal gambling, which had existed for the past twenty years. This story, "Gamblers have the money," explored the arrests of three men after an illegal lottery game. In the same neighborhood in which they lived (Nigger Alley), two Chinese men and one African American man operated a lottery on Los Angeles Street. King Lee, Wong Sin, and C. Landy were charged and each posted $50.00 bail. In a similar but unrelated event, a man named Dock Goon, who operated of a lottery on a nearby street, posted a fifty-dollar bail for his crime. These violations fell within the restrictions set out in the state constitution.[53]

Chinese Exclusion

California restricted Chinese and Japanese immigration several years before the Exclusion Act was in place, even though the first census of the County of Los Angeles listed only two Chinese men. This law intended to prevent unwilling importation of people from China and Japan. In 1872, an anti-immigration law stipulated that anyone who attempted to bring immigrants from either of these countries (or any island near China) needed to obtain a permit and proper immigration papers stating that the person came to the state on a voluntary basis, and that he (or she) was of good character. These papers required the signature of the immigration commissioner. Anyone who violated this law was fined between $1,000 and $5,000, or sentenced to 2–12 months in the county jail.[54]

By 1880, a noticeable increase in the Chinese population occurred throughout the entire state, including in Los Angeles. For a short time, the Chinese population was able to participate in every aspect of the local community, even after the 1871 riot and massacre. Most worked in the domestic sector, typically as cooks, gardeners, or servants. Some worked alongside whites, Latinos, and the few African Americans. Taking menial jobs and working through the social hierarchy, Chinese Angelenos found themselves in a very similar position as African Americans who arrived earlier. Some even rose up through the ranks and opened their own businesses.

For about a decade, Chinese people shared a significant place within the city. Then, beginning about 1880, they suddenly became targets of a vicious strain of racial violence and hatred. The local newspaper headlines began announcing the radical change in the racial landscape brought by the influx of Chinese people—in generally unflattering terms. White Angelenos increasingly found themselves competing for jobs against Chinese laborers in various sectors of the mainstream community, and resentment ensued. By 1880, Chinese exclusion had become the major political topic. The *Daily Times* published articles expressing the desire to eliminate Chinese residents. The newspaper also printed dehumanizing stories about the Chinese almost every day.[55]

As the general population began reading more demonizing information about the Chinese, and taking it as fact, whites increasingly supported notions of exclusion. Proponents of the *Chinese Exclusion Act* (1882) gained support throughout the city, the state, and finally, the country. In a very short time, the Chinese had sunk to the bottom of the city's racial hierarchy, below African Americans, Native Americans, and Mexican Americans. The primary difference between these four groups, however, was that the Chinese truly immigrated in large waves to the region, and to the country, ringing nativist alarm bells and raising hackles.

The initial attempt to restrict Chinese labor occurred in 1880. The "Treaty Regulating Immigration from China" passed on 17 November. It forbade Chinese laborers from entering the country, and those already residing in the United States risked deportation.[56]

Chinese people employed as skilled laborers maintained their status. Article II stated: ". . . as teachers, students, merchants, or from curiosity, together with their body and household servants, and Chinese laborers who are now in the United States, shall be allowed to go and come of their own free will and accord, and shall be accorded all the rights, privileges, immunities and exemptions which are accorded to the citizens and subjects of the most favored nation."[57] The third article of the treaty, however, empowered the United States to deal with and determine whether any of these classes of Chinese people endangered the mainstream community. If so, the government had the authority to regulate any threat they felt the Chinese posed.[58] *The Chinese Exclusion Act* of 1882 was the tool used to execute this treaty. The Act itself opened the door for whites to target Chinese people.[59]

As Chinese Exclusion moved to the forefront of local politics, white Angelenos depicted them as physically dangerous. New stories emerged about "Chinese gangs." Officers Sands and Celis arrested six men known as the "Ching fo-to gang" on 7 January 1882. There was no indication in the newspapers of the alleged crimes the men committed, nor was any information given about the length of time the police wanted them. The men had a small amount of money on their persons, and were immediately placed into custody. The wording (and omissions) of such articles helped to portray the Chinese as innately criminal.[60]

On 26 January 1882, the *Times* took an even stronger approach to excluding the Chinese. An article entitled, "Chinese Criminals: Chinese and Hoodlums Compared and John [*sic*] Ahead" portrayed violent crimes as a trait inherent to the Chinese. The article stated that they committed more murders in Los Angeles than any other ethnic or racial group. The newspaper also accused them of having criminal and essentially violent tendencies. It stated, "Crime seems to be closely connected with the character of the Chinese, who, lacking in a sufficient degree of moral restraint, are generally but too willing for suitable consideration to enter into any wicked scheme."[61] The *Times* determined that no one understood the extent of the threat the Chinese posed except city detectives, possibly, and, "the press reporters, who have superior information."[62] The newspaper claimed to have more information than almost anyone else, leading its readers to believe that the *Times* accurately portrayed its subjects.[63]

The newspaper's assessment of Chinese neighborhoods, regardless of what city in California they were located, indicated much more violence and criminal activity comparatively, and police and court records supported this notion. "Chinese Criminals" compared crimes committed by whites to that of the Chinese. It alleged the Chinese committed more crimes throughout the entire state. Most Chinese people accused of crimes faced felony and murder charges. The city aimed to find new ways of controlling them. Finally, the article stated that, "A secret organization of so-called Chinese Free Masons is to-day in existence wherever there is a settlement of these strange people, in comparison with which the hoodlums and the white criminals seem utterly tame and insignificant."[64] The newspapers were going to great lengths to sow fear in the minds of white Angelenos.[65]

The *Los Angeles Daily Times* continued to increase anxiety about the Chinese. On 5 March 1882, only two months before implementation of the *Exclusion Act*, the *Times* printed an article titled, "Chinese Curse." It stated that the presence of the Chinese was actually a curse on California and on Los Angeles. (Curiously, the story also noted that local whites believed that the flow of Chinese emigration was slowing. In Los Angeles, 1,144 people reported China as their place of birth according to the 1880 census.)[66]

The *Daily Times* constantly attacked the Chinese work ethic and Chinese culture. By likening Chinese laborers to slaves, white Angelenos stripped them of their humanity. Ironically, the plight of the Chinese immigrants provided a temporary "relief" for African Americans during this period, insofar as whites did not aggressively target black residents with the same level of race hatred.[67]

The position of Chinese people in Los Angeles worsened over time. A 25 January 1882 *Los Angeles Daily Times* article, for example, told the story of a Chinese man who offended a white man by speaking profanely to his wife. The man, George Atwood, assaulted the Chinese man (whose name was not reported), and was arrested. The newspaper took a position on this case stating, "This is a very common thing with Chinese washmen, and they are served right whenever they run up against such a man as Atwood. They should be thrashed into decency if they cannot conduct themselves properly without it."[68] Atwood suffered no consequences for his actions.[69]

While white Angelenos supported Chinese Exclusion, they welcomed ethnically white immigrants. The *Daily Times* even celebrated the increase of people coming to Los Angeles from other parts of the United States as well as from Europe. In comparing Chinese immigration to European, one story noted, "The objections to Chinese immigration are not applicable to European immigrants who assimilate with us."[70] Senator John Frank Miller of California declared his belief that the Chinese refused to conform to American culture; contained uncivilized traits and characteristics; and were therefore, unqualified to live in this country, or to become citizens. Miller also referenced their "violent" nature.[71]

The increase in the adult community raised further concerns. Senator Miller pointed out that there were equal numbers of Chinese men and white men in California, old enough to bear arms, which was far too many. He believed that the country needed to stop the flow of Chinese immigration before they attempted war within the United States. Although Senator Miller believed that the country—and California specifically—received the outcasts from other regions around the world, he focused his resentments against Chinese immigration alone. Describing the Chinese as criminal, violent, and even uncivilized, he attempted to justify his calls for Chinese Exclusion.[72]

While this debate went on in Washington, D.C., Angelenos continued targeting the Chinese. Soon, much of the city's crime and antisocial behavior became associated with the Chinese, either directly or with their neighborhood. Chinese Exclusion allowed African Americans to remain amongst the higher echelon of people of color within the city's racial hierarchy, which, in turn opened opportunities for middle class black Angelenos.[73] Even after Exclusion, the Chinese remained targets of racial animus.

The *Times* continued targeting Chinatown in several exposés. If, say, a fire broke out within the neighborhood, rather than citing structural conditions as causes, the newspaper often blamed the Chinese. Some were accused of setting their own businesses on fire, while other blazes were blamed on overcrowding, drug abuse, and violence. On 24 October 1886, the paper described one fire: "The building was occupied for a Chinese store, restaurant and theater, lodging house, opium den, and what not. The Mongolians who had been packed away like peas in a pod came rolling out in short order, seeming satisfied to get away with very few of their effects."[74] A year later, another fire broke out, and this time rival Chinese gangs were blamed. It was believed that two men, Ah Jim and Ah Sam, were hired to set a store owned by Wah Cheng on fire. The two men were arrested, as witnesses testified they heard the two men plotting the blaze. There were also several eyewitness accounts of the men setting the fire. After police arrived on the scene, one of the men attacked an officer. The police knew at that point that the men would definitely be sent to prison. The paper reported, "One of the two charges against the men will stick, and if they are convicted on either the arson or assault charge, it will be enough to send them to San Quentin for a long term of years."[75] Accusations of setting fire in their own community and violence continued through the turn of the century.[76]

Attempts to Close Nigger Alley

The city made great attempts to close the neighborhood known as Nigger Alley, thereby displacing several working class and people of color. Although it was predominantly a Chinese neighborhood, white immigrants also lived on adjacent streets, and some owned buildings on the block. It was not long before people of all races, ethnicities, and economic backgrounds intermingled, which also led to small-scale coalition building in order to prevent the city from closing the street, as several white business owners were determined to protect their properties, many of which, housed Chinese-owned businesses.

In 1887, the Superintendent of Streets began a campaign to remove Chinatown. His plan was to extend the streets, which would destroy structures, forcing home and business owners to move their buildings. The plan was to abandon its newly acquired property, thereby making it easy for construction and rendering the remaining properties virtually worthless. Some people allowed the city to buy them out, at a rate of $12,000.[77] Others refused to cooperate, sparking a legal battle that lasted for a decade. One city council member said, "We are about to extend Los Angeles Street, and I will tear down all that part of the long festering rookery that stands in the way."[78] When asked what would become of the neighborhood, he replied, "That falls to the property owners on the present east line of Los Angeles Street and Nigger Alley. The city having moved the street from them, they acquire the right to move their property up to the new line or build new property on that line."[79] This only resulted in increased racial and ethnic animosity, as it was obvious that the city was strong-arming people of color as well as white immigrants.

One business owner, Mrs. L. M. Bigelow, sued the city, since the street expansion ran over her property line. Bigelow "owned the corner of Nigger Alley opposite the Plaza, in Chinatown."[80] She began constructing a two-story brick building on her property, but the city stepped in to force her to stop. When that failed, the fire marshal was sent in to intervene. He deemed the building a fire hazard because it only had eight-inch walls, but the new fire codes required twelve-inch walls. Bigelow would not back down.[81]

M. J. Newmark and Pierre Laronde joined her, arguing that abandoning Nigger Alley would cause their property values to depreciate by $25,000 to $50,000. Laronde was granted a court order that intended to keep the city from vacating the property. Bigelow, meanwhile, adhered to the original agreement with the city, clearing the way for construction, but was not allowed any new construction. The city also did not allow enough space for new structures. She too claimed great profit loss because of the plan. Because this matter had not been resolved within a year, Mrs. Bigelow decided to be proactive and enlisted other business owners to join in her lawsuit against the city, whom they fought with for the next ten years.[82]

Bigelow hired a work crew and began construction for her 2-story brick building. The *Los Angeles Times* reported, "Property holders in that section of the city have made up their minds to improve as rapidly as possible for the reason that the city is moving south at a very rapid rate, and they know that something must be done to hold business in the district north of First street."[83] Mrs. Bigelow held firm, and continued fighting. In late June 1889, she filed a lawsuit in the United States Circuit Court for damages. She claimed that she was being harassed by the city, and that as a citizen of Britain, she was being treated unfairly. It was her belief that her British status protected her from California and American laws, and therefore filed suit in federal court.[84] Although Mrs. Bigelow's fight with the city stands out, she was not alone.

Bartolo Ballerino was often referred to as the city's notorious "crib king." Peruvian-born, Ballerino moved to Los Angeles in 1849. In 1856 he married Maria, a white woman of Mexican descent who was born in California. She was a housewife. Together, they had two daughters and three sons. Neither of his daughters (Rachel and Nellie) worked, and two of his sons did. Phillip was a clerk while Frederick worked as an apprentice. Ballerino's businesses allowed him to purchase his home outright. He reaped all of the benefits of being classified as white, and even lived in a predominantly white neighborhood on Pico Street between Central Avenue and San Pedro.[85] Having businesses in Nigger Alley meant that he was subject to the same hostility as the hundreds of people of color who lived there. It also availed him to exploit the community, and its residents.

He owned a saloon with a brothel, and constantly clashed with law enforcement. In addition to closing the neighborhood, the city attempted to curb drinking and gambling by reducing the amount of liquor licenses it granted. People were denied unless they served food along with the liquor. Otherwise, a business owner could lose his or her license. Ballerino's was revoked at the beginning of 1900, but he was not to be deterred.[86]

The Development of the Underclass   125

Ballerino unapologetically continued to run his gambling houses and saloons without a liquor license. In 1905 he was accused of kidnapping women. Several parents reported that their daughters were being taken away. The police raided the Lilly Club in Ballerino's International Hotel, located in Nigger Alley near South Spring Street. According to the *Times*, "Most of the men found there are of the class that live off of the earnings of fallen women, and they probably will be prosecuted on charges of vagrancy."[87] Two and a half months later, a Greek man staying at the hotel was robbed. The paper reported that the man stepped out for a while, and returned to a disheveled room with some of his belongings missing. Blaming the owner, the paper underscored the unsafe and unsavory elements of the neighborhood.[88] Even elite and middle-class African Americans, primarily involved in social reform, supported cleaning up the neighborhood, in order to strengthen their own status within the city's hierarchy.

Meanwhile, white Angelenos aggressively attacked the reputation of the black Angeleno community, escalating racial tension between each group. As the African American population increased, particularly in relation to other racial minorities, the spotlight on their social problem grew even brighter. Both the Gwin Act of 1851 and the Chinese Exclusion Act of 1882 restricted the numbers of Mexican and Chinese residents of Los Angeles. By 1900, on the other hand, the number of African Americans had increased so greatly that they surpassed that of the Chinese by more than one thousand, making them easy targets of racial opposition and violence.[89] As Los Angeles continued growing, racial interaction intensified, resulting in increased racial violence.

African Americans and the News of the Day

In 1882, Harrison Gray Otis acquired the *Los Angeles Daily Times*, making him one of the city's most influential people, shaping the opinions of many Angelenos. The readership of the *Times* and other local papers became part of an elite class, privy to a certain amount of information that others received differently due to the low literacy levels of the city. The *Times* shaped middle class opinions about very specific aspects of its community. It portrayed Los Angeles as a haven for whites, while dehumanizing people of color. In fact, the *Times* took special care in advising potential residents that the city as a whole was intolerant of racial mixing at any level. An early target of this intolerance was African Americans.[90]

One of the more controversial stories published in the *Daily Times* on 25 January 1882 was about a black man accused of abandoning his white wife. The two settled in Los Angeles together, and shortly thereafter, began having marital trouble. The woman accused her husband of abandonment and adultery with several African American women not long after they wed, and sought dissolution of the marriage. The *Times* reported that witnesses identified the husband at several gambling halls with these other women, and the article pointed out the ways in which the man abused his marriage and his wife and failed to act responsibly. Then, it discreditably used this one incident to claim that such behavior exemplified that of the entire race.[91]

The *Times* and other mainstream newspapers maintained a monopoly of sorts on community information. On 12 April 1906, for example, the *Los Angeles Times* printed an article about an African American woman who attacked a police officer. The story, "Negress Bites Patrolman, Escapes," stated that, "A negro woman, laboring under the strength of a jag, escaped from Patrolman Briest on Boyle Heights last night by biting him to release his hold on her arm."[92] Hence, African American women were included as a focal point of local media coverage.

Although many Angelenos relied on various ways of getting and transmitting information, African Americans continued sharing news verbally until 1896 when Jefferson L. Edmonds became the premier spokesperson for Los Angeles, promoting racial uplift and opportunity by creating the first local African American paper. Los Angeles proved to be the "Promised Land" for Edmonds who was born into slavery in 1845 on a tobacco plantation in Virginia. He migrated to Mississippi in 1875 where he was educated in the segregated school system. He arrived in Los Angeles in 1888, and soon recognized the need for a black-owned weekly newspaper.[93]

Edmonds used the press as a platform for promoting Los Angeles as a place of black opportunity. In 1896, he published his first installment of *The Pasadena Searchlight*, a weekly publication, which quickly failed. Four years later, Edmonds published *The Liberator*, a monthly African American news magazine. His paper highlighted the positive aspects of Los Angeles, as he understood them.[94]

Historian Lonnie G. Bunch noted the ways in which Edmonds utilized his resources to entice black people into settling in the region. He explained, "Using the Liberator, he effectively crafted an optimistic, middle class vision of what black life could become in Los Angeles."[95]

Similar to the ways in which the *Times* promoted middle class values for whites, the *Liberator* both supported those values, and lured more African Americans to the city. Edmonds adopted notions of Progressivism as a way of fighting racial discrimination. He also used the *Liberator* as a tool for educating the African American community to fight for equal access to education and to overcome and combat racial oppression.[96]

Edmonds entered an ideal situation to get involved in organizing on a political scale to assist the African American community. The advent of his newspaper enabled him to reach his goals. The small, but growing African American community now had a monthly publication, which focused on current events, crises, economic concerns, and political opportunities. His paper served to combat the disparaging stories about the African American community that only increased at the beginning of the twentieth century.

As the African American population continued to increase, and other communities of color decreased, the *Times* focused its attention on black crime. Prior to this time, stories about crime and criminality in the black community were much fewer and farther between. One difference worth noting is that African American women appeared in many more of the newspaper's stories than any other group, as if to say that black women posed as much of a threat on the greater Los Angeles community than non-black men. These stories underscore the systematic attempt of white Angelenos to subjugate people of color.

On 3 January 1907, the *Times* examined a case involving a group of six African American men and women for mail theft. This was a serious federal offense, and the three women absconded to northern California to avoid facing charges. They were caught, and returned to Los Angeles to stand trial. Although this story merely places black women into the criminal element, others portrayed them as much more violent.[97]

An African American woman was arrested for fracturing her husband's skull. One evening, he had come home drunk, and the couple (who lived in a boardinghouse) had a fight. Since he returned from work at a late hour, she refused to sit with him while he ate, as she wanted to get up early the next morning to go to work. His meal was already prepared and she even laid his clothes out for the next day. On the way to bed, the woman stopped at another man's room for a moment. Her husband caught the two of them talking, and they began fighting. He threatened her with a knife, but she got the better of him. She somehow managed to knock him down, causing the injury to his head. She sustained a cut on her hand, which would seem to corroborate her story. The police, however, took him to the hospital and her to jail.[98] The story as printed underscored to its white readership that black women were also dangerous and violent.

The paper did not limit its focus on working class black people. J. G. Fleenor was a black real estate agent in Los Angeles. He was accused of committing over one hundred crimes, and was known as the "barefoot burglar." Police said he used his business to gain access to houses by telling the residents that he wanted to list or appraise their properties. Once inside, he would carefully study the floor plan of the home, noting all of the exits. He would then watch the property, noting the habits of the residents, and figure out a good time to return in order to commit his crimes. This usually took about a week. Since the majority of the homes contained working families he waited until everyone was gone. Once inside, he stole their jewelry and other small items of value.[99] After his arrest, Fleenor confessed, but when the case went to trial, he said that the police officers forced him to drink whiskey, which made him confess. It took the jury seven minutes to find him guilty of first-degree burglary, and he was sentenced to the State Prison.[100] The *Times* covered this story over several months, making it a relatively high-profile case, until a black man was accused of sexually assaulting a child.

In June, a man named Clarence Tribley was arrested for assaulting—and probably raping—a 9-year-old girl named Laura Akers. His bail was set at $500, an amount he would never afford to pay. This was considered the most brutal crime ever committed in the county. According to the *Times*, "The assault upon a little girl on the Monrovia road, years ago, by a Chinaman, who was torn to pieces by the child's relatives, does not compare in horror with the assault on Laura Akers."[101] During the trial, the little girl was at home under the care of her doctor, and Tribley was facing life in prison.

Although an African American man named A. Curtiss captured the assailant, the city maintained that the migrant black community was a threat. Police began watching incoming trains for black migrants from the South. It was believed that black criminals were fleeing southern communities with lynch laws. Police captain Flammer wrote, "Los Angeles is a paradise for the negro. We have many cases where bad negroes from the southern states come to Los Angeles to continue their depredations. In the first place the climate attracts them here, and again it is far away from where they are known."[102]

The purpose of this story was to ensure for white people that the police were ready to capture unwanted African Americans as soon as they arrived in Los Angeles. It also served as a warning for black people about encouraging southern migration. Both the police and the *Times* painted African Americans in the worst light possible, making it easy for white Angelenos to distrust and even fear black people. These kinds of stories promoted and justified racial hostility toward black people, no matter their status in the community, nor their willingness to work with the white community. This is especially true when one considers the resistance to black people becoming members of the police department.

Local Law Enforcement and Black Participation

African Americans in Los Angeles made slow but steady progress joining the ranks of the Los Angeles civil service. In 1869, the first paid police force comprised six local officers. Its first bona fide police chief was appointed in 1876. Just ten years later, the Los Angeles Police Department (LAPD) employed its first African American, Robert William Stewart. This marked an historical and rather large accomplishment for the African American community. But progress then slowed. Between 1886 and 1911 the LAPD only reluctantly increased the number of African American police officers. Around 1895, a man named Randolph became the second black police officer. In 1910, four black Angelenos listed in the census—William S. Stevens (27), Phillip Bomar (34), Lindsay Russell (44), and William Glenn (34)—reported their occupations as policemen. An additional four officers who were not listed in the census— Allen Watson, Frank White, Littleton McDuff, and Paul Stevens, may have not lived in the city at the time it was taken, or may not have been counted. Two more black men joined the police force in 1911. Out of 505 officers, only eight were black.[103]

Then, progress improved. By 1914, the number increased to fourteen.[104] In 1917 the force promoted its first black detective sergeant; Littleton McDuff became the highest ranking black member of the LAPD. In 1923, the first African American detective lieutenant, William L. Stevens, was assigned. The first female African American police officer, Georgia Robinson, was hired in 1919. By 1920 Los Angeles had become much more progressive in hiring African American men and women police officers than most cities in California and across the country.[105]

Qualifications for the LAPD stressed physical stature and ability. All candidates were required to have resided in the city for a minimum of two years. Members of the LAPD were not permitted to drink alcohol, smoke, or play cards or billiards while in uniform. (A number of officers however, including the second Chief of Police Emil Harris, owned saloons.)[106]

Despite the relatively progressive nature of the LAPD—at least by 1920—black Angelenos' relationship with local law enforcement was adversarial at best. Some black migrants adopted many of the city's ideologies, including taking a firm stance against crime. Despite the difficulties caused by racial tension and prejudice, and despite the bias against them shown in the press and local government, many black Angelenos supported the city's fight against criminal behavior.

By the turn of the century, the "California Dream" in Los Angeles was luring people into the region from all parts of the country. Looking to overcome its history of "wild west" violence, Angelenos (mainly white Angelenos) created a narrative that the city was safe and free of undesirable elements—and used oppression of immigrant communities of color to maintain that narrative. Through the years, white Angelenos systematically marginalized minority groups, beginning with the Native Americans, then Mexicans, then the Chinese, and finally African Americans. In doing so they helped to create the very underclass that they claimed to be fighting. However, the people and communities of color in Los Angeles did not go away, or yield in defeat. Instead, many used these undercurrents of hostility to come together and overcome prejudice and hate.

5

They Were All Filled with the Holy Ghost!

The Early Years of the Azusa Street Revival

In 1907, an entire family by the name of Cummings attended a prayer meeting in Los Angeles. Everyone, including the parents and small children, received the baptism of the Holy Spirit and began to speak languages unknown to them. Soon after, they planned to travel to Africa as missionaries. Participants prayed for and "laid hands" on them to ensure safe travel. These acts exemplify some of the many characteristics of the Azusa Street Revival that occurred in Los Angeles between 1906 and 1912.[1]

The revival started with a group of black working-class women and quickly spread across Los Angeles and the rest of the nation as black and white ministers began organizing churches across the country. In many ways, it captured the spirit of Los Angeles as a multicultural and multi-ethnic setting. Initially attended by black laundresses, the Azusa Street Revival appealed to anyone who believed it was possible to receive certain "gifts" from the Holy Spirit, regardless of their race, gender, or class. This revival was a catalyst of the modern Pentecostal movement.[2]

The revival movement was remarkable not only because of its eventual global impact, but also because of its "rituals of equality." Laypeople, for example, served in every capacity of the movement, from leading prayer, to the "laying on of hands," to managing the movement's publication, *The Apostolic Faith*. This chapter examines the Azusa Street Revival within the larger context of other national revival movements such as the First and Second Great Awakenings of the late eighteenth and mid-nineteenth centuries. This chapter also reconstructs the events that led up to and comprised the Azusa Street Revival, the important role of women and laypeople during the early years of the revival, and the impact of the movement and its broader implications for race relations in Los Angeles.[3]

Early Revivals

The revival in Los Angeles has to be seen in the context of earlier religious revivalist movements in North America. The Great Awakening was a revivalist movement that spread from the British Isles to the northern and southern colonies between the 1730s and 1770s. Led primarily by George Whitefield, Jonathan Edwards, and Gilbert Tennent, these revivals were evangelical, and found their home in many of the already established Baptist, Puritan, and Presbyterian denominations. Most revivalists accepted the Calvinist version of salvation, that only God controlled one's salvation, rather than personal acts or deeds. The revivals consisted of people of varying backgrounds and social status (with the exception of enslaved people), and were known for the enthusiastic preaching and worship styles of the preachers and congregants.[4]

The Second Great Awakening (1790–1830s) differed not only socially, but also doctrinally. Revivalists rejected Calvinist predestination, and embraced Wesleyan and Arminian notions that everyone was entitled to salvation, which was determined by one's actions. Wesley also asserted a social responsibility for converts. Second Great Awakening leaders such as Timothy Dwight and Lyman Beecher, for example, stressed conversion of the unsaved. Revivalists adopted social causes such as healing the sick, temperance, and abolition, essential to nineteenth-century reform efforts. African Americans were not exempt from participating. Young unmarried women also played a crucial role in these revivals, and in New England were more heavily represented in membership than men. Finally, unlike with the earlier revivals, many new denominations such as the Latter Day Saints, the Seventh Day Adventists, and numerous Holiness churches organized as offshoots of these revivals.[5]

While the Pentecostal churches grew out of the Holiness movement, the two are not always interchangeable. Holiness and Pentecostal churches adopted characteristics of these early revivals as well as aspects of Reformation theology. John Calvin was among those who had changed the way Christians viewed their relationship with God by postulating that certain people were predestined (chosen) for salvation. After accepting the call of salvation, they would perform "good works," which were also predestined. John Wesley challenged this notion in the 1740s, believing that people were allowed to "choose salvation," and would perform "good works" accordingly. But Wesley did agree with Calvin and Martin Luther that God's grace was the main factor in salvation (whether one is predestined or not). He claimed that salvation discouraged believers from acting in a sinful manner, and motivated them to perform good works.

Most Protestants fall on either side of this debate, but many Pentecostals adopted a combination of both Calvinism and Wesleyan theology.

While both Calvin and Wesley believed in predestination, Wesley believed that a person is drawn to God through biblical preaching and teaching. He or she is "the chosen" and, in return, "chooses" God. Biblical learning also contributes to the believer's choice to do good works and to have a tremendous amount of faith. Wesley also placed great emphasis on the work of the "Holy Spirit." He stated that the "baptism of the Holy Spirit" was essential to one's salvation, and that the evidence of this was glossolalia, or "speaking in tongues." These beliefs became a cornerstone for Pentecostal theology.

Pentecostalism Defined

Churches commonly referred to as Holiness or Pentecostal place great doctrinal emphasis on the biblical Day of Pentecost (Acts 1), when the gift of the Holy Spirit (Ghost) was bestowed upon the apostles. This is also known as receiving the "baptism of the Holy Spirit (Ghost)." The belief that one receives the baptism of the Holy Spirit (Ghost) means that God has sent His Spirit to dwell within our human bodies. The "evidence" of this baptism is that the person speaks in a tongue, or unknown language.[6]

Historian William E. Montgomery has argued that the Holiness movement evolved in response to the conservative directions of the First and Second Great Awakenings. As the Baptist and Methodist denominations became more theologically conservative, they discouraged the level of emotionalism the revivals once evoked. The Holiness movement "incorporated a high level of emotional excitement, an ascetic doctrine that substituted the reward of spiritual salvation for material success and earthly pleasures, and a strictly literal interpretation of the Bible. Its adherents placed a great value on the sanctification, or 'holiness' in attitude and behavior, that was manifested in old-time revivalist religion."[7] Montgomery also noted that members of the Holiness movement were typically of the lower classes, excluded from elite social institutions. The movement appealed to African Americans particularly, because of its similarities to African religious practices. The Holiness movement, therefore, served as the social, cultural, and spiritual foundation for the Pentecostal movement.[8]

Most Pentecostals recognize the Azusa Street Revival as its foundation. Although they may differ in practice, each denomination contains churches that adopted the idea of the "baptism" of the Holy Spirit, and speaking in tongues. The doctrine of the Holy Ghost is called Pneumatology. The purpose of the Holy Ghost is to equip and empower "the believer, making him a more effective witness for the service in the world."[9] In this church, salvation becomes a process. First, a person confesses to having been a sinner, but now proclaims belief in Jesus. Next, the person enters sanctification, or the "continuous operation of the Holy Ghost, by which He delivers the justified sinner from the pollution of sin, renews his whole nature in the image of God and enables him to perform good works."[10]

One knows that he or she has received the baptism of the Holy Ghost when that person is enabled to speak in unknown languages, just as the apostles did according to the Book of Acts. Again, this happens after one is "justified" and "sanctified." Once the baptism has occurred, the believer is generally equipped to speak in other languages. Pentecostals also believe in other "spiritual gifts" such as prophecy, healing, wisdom, knowledge, and faith. Pentecostals are fundamentalists; total-immersion water baptism, and the baptism of the "Holy Spirit" with speaking in tongues as the evidence, are some of the main characteristics of the religion. Sociologist and anthropologist George Simpson noted that Pentecostals use the biblical apostolic church as their model. This was the original vision of the revival's leader, William J. Seymour.[11]

Pentecost in Los Angeles

The Azusa Street Revival united people of various religious backgrounds, nationalities, and racial heritages. In addition to feeling God's power and that of the Holy Spirit, participants received spiritual "gifts" that enabled them to conduct ministry throughout the world. In many ways, the Azusa Street Revival served as a training ground for people who, not unlike the Cummings family, were serious about practicing Christianity and learning the significance of Christian discipleship. Perhaps more significant is the lasting impact of the movement that began in Los Angeles.[12]

In many ways, Los Angeles was the best place for the Azusa Street Revival. The city appeared to be "heaven on earth." Migrants viewed it as a social and cultural mecca, full of tremendous opportunity and promise. By 1906, Los Angeles was becoming one of the fastest-growing cities in the nation, and many people truly believed they could take advantage of everything the city had to offer. Although many people associated these ideas with California specifically, a revival could not have occurred with the same intensity in San Francisco, for example.

On 18 April 1906, nine days after the revival began, a devastating 7.9 magnitude earthquake struck San Francisco. People from Oregon to Los Angeles and as far as Nevada felt the impact, yet the majority of the damage occurred in San Francisco. The next day, the *Los Angeles Times* estimated an initial death count of seven hundred people. Many religious enthusiasts understood the tragedy as a sign from God that the world would soon end. One revivalist, Frank Bartleman, for example, wrote that after the earthquake people feared God. The earthquake occurred three days after Easter, when Christians still felt the spirit of celebration of the Resurrection of Christ.[13]

To Bartleman, the earthquake directly affected the movement's overall success. He explained that as the region felt the aftershocks of the quake, many sought answers. It appeared to Bartleman, as it did to many others, that the world would soon end, and that God was casting judgment upon His people. They understood it as an opportunity to seek His forgiveness. Several preachers, including Bartleman, immediately began proselytizing. While many people accepted the possibility of the world ending, many also showed an interest in revivalism, and even Pentecostalism.[14]

Los Angeles possessed one final quality that made it an appropriate location for such a revival to occur. The city provided a viable stage for new religious traditions to take place without fear of interference or racial violence. Given the city's racial tensions, it still was a relatively better place for African Americans to live than other parts of the country, especially the South. By 1900, almost 40 percent of the African American population in Los Angeles was southern-born. An additional 20 percent had migrated from Texas, while another 14 percent came from states throughout the Midwest. In many states where out-migration occurred, lynching threatened the lives of most black families. Los Angeles, however, managed to suppress notions of racism, and presented itself as a safe haven for immigrants and new migrants. This also allowed, and in some ways encouraged, people in the city to enjoy more social and religious freedom. Indeed, throughout the course of the revival, African Americans and other people of color never experienced the kinds of physical danger faced by their southern and northern counterparts.[15]

Many southern black migrants in Los Angeles brought certain religious customs, derived predominantly from West African, Baptist, Methodist, and other traditions. In West Africa the religious practices oftentimes included spirit possession and rhythmic dance. Historian Sterling Stuckey identified the "ring shout" as a widespread religious practice in West and Central Africa that was transferred to various parts of the Americas. Religious ceremonies included dancing, singing, and moving in circular patterns, and some experienced ecstatic states and spirit possession associated with the religious practices of enslaved African Americans' traditional religion. Slave religion encompassed several aspects of African religions, particularly shouting, dancing, and music. Thus, southern black migrants found a religious space that celebrated their cultural characteristics rather than suppressing them. Participants of the Azusa Street Revival danced, sang, and shouted as the "Holy Spirit" allowed.[16]

Scholars of the Azusa Street Revival have neglected to investigate the reasons why it occurred in Los Angeles. Rather, they have focused on the doctrinal aspects of the movement. Some have viewed it as an event that took place in a spiritual vacuum. Revivalist Frank Bartleman noted that other churches around Los Angeles were also waiting for a Pentecostal experience, yet did not experience one. He blamed their lack of willingness to work with one another to earnestly pray and wait for the "Holy Spirit" to fall. The earnestness of the original group allowed for such a movement to occur, which forced other Holiness churches to come together at Azusa Street. This sincerity, in turn, prompted people from around the world to attend the revival meetings. As people heard the testimonies from Azusa Street, they wanted to experience Pentecost firsthand, often believing that it was essential for them to travel to California.[17] While some scholars have accepted Bartleman's account of the earnestness of Seymour and his followers, the revival took place in Los Angeles for many more reasons.

The movement itself reflected and represented the city's sociopolitical dynamics. Although a small group of African Americans began the meetings, the revival had a multicultural and international appeal, just as Los Angeles did. Since middle-class Angelenos continued pushing people of color and some ethnically defined whites toward the margin, the working-class neighborhoods became multiracial districts comprised of people who shared certain social and economic disadvantages. This becomes increasingly evident during the revival, when most participants resembled those who lived in the surrounding community. Los Angeles continued to promise equality, success, and hope. The Pentecostal movement provided many of the same things, but only in the context of the revival. When people arrived in Los Angeles, they hoped to find paradise; instead, they found "heaven's ghetto."

Economic status played a pivotal role in both the beginning and the decline of this movement, as many of the participants were among the working class. Revival leader William J. Seymour, along with the movement's founding families, lived on the periphery of downtown Los Angeles. These families did not own the premier property in the city, and most of them worked in unskilled occupations. Seymour was not only black, but illiterate, which was a social issue elite African Americans spent years combating. Observers of the revival viewed the movement entirely as a lowbrow phenomenon. This, in turn, motivated the unstructured, unscripted elements that contributed to the decline of the movement. Although members believed in waiting for God to "move" in their services, it made the church vulnerable to criticism and to influence from outsiders who had different spiritual, and perhaps social, agendas. The revival, in many ways, mirrored the African American experience in Los Angeles.

Not only did class stratification impact the Pentecostal movement, it was key to the problems of black Angelenos. In many ways, the Azusa Street Revival served as not only a religious refuge, but also a space for African Americans and those of lower class status to escape the impositions of middle-class Christian practices. As in earlier revival movements, participants of the Azusa Street Revival were drawn to its cultural and spiritual retentions. They felt free from the pressures of the middle class that tried so desperately to suppress the lower-class elements of the city. While the middle class had created several programs that it believed were beneficial to working-class people, the revival served as a form of resistance of such reform programs. Since the Azusa Street Revival maintained a level of egalitarianism, participants felt neither spiritually nor socially subordinate, regardless of racial or socioeconomic background.

Founders of the Azusa Street Revival

Scholars of Pentecostalism and of the American religious tradition debate whether to credit Charles Fox Parham or William Joseph Seymour as founder of the modern Pentecostal movement in America. Both played instrumental roles in spreading the movement.[18] By considering the relationship between the two, one better understands the role of each and his contribution to the denomination. To begin, Parham, a white male, was born in Iowa in 1873, and was "called" to ministry at the age of nine, when he began studying the Bible. In 1889, he enrolled in Southwestern College, a Methodist school in Kansas. After a period of "spiritual confusion," Parham decided to leave, claiming that it was a hindrance to his doing God's work. In 1892, he received ordination from the Methodist Church and began preaching. Parham's messages conflicted with Methodist doctrine, forcing him out in 1894. Two years later, he married Sarah Thistlewaite and the two began traveling and preaching together. After the Parhams' first child was born in 1897, the minister developed heart disease. Parham began praying for "divine healing," and recovered. This encouraged him to commence a ministry of healing, and he opened the Bethel Healing Home in Topeka, Kansas, in 1898.[19]

Parham soon adopted Holiness theology. He met Frank W. Sanford, the head of a "Spirit in Holiness" Center in Maine, and, along with eight of his colleagues, enrolled in 1900. The group found themselves locked out of their facility upon returning to Topeka. Parham gained the use of another building (an unfinished mansion) just outside of town. Parham named his new facility, which opened on 15 October 1900, the "College of Bethel," and admitted approximately three dozen students. While Parham received a number of Holiness believers, most of his students came from Methodist, Baptist, or Quaker backgrounds. Parham taught his students about the importance of a "Spirit Baptism" and the "outpouring of the Holy Spirit." On New Year's Day 1901, Parham's first student to experience the "outpouring of the Spirit" was a woman named Agnes N. Ozman.[20] Soon after, other students prayed for a "Spirit Baptism" and were "filled." As word spread about Parham's teachings, he began receiving invitations to preach in Oklahoma, Kansas, and Missouri. By 1905, he and some of his followers had moved to Houston, where they opened another facility. A man named William Joseph Seymour approached Parham about becoming one of his students.[21]

William J. Seymour was born on 2 May 1870 in Centerville, Louisiana, to former slaves, Simon and Phillis. Simon Seymour was a brick maker, while Phillis stayed home and tended to their four children. William was the oldest brother to Simon Jr., Amos, and a sister who was nine and a half years younger.[22] By 1900, Simon Seymour had died, leaving Phillis and her children to care for themselves. Phillis owned a farm in St. Mary Parish, Louisiana. All of her sons worked with her cultivating the property while her daughter Emma attended school. Phillis had two other children by 1900. At the time, Jacob, Isaac, and Emma were in their teens, and William, Simon Jr., and Amos were adults. Phillis continued caring for her family well into the twentieth century.[23]

William J. Seymour decided that, as an adult, he needed to get out on his own. In 1895, he took a job as a waiter in Indianapolis, where he joined the black Methodist Episcopal Church. Soon, he became an ordained minister through the Church of God in Anderson, Indiana. From 1900 until 1902, Seymour lived in Cincinnati, where he actively participated in the Holiness movement.[24]

In 1903, Seymour moved to Houston, where he attended a Holiness church led by an African American woman named Lucy Farrow. She later left this church to work in Kansas, but in 1905 Farrow returned to Houston. She invited Seymour to a meeting, and introduced him to radical Holiness teachings, which emphasized the concept of "entire sanctification" as well as the "outpouring" of the Holy Spirit. Farrow worked as Charles Parham's governess, and often accompanied him to the African American meetings in Houston, where Parham introduced Seymour to the concept of "tongues."[25]

Seymour tried enrolling in Charles F. Parham's school, to learn more about radical Holiness doctrine, but Parham was unwilling to admit him because he was black. Eventually, Parham permitted Seymour to sit in the hallway and listen to the lectures. This was Parham's only stipulation to the agreement to admit Seymour. Seymour happily attended classes in the halls, and soon became pastor of his own African American Holiness mission in Houston. Within a few months, Seymour accepted an invitation to travel to help some of the Holiness missions in Los Angeles.[26]

An African American woman, Neeley Terry, visited the Houston mission and solicited Seymour's help with her black Baptist church's doctrinal divide. Julia Hutchins, a member, was teaching the equivalence of "Sanctification" and the "Baptism of the Holy Spirit," as a second act of grace that every believer was entitled to and possessed.[27] Since this belief contradicted traditional Baptist doctrine, the church forced Hutchins and her followers out. They moved to the downtown area of Los Angeles, into a storefront on Santa Fe Street. Terry, upon her return to Los Angeles, convinced her congregation that Seymour was an appropriate choice for an associate pastor. He gladly accepted the invitation and arrived in Los Angeles in 1906.[28]

Seymour preached about the importance of the Holy Spirit "baptism" and the concept of "speaking in tongues." Julia Hutchins disagreed with his teaching, stating that "speaking in tongues" was only one of the evidences of a Holy Spirit "baptism," rather than the *only initial* evidence, as Seymour believed.[29] She locked the doors of the church and forced Seymour and his followers out. Seymour relocated his prayer meetings to the home of the person with whom he resided, Edward "Irish" Lee. Soon after, the group moved to 216 North Bonnie Brae Street, not far from the Lees. The address was the home of an African American Baptist family, Richard and Ruth Asbury. Though they entertained a different set of religious beliefs than Seymour, the Asburys empathized with him, and allowed meetings in their home.[30]

African American laundresses and their husbands primarily attended Seymour's meetings. Though Seymour was initially unsuccessful, he continued teaching, and often wrote to Parham for advice. Meanwhile, the Lees invited members of their own church to meet Seymour. In April 1906, Parham sent Lucy Farrow, now Seymour's good friend, and J. A. Warren to help.[31] Edward Lee became ill, and asked Seymour to pray with him for "divine healing." Soon, he asked Seymour to pray with him for a "Spirit Baptism," which Seymour himself had not yet experienced. Believing that Lee could be "filled" with the "outpouring" of the Holy Spirit, Seymour prayed until Lee began to speak in other languages. Seymour immediately rushed to the Asbury home and shared his excitement. There, Seymour and several others spoke in other languages.[32]

The Asburys' daughter, Willie Ella, went to tell others about the occurrences at her parents' home. Soon, many people from the neighborhood arrived at the house to witness these events for themselves. They gathered on the Asburys' porch, where Seymour and his followers met them for prayer and preaching. The crowd became so large that the porch separated from the foundation. Many observers across the street also experienced a "Spirit Baptism." Seymour realized that he needed to move his prayer meetings to a larger venue.[33]

The Stevens African Methodist Episcopal Church congregation had abandoned a building at 312 Azusa Street, also located in downtown Los Angeles.[34] Theologian Robert Owens defined the dimensions of the building as a "small, rectangular, flat-roofed building, approximately 2,400 square feet (40 x 60) sided with weathered white-washed clapboards. The only sign that it had once been a house of God was a single gothic style window over the main entrance."[35] Seymour and his followers purchased, cleaned, and repaired the building, making it suitable for services. They turned the ground floor into a chapel, and used the second story as an "upper room" where people would "tarry" for the "outpouring" of the Holy Spirit as the apostles did on the Day of Pentecost.[36]

Almost a year after the revival began, one visitor, Arthur B. Shepherd, described the "upper room" experience. He said he "tarried" in the room until he felt the "baptism" of the Holy Spirit. He likened it to a near-death experience: "Slowly, surely my life seemed to ebb away, until at last unconsciousness took place. How long I lay I do not know, but the first thing I was conscious of was a new life flowing in. Soon, my jaws and tongue began to work independently of my volition and the words came, a clear language."[37] Seymour named the building the "Apostolic Faith Mission," and people traveled from all parts of the world to experience the modern Pentecost.[38]

Immediately, the Apostolic Faith Mission proved inadequate to hold the crowds it drew. The police regularly attempted to close the meetings because of the overflow of traffic and loud noise. The Los Angeles Fire Department also responded to reports of explosions and a mysterious "glow" being seen from the building. Other agencies that attempted to interfere with the mission included the Child Welfare Department, since unattended children were seen playing around the building, and the Health Department, which investigated unsanitary conditions. Since the number of people using the building was so great, members endured cramped quarters. Moreover, this event began during the spring and summer months, during warm or even hot weather conditions. The mission did not have air-conditioning, with approximately one hundred people regularly squeezed into a room designed to hold between thirty and forty. The above-mentioned agencies were not the only organizations that shared negative feelings about the mission.[39]

The religious community initially rejected the movement. According to Owens, the majority of the Holiness movement opposed the Apostolic Faith Mission because of their position on "speaking in tongues." They accused revival participants of practicing devil worship, witchcraft, and sexual immorality. More importantly, most of the original participants of the Azusa Street Revival were of the lower and working classes, many of whom were illiterate and uneducated. Even the *Los Angeles Daily Times* reported that the revival clearly was a lower class phenomenon. This, however, did not prevent the revival from continuing.[40]

The more attention the mainstream media paid to the revival, the more people came to witness it. Seymour addressed this in the mission's newspaper in September 1906. He noted the amount of negative publicity from the "secular papers," and said people understood that God's presence was there, otherwise, fewer people would have participated. Seymour concluded that "they have come and found out it was indeed the power of God."[41] Members at the Apostolic Faith Mission clearly used the bad publicity to their advantage.

The negative attention from the *Los Angeles Daily Times* only increased people's curiosity for the revival, and more came to visit. Most who attended the revival did so only to see the phenomenon that was taking place, but many also became active participants in the revival. In fact, so many people attended meetings at the mission that services often ran late, one overlapping with the next. Service was often held twenty-four hours a day. They began with prayer, praise and testimony. Then someone prophesied to the congregation, before singing commenced, both in English and in unknown languages. After someone preached a message, the Holy Spirit "moved" throughout the room. Up to one hundred people at a time approached the altar for prayer, then a member read letters from people seeking the Holy Spirit "baptism," and finally, praise resumed. The mission relied entirely on a spontaneous "move" of God.[42]

When sermons were preached at the mission, anyone could be "anointed" to speak. Often, the congregation continued in prayer, praise, and singing until someone "received" the message. Seymour also preached on many occasions, focusing primarily on the significance of Jesus and salvation. Still, participants at the mission relied on God to minister. Many were "anointed" with "spiritual gifts" that proved useful in spreading the revival as well as the modern Pentecostal movement. The majority had no theological training, and a large number were women.[43]

While Seymour never supported the ordination of women, he surrounded himself with them and relied on them to help run the mission. He married one of the original members from the house on Bonnie Brae Street, Jennie Evans Moore, a young African American woman. Moore was born in 1883. She married Seymour at the age of twenty-five. Although she had actively participated in the mission from its inception, she and Seymour waited to marry until 13 May 1908, two years after the revival began. They adopted a daughter and resided on the second floor of the Apostolic Faith Mission.

Moore played a pivotal role at the mission. During the first few meetings at the Bonnie Brae Street house, Moore had received her "spirit baptism" and spoke in other languages. In fact, she was the first woman in Los Angeles to experience a Holy Spirit "baptism." Her testimony appeared in *The Apostolic Faith*. She wrote: "On April 9, 1906, I was praising the Lord from the Depths of my heart at home, and when the evening came and we attended the meeting, the power of God fell and I was baptized in the Holy Ghost and with fire, with the evidence of speaking in tongues. . . . I sang under the power of the Spirit in many languages, the interpretation both words and music which I had never before heard, and in the home where the meeting was being held, the Spirit led me to the piano, where I played and sang under inspiration, although I had not learned to play."[44] Moore and the others believed that one of the languages she spoke and sang in was Hebrew. She also helped to recruit people for the mission.[45]

After her own experience at the Asbury home, Moore returned to her former church to share her testimony. They rejected her. She enlisted Ruth Asbury to visit another church. There, Moore spoke in "tongues" and Asbury explained the biblical basis for it. The entire congregation followed them to the house on Bonnie Brae Street. This kind of occurrence became so common that it caused many churches to close down after losing their parishioners. Established churches often asked police to stop the revival, but were unsuccessful. Moore's experience at the mission was not without controversy.[46]

As Seymour continued surrounding himself with women, he found himself in the midst of a love triangle. A Caucasian woman at the mission, Clara Lum, opposed Seymour and Moore's relationship. Lum probably hoped to become romantically involved with Seymour, who rejected her. She had played an integral role in helping the movement spread. She not only held the mailing list for *The Apostolic Faith*, but also was one of its publishers. Among her other responsibilities, Lum read testimonies at the meetings, was given the "gift" of interpreting "tongues," and published testimonies in the newspaper.[47]

Her affections spurned by Seymour, Lum retaliated. She left the mission, taking the mailing list with her in 1909. She later joined another mission in Oregon, and published her own newspaper under the same name. For this reason, *The Apostolic Faith* in Los Angeles only lasted for two years, from 1906 until 1908. During those years, however, Clara Lum had dedicated herself to the movement, and due to the publication's large mailing list the Apostolic Faith Mission had maintained both national and international readership, which in turn brought more people to the Los Angeles mission during her time there.[48]

Lucy Farrow also played a crucial role in the movement. Not only did she invite Seymour to Los Angeles in September 1906, but she printed her testimony about receiving the "gift of laying hands." The article read, "Mrs. Lucy Farrow, God's anointed handmaid, who came some fourmonths [sic] ago from Houston, Texas, to Los Angeles, bringing the full gospel, and whom God has greatly used as she laid her hands on many who have received the Pentecost and the gift of tongues."[49] When people approached the altar, Farrow prayed with them, thus utilizing her "gift."[50]

Though Seymour had met Farrow in Houston, she was a former slave, originally from Norfolk, Virginia. She planned to begin a mission in Africa, believing that the Lord was "calling her back" to her ancestors' birthplace. In December 1906, Farrow reported that while she was in New York preparing for her trip she saw approximately "two hundred souls saved and most speak in tongues."[51] She settled in Johnsonville, Liberia, near Monrovia, where she preached and ministered until August 1907. Members at the Apostolic Faith Mission financed her trip. One of the people with whom Farrow was traveling was Julia Hutchins, the same woman who had locked Seymour and his followers out of her church for preaching about "tongues."[52]

Even though Hutchins had originally disagreed with Seymour's teachings, she became an avid supporter. Her own testimony admits her hesitance in accepting Seymour's doctrine. She also believed that when she finally did, she received "gifts" similar to her colleague Farrow. In October 1906, Hutchins "received the baptism with the Holy Ghost and the gift of the Uganda language, the language of the people to whom she is sent."[53] Hutchins's husband also experienced a "Spirit baptism." She stated, "The Lord reclaimed my husband and sanctified him wholly and put the glory and shout in him."[54] Together, the two traveled to Africa.[55] Many women who embarked on foreign missions traveled with their husbands and families. Hutchins's niece, Leila McKinney, also received her "spirit baptism" and was "anointed" to travel to Africa and "testify to those people and teach the children about the blessed Lord, and to work for the Lord."[56] Hutchins believed she was "called" to Africa for a mission, and her husband, her niece, and several others were to accompany her.[57]

Even while traveling on a mission, members believed God spoke through them on every segment of the journey. Hutchins was in New York with Farrow awaiting transport to Liberia when she wrote to *The Apostolic Faith*, "The last meeting we had with the people was beside the train that brought us away. Under the shed there was where the Lord used me in that city. He sang and preached through me and some confessed their sins and asked, what shall I do to be saved?"[58] Inherent in what she said was that women, just as men, were "called" to preach without having to undergo an ordination process. This also illustrated the ways in which people were "anointed" to deliver messages at the Apostolic Faith Mission. Hutchins continued, "While on the train, we preached the Word and some received it with joy."[59] She traveled from Los Angeles to Chattanooga and to New York on her way to Africa. She frequently sent letters to the Apostolic Faith Mission. Hutchins and her companions never missed an opportunity to share the Word of the Lord.[60]

Florence Crawford was another exceptional woman who played a significant role in the success and decline of the Azusa Street Revival. Crawford was a Caucasian whose primary responsibility at the Apostolic Faith Mission was to oversee the publication of *The Apostolic Faith*. Most of her missionary work took place along the Pacific Northwest in places such as Portland and Salem, Oregon; Oakland, California; and Toronto, Ontario. In October 1906, Crawford reported to *The Apostolic Faith* that in Oakland sixty-five "souls were saved."[61] Just over a year later, she went to Oregon for missionary work. She wrote that in Salem, "The slain of the Lord lay so you can't move about the altar. The altar is full before the meeting is half over."[62] Crawford's dedication to the mission interfered with her personal life, and unlike her female counterparts, Crawford and her husband divorced. She opened her own mission in Portland.[63]

While in the Northwest, Florence Crawford continued assisting with the publication of the paper, and often sent in testimonies of people at her mission in addition to messages she received from God, either through visions, or prayer. Like Clara Lum, Crawford disapproved of the union between William J. Seymour and Jennie Moore. She believed that the church would experience the "rapture" soon, and that Seymour had failed to recognize his priorities as a leader. Crawford also rejected Seymour's doctrine regarding sanctification as a second work of grace. She decided to transfer *The Apostolic Faith* to Oregon, where she and Clara Lum continued publishing it. Without the mailing list, Seymour was left unable to reach his audience.[64]

Robert Owens and historian Robert Mapes Anderson assert that the loss of the mission's publication caused the initial breakdown of the Azusa Street Revival.[65] Owens notes that this was the first of two major blows to the revival. Seymour and Moore traveled to Portland to recover the mailing list, but were unsuccessful. By 1908, *The Apostolic Faith* had reached at least 50,000 people.[66] Though the revival never fully recovered, the laity continued establishing missions at home and abroad.[67]

Ministry, Spreading the Gospel, and Women

A regularly occurring phenomenon of the Azusa Street Revival involved women attending meetings first, with their husbands following soon after. Numerous women received salvation before their husbands. In similar ways that women bore the responsibility for attending to their children's education, so too, scholars have observed, did black women set the religious climate, not only in their homes, but also in their communities. Sociologist Cheryl Townsend Gilkes points out, "Women are responsible for the care and cultivation of tradition."[68] Historian Brenda E. Stevenson notes that among the various responsibilities slave women held, they also "promoted religious practice in their quarters."[69] Historian Bettye Collier-Thomas explains that the church played an essential role in the lives of African Americans. The black church, therefore, gave women a platform to address a myriad of social issues.[70]

The black church depends on its female members who utilize the church as a space for them to address sociopolitical issues involving the entire community, such as racism and sexism. In her seminal work on black women in the Baptist Church, historian Evelyn Brooks Higginbotham points out that black women "had a crucial role in the formation of public sentiment and in the expression of a black collective will."[71] She and others have noted that black women are at the heart of the black church, regardless of whether they have official ministerial roles and titles. The Azusa Street Revival was no exception. Women, black and white, played integral roles in the revival.[72]

William J. Seymour's position on women working in the ministry was patriarchal. He stated, "All ordination must be done by men not women. Women may be ministers but not to baptize and ordain in this work."[73] Given such limitations, women served as ministers at The Apostolic Faith Mission and throughout the world. One issue of *The Apostolic Faith* reported that "God wants men and women that will preach this Gospel square from the shoulder."[74] Women such as Florence Crawford, Jennie Moore, and Lucy Farrow represent some who served as ministers. In Portland, Oregon, and in northern California in Florence Crawford's missions, women were primarily responsible for taking care of the new converts. Jennie Evans Moore joined the board of trustees for the mission in 1915. She replaced Seymour as pastor of the Apostolic Faith Mission after he died in 1922 until she was hospitalized in 1935. She died on 2 July 1936. Yet these were only some of the women who established and led missions and traveled throughout the world.[75]

Sister Wettosh, a German woman, set out to "carry this Gospel" to Reno, Nevada.[76] At a mission in Central Africa, a slave woman began to spread the Gospel after her son was "healed" from smallpox. Brother Samuel J. Mead reported that she was winning more souls than he was.[77] The Garrs of Los Angeles left their home in Los Angeles to preach in India. They also held meetings in Chicago and in Danville, Virginia.[78] A woman named Anna Hall traveled from Houston to Los Angeles to preach at the mission. Believing the Lord called her to that city, she wrote, "The voice answered. 'Yes and I have come to tell you that Jesus is coming. Go forward in my name, preach the Gospel of the Kingdom, for the King's business demands haste.'"[79] A Sister Leatherman also believed she was "called" to work in Jerusalem, and held meetings in Oakland, California, before her departure.[80] A Louisa M. Condit and Mrs. Rushnell also traveled to Jerusalem to preach.[81]

Lizzie Frazier, who sometimes led meetings, was excited about these women's work and was motivated to travel to India with a group of missionaries. In Benton Harbor, Michigan, a Sister Robinson taught members about Pentecost, and "laid hands" on people as they received the "baptism" of the Holy Spirit.[82] A Sister Ladd led her own mission in Des Moines, Iowa.[83] M. Eila Judy was a teacher from the Blind School of Columbus, Ohio, who visited the Apostolic Faith Mission while on vacation. She was instrumental in "winning souls."[84]

Ophelia Wiley was another woman who preached. The October 1906 issue of *The Apostolic Faith* included a sermon that she wrote called "A Sermon from a Dress," which addressed the ways in which one removed sin from his or her life. She exhibited tremendous oratorical skill. One day, while preaching to a group of people, an officer tried to interrupt, but once service started, "the saints began to pray," and continued the meeting undisturbed until they finished.[85] The members were so involved in the act of prayer that an officer of the peace, or anyone else, could not interrupt them. A Mary Perkins published a sermon about salvation titled, "Whisperings of the Comforter."[86] It was not uncommon for sermons to be published in *The Apostolic Faith*.[87]

A Sister McClain wrote that she and her husband planned a trip to Michigan to preach and to hold meetings. They planned to take their three children, and one of her daughters would provide lodging. McClain stated they expected to "preach the word till He comes."[88] Many women who traveled with their husbands had the authority to preach. In Los Angeles, a Mrs. Lopez and her husband assisted by translating sermons into Spanish. Most of the time, the couple assisted at the altar, where people sought prayer, salvation, and the "baptism" of the Holy Spirit.[89]

The woman known as "Mother" Wheaton often visited prisons, introducing the plan of salvation to inmates. She worked in both the United States and Europe.[90] In Osterville, Washington, a K. E. Andrews opened her home for prayer meetings and Bible study. She said, "The Lord set me apart for His service and soon gave me a commission."[91]

Salvation

William J. Seymour's *Doctrines and Discipline of the Azusa Street Apostolic Faith Mission* defined salvation as a "new birth." Seymour asserted that one received salvation through the blood of Jesus Christ, and when a person received it, he or she knew it. When a person lost it, he or she recognized it as well. The only way for a person to receive salvation, according to Seymour, was by repenting and believing in the gospel of Jesus Christ.[92] He did not believe a "Holy Spirit" baptism was a prerequisite of salvation.[93] Finally, Seymour viewed salvation as available to all believers, regardless of race, class, gender, age, or religious background.[94]

Seymour defined justification and sanctification in his *Doctrines and Discipline*. He noted that justification was the first work of grace, and defined it as "the act of God's free grace by which we receive remission of sins."[95] Sanctification, according to Seymour, was the second work of grace, defined as "that act of God's grace by which He makes us holy in doctrine and life."[96] He explained sanctification as a process by which a person was spiritually cleansed in the manner of the apostles before the biblical Day of Pentecost. This meant, according to Seymour, that one was incapable of "receiving" the Holy Spirit if one was unclean. Once a person was "filled" with the Holy Spirit, he or she became empowered and equipped for Christian service.[97]

The December 1906 issue of *The Apostolic Faith* reported that people were coming from "thousands of miles" to Los Angeles seeking salvation.[98] In September of that year, at the beginning of the revival, the paper had reported that 160 people in Los Angeles had received salvation. It compared these events to the biblical movement: "more than on the Day of Pentecost, have received the gift of the Holy Ghost and the Bible evidence, the gift of tongues, and many have been saved and sanctified, nobody knows how many."[99] The paper also reported that the spirit of the revival manifested in many homes throughout Los Angeles and that "God has been melting and saving and sanctifying and baptizing with the Holy Ghost."[100]

In the January 1907 issue of the newspaper, Seymour noted that people were traveling from thousands of miles for the "outpouring" of the Holy Ghost. He said that wherever they traveled after leaving Los Angeles, the Spirit was "poured out."[101] A Tom Qualis wrote to the mission stating that he traveled three hundred miles from Fresno, California, to feel the presence of God. Some made the sojourn from closer locales, as one man traveled from Redlands, California, and others from as close as Pasadena, only twelve miles away. Still, participants arrived from various cities and states across the country. Soon, people sent in testimonies about their own salvation and sanctification experiences.[102]

Daisy Bateman's story was published in the December 1906 issue as "Mrs. Daisy Bateman's Testimony." She had felt overjoyed when she received word about Pentecost in Los Angeles. Bateman had already experienced salvation, but not sanctification until the revival. She wrote, "Last April He sanctified my soul, took all inbred sin out and gave me a clean heart fit for the Lord's use."[103] Julia Hutchins noted that her own justification occurred on 4 July 1901, but it was not until 28 July that she was "sanctified."[104] At an Oakland mission where Florence Crawford and a Brother and Sister Evans worked for five weeks, approximately "sixty-five souls received the baptism with the Holy Ghost, thirty sanctified, and ninety converted."[105] Through the process of sanctification, one was "cleansed," and thus equipped for ministry. This also included "deliverance" from addictions, among other unlawful habits.[106]

Many people acknowledged the tremendous work Seymour and his followers accomplished. One Mary Galmond sent a letter from Pasadena praising the Azusa Street Mission and Seymour specifically. She believed more people had converted and received salvation in Los Angeles under

Seymour's leadership than in the five years prior.[107] The "Spirit" had healed a man named Harmon Clifford of alcohol abuse. The process took only an hour and a half at the mission. Clifford felt so strongly about this healing, he had traveled north to Oakland, where he ministered to others.[108] On 1 May 1907, a Jewish man testified at the meeting about his own conversion experience, while a young boy stated that he was glad for his own salvation. Not only were people experiencing salvation, several accounts of "deliverance," especially from substance abuse, were recorded.[109]

The November 1906 issue of *The Apostolic Faith* reported that the Lord was saving "drunkards and taking the appetite for liquor and tobacco completely away."[110] Bridget Weich shared her testimony of deliverance from drug addiction. She said, "The Lord took me out of an awful pit and set my feet on the solid rock and established my goings and put a new song in my mouth. He sanctified me and baptized me with the Holy Ghost and gave me the gift of tongues."[111] In the same issue, a man reported that he was free from a morphine habit and had lost the desire for the drug.[112] The February and March issue contained a story about a "poor" woman addicted to cocaine that came into a meeting in South Carolina. She was "convicted of her sins, and as a second definite work was sanctified, and has obeyed God confessing Christ in baptism."[113]

Even ministers who visited the mission confessed their own indiscretions. A Baptist preacher in San Francisco, for example, traveled to Los Angeles to experience the modern Pentecost. He confessed his wrongdoings and asked for forgiveness from God. Observers stated, "He gave up his tobacco and seemed wonderfully happy in the Lord."[114] Although the man was a preacher, the manifestation of God was so powerful at the revival that even he could no longer hide his transgressions. Not all revival participants sought "deliverance," however. Many came simply for the conversion experience and salvation.[115]

Meeting attendees included people from various Christian denominations, including Catholics and Jews. G. A. Cook reported in *The Apostolic Faith* that one woman, a Free Methodist, was "baptized" with the Holy Ghost. This profoundly affected her household. He wrote, "She began to sing at home in tongues, and her husband got under such conviction he could scarcely do his work, and in a few days came to the altar and was beautifully saved."[116] Her experience was not dissimilar from other women who attended the meetings without their husbands.

Often, husbands would follow, either to investigate their wives' involvement or because of their own "convictions." This also led to an increase of membership and participation at the mission. Still, *The Apostolic Faith* constantly printed reports of people seeking salvation, justification and sanctification.[117]

Sister Ladd headed a mission in Des Moines, Iowa, where she noted many people receiving "the Pentecost and Bible evidence." At her mission, many were "saved and sanctified."[118] At another meeting, in January 1907, a young woman received salvation who "had been under deep conviction for several days. When once surrendered, she seemed to sweep with one bound from the altar of burnt offering into the most holy place, from the cross to the Pentecostal chamber, sealed with the Bible evidence."[119] Women not only played a significant role in helping others experience salvation, justification, and sanctification, but also were active participants, often experiencing and receiving miracles such as "divine healing."[120]

Healing

Charles Fox Parham taught "Divine healing" to his students, and William J. Seymour fully accepted the notion, and healing became a significant characteristic of the revival. Stories of people either being healed or having the ability to heal through prayer or the "laying on of hands," almost outnumbered stories of people experiencing salvation, justification, and sanctification. The first issue of *The Apostolic Faith* noted many people healed from defective sight, and that their ability was "completely restored." It also stated, "The deaf have had their hearing restored."[121] One man even came to a meeting seeking healing of deafness. God restored his eyesight as well.[122] The newspaper reported many examples of healings: "Soon after we arrived, a lady sick with dropsy came to the meeting. She got out of bed to come; had been sick a long time.... She immediately shouted that she was healed. I felt the healing power flow into her body.... She walked down town and told her neighbors about the wonderful things the Lord had done for her."[123] Many people were cured of other infectious diseases. In Los Angeles, a Mrs. S. P. Knapp who suffered from tuberculosis received "divine healing" on 12 August 1906.[124] Another woman received healing for consumption when she had lost all but part of one of her lungs.[125] Several other people were "divinely healed" of similar ailments.[126]

Men also received healing. Tom Anderson, for example, was a member of the church living in Los Angeles during the revival. He testified about being cured of an illness that had lasted approximately six and a half years. He said that doctors had failed to heal him, but when he attended the revival meetings, God cured him immediately. Anderson's testimony was not unlike that of others, regardless of whether they were regular members.[127]

Mrs. J. Kring was "healed" from having cancer in her lungs on 8 August 1906. Her doctor had told her she had no hope, and diagnosed her condition as terminal. Her testimony read, "One lung was entirely closed up. When she was prayed for, the Lord immediately touched her body and healed her."[128] Kring was so overwhelmed with joy that she spent the rest of the evening shouting as if she had never been ill. Another woman had been suffering from hemorrhages in her lungs for many years. Before she came to the revival, she had experienced seven consecutive hemorrhages. In fact, the woman was too ill to attend the revival, but members there prayed for her. She immediately was healed, and finally left her bed.[129] Margie Downing also experienced "divine healing." Diagnosed with cancer, the doctors told her that they could not help her. Her physicians told her that she could expect to die at any time. Her entire abdominal parts were "a mass with cancer. The hole eaten by the cancer was deep enough to hold a quart of water."[130] Miraculously the hole filled up with new flesh. Conditions such as lung cancer, tuberculosis, and consumption were ailments that many were "cured" of. Other ailments included metal illness, bone disorders, hernias, as well as general sickness.[131]

A woman in San Pedro, California, was very ill, and suffered from great physical pain. She was almost unconscious and appeared nearly dead. *The Apostolic Faith* reported that she was "almost insane." Women laid hands on her, while others prayed, and she was able to cook dinner the same day.[132] In Whittier, California, physicians considered another woman helplessly ill. She suffered for eighteen years and had been bedridden for fourteen of them. Someone "laid hands" on her body as others prayed for her, and her ailment dissipated.[133]

E. Thomas complained of a terrible sprain that caused her bones to realign, which gave her great pain and discomfort. She attended a prayer meeting and was healed. God also "divinely healed" people of epilepsy, which sometimes, was attributed to demon possession, and also happened to a woman who suffered from seizures. Another woman's son was "divinely healed" from them. People even received cures for emotional instability. During the revival, many participants blamed the devil for attacking one's physical, emotional, or metal health. In the above two cases, the women were prayed for and "demons" were "cast out" of them, which resulted in their recovery.[134]

Laypeople actively participated in the healing process of others. Often, their role was to pray, and to "lay hands" on the sick, who miraculously were "healed" because of the "power" they received from the Holy Spirit. As May Evans wrote, Florence Crawford and a Sister Junk witnessed the healing "power" of God when He revealed to them that He had come to heal her. She believed she "felt the healing work of Jesus."[135] Similarly, one Sister Seeley from Los Angeles, who suffered from rupture (hernia) for over eight years and was completely dependent on medication, sought "divine healing" at the Azusa Street Mission. While Seymour prayed, Seeley "felt a thrill of joy through her being"[136] From that time, she no longer needed to take her medication, and felt perfectly healed.[137]

After visiting the Azusa Street Mission, a man named Joseph Robbins returned to Columbus, Ohio, and started a ministry of healing. In May 1907, he wrote that the Lord gave him "healing" power, and "laid hands" on two people at a meeting of his own. He said he had only needed to thank God, and the people had instantly became healed. He also explained that many people received "divine healing" under his leadership.[138]

Another aspect of "divine healing" involved "blessed" handkerchiefs. Sometimes called prayer cloths, people prayed for and "blessed" them, then sent them to people in need. One woman received a handkerchief from her ill brother who lived across the country. He asked her to have it blessed as they did in the Bible. She brought it to the Apostolic Faith Mission and asked the Lord to reveal whom to give it for prayer. She said the Lord led her to a woman named Sallie Trainor, who took the handkerchief upstairs, knelt down, and prayed. When the Spirit "came upon her" she received "power" and prayed in tongues. She then kissed the cloth "three times as the Spirit seemed to lead her."[139] The woman sent the handkerchief back to her brother who was miraculously healed.[140]

Healing served as a catalyst of the revival and of the modern Pentecostal movement in general. Many Pentecostals, as well as other Christian believers, consider "divine healing" a "spiritual gift."[141] Laypeople actively participated in healing practices including "the laying on of hands" and prayer. While women often were responsible for helping other women, they assisted in helping men receive "divine" healing. Likewise, men prayed for women. Not only did members of the laity participate in healing and salvation ceremonies, but they played a major role in the practice of "speaking in tongues" during the revival.[142]

Speaking in Tongues

Many Pentecostal denominations debate "speaking in tongues" as requisite for salvation. Seymour rejected this notion, and disagreed that it was the *initial* evidence of receiving the "baptism" of the Holy Spirit. Yet he believed that anyone could "speak in tongues" if they had faith, and asked the Lord for that "gift." The entire concept of "speaking in tongues" is quite complicated, because there are many ways that it can be done. People at the mission mostly spoke in languages known to men, just as the disciples did on the Day of Pentecost. For example, a person who never spoke Italian may suddenly be able to communicate in that language. This was one of the most common ways people during the Azusa Street Revival utilized the "gift of tongues," making it easy for them to communicate with the immigrant communities of Los Angeles in addition to traveling abroad. Because so many people came to the mission from different countries, speaking all languages, someone usually translated the "tongue," proving its validity.[143]

Other forms of "speaking in tongues," however, may not be interpreted and are considered "heavenly" language, or the language of angels. That occurs when one is praying in a language that he or she may not even understand. They may understand its function—praying to God in a language only He knows, so that the devil may not hinder one's prayer. For every believer, each tongue is different. It is also possible for several people to speak in tongues that sound similar, but there is no real way of knowing whether they are saying the same thing. The only time there is a translation is when either someone within the congregation or the preacher himself offers a prophetic message in tongues. If it is a true prophecy—a message from God, it will be interpreted into a language that everyone understands. If it is not, no interpretation is given.[144]

Seymour noted that all of "God's children" could pray and ask for a Holy Spirit "outpouring" if they had faith. He believed that people underwent a "cleansing" process of justification and sanctification, then received the "gift" of the Holy Spirit and spoke in unknown languages, as the Holy Spirit led them. He explained that the Apostolic Faith Mission members did not base their entire faith on the premise of "speaking in tongues," but that it was merely one sign of being "baptized" with the Holy Spirit. Furthermore, according to Seymour, one knew when one received the Holy Spirit because he or she also received "wisdom, power, truth, holiness."[145] Seymour stressed that "speaking in tongues" did not necessarily show outward profession of what a person possessed on the inside but stressed the importance of knowledge and "power." Still, Seymour believed that people, including himself should pray for the ability to "speak in tongues" as an essential characteristic of being equipped for ministry.[146]

The Apostolic Faith reported "speaking in tongues" more than any other spiritual gift. One woman, a Miss Tuthill, who spoke Italian, met a man considered a skeptic. Though he was unaware of the language she was speaking, Miss Tuthill communicated with him. She approached him, referring to him by his full name, which no one else in town knew except him, and told him about specific incidents that had occurred in his past. She even knew about his current circumstances and spoke with him "until he cried for mercy and fell on his knees seeking God."[147] This type of occurrence was not uncommon for the revival.[148]

People spoke many languages, often addressing the immigrant populations in Los Angeles. Anna Hall visited a Russian church in Los Angeles and addressed the congregation in their native language. Many happily received the message from God, and embraced her with great joy.[149] In Oakland, Sister Leatherman went into the streets to talk about the "gift of tongues." While she spoke, a man in a Turkish fez approached her. He asked her where she had received her language training, and told her she spoke Russian almost as well as natives of the country. Coincidently, he was a well-educated man from a Turkish college in Constantinople. Leatherman responded that she had never received training in Russian, but credited the Holy Ghost for enabling her to communicate in that language. The man interpreted for her. Leatherman's experience reflects those of many. This was one way people understood what languages they spoke, and helped them to understand their "calling," especially when they traveled to foreign missions or even when they met people from other countries at home.[150]

One woman "received" the Chinese language and communicated with many Chinese people around the city. The Apostolic Faith reported that "she speaks to them as she passes them on the street, or as they come into the house and they listen in astonishment and say she is telling them about God."[151] Mrs. Garr also "received" the Chinese and Tibetan languages and spoke them daily.[152] In Pueblo, Colorado, the woman who was leading the local mission "received the baptism of the Holy Ghost" and began to speak Chinese as well. In Minneapolis, Minnesota, a woman "spoke in tongues" and was able to speak many languages. The newspaper stated, "Some understood her when she spoke the Polish and others recognized several sentences spoken in Bohemian. I recognized the Chinese when she spoke that and another recognized the Italian. She sang beautifully in the Norwegian tongue."[153]

People often believed that receiving other languages qualified them not only for communicating with the immigrant communities throughout the city, but also for traveling abroad to spread the message of the modern Pentecostal movement. One man reported that he received the French language without any training. He then saw a vision of France in danger of destruction, and decided to travel there. Believing he was fully equipped for ministry and was confident about communicating with the French, he immediately left for Europe. Participants often used the revival as a tool for equipping themselves to spread the message of God, and to further the movement.[154]

A Swedish woman, Jennie Jacobson, was in America for only two months when she "was given the gift" of the English language. Unlike many others, Jacobson also understood the words she spoke. Later, she became an instrumental force in the foreign missions ministry. One Sister Shiply spoke many languages, including that of the Klamath Indians, and also sang many of their songs. Not only did people translate languages, many "spoke in tongues" that no one deciphered. They knew, however, that these were other languages.[155]

Lillian Keyes was able to "speak in tongues" as well as interpret what she said. Although the specific dialect was uncertain, she still translated the language into English for people to understand.[156] She also received the ability to sing in other languages. Mary P. Perkins also reported that she spoke in different languages. She "spoke in tongues" regardless of whether she was at a meeting or at home.[157] Maggie Geddis of Brooks, California, spoke several languages, and Mrs. James Hebden from Toronto was able to communicate in three different languages, which she considered a "gift" of the Holy Spirit.[158]

In Durham, North Carolina, several African American people received the "gift" of the Holy Spirit, and communicated in other languages. One schoolteacher spoke in other languages for an extended period.[159]

"Speaking in tongues" took on other forms, such as sign language. One woman not only was able to speak in other languages, but also "received" the ability to communicate with the deaf. Even though many deaf and blind were healed, some were not. The Holy Spirit equipped this woman, as well as others, to minister to the deaf. Many people were also prepared to go anywhere to minster to others.[160]

No one saw the vision of spreading the Pentecostal movement more clearly than William J. Seymour. He considered the events at the Apostolic Faith Mission to be encouraging, if not crucial to getting people involved in sharing God's message with others, not only across the country, but also throughout the world. In January 1907, Seymour addressed this topic: "the good tidings has spread into two hemispheres."[161] According to Seymour, "God is working with them, granting signs and wonders to follow the preaching of the full Gospel."[162] He stated that many people worked "in the field," and a large percentage of them worked in foreign countries. This, in turn, motivated people from various parts of the world to travel to Los Angeles to experience the Pentecostal movement, and more importantly, the outpouring of the Holy Spirit.[163] Many also received the "gift of prophecy."[164]

Prophecy

Another important aspect of the Pentecostal movement was the gift of "prophecy." A woman named Sue received this "gift" in 1896 and predicted certain events. She foretold things that happened, such as the Japanese victory over the Russians, even before the war began. She also envisioned an earthquake in San Francisco in 1905, one year before it happened. She stated that an earthquake would hit Los Angeles as well.[165] Mrs. Hebden, in Toronto, also received the "gift" of prophecy. She saw visions in the clouds, and interpreted their messages.[166]

Members of the revival also met people who prophesied to them, and accepted their predictions as messages from God. In May 1907, Seymour and his followers prepared for a camp meeting outside the Los Angeles city limits. Three people shared a vision regarding the location of the meeting. A woman who offered assistance confirmed these visions. While searching for a location, the group stopped at the woman's home to ask if they could drink from the well in her yard. She told them that she was seeking "Pentecost." R. J. Scott decided that the area near her home was the place to hold the meeting. Women bore the responsibility for caring for the children at the meetings. As a result, children received salvation as well as "spiritual gifts" of their own.[167]

Children in the Movement

Seymour defined the "Duty of Children" in his *Doctrine and Disciplines*. He explained that children "are a blessing and a gift from God."[168] Their duties, according to Seymour, not only included obeying God, but the instruction to "seek God early; they should attend to parental teaching; they should obey their parents; they should take care of their parents."[169] Specifically, God's children were to follow God's law in order to receive God's blessings. Another requirement for children included loving one's parents.[170] Children played such an important role during the revival; *The Apostolic Faith* constantly printed their testimonies.[171]

Viola Price, a young African American orphan, experienced Pentecost at the age of eight. She also "spoke in tongues."[172] The November 1906 issue of the newspaper explained, "Little children from eight to twelve stand up on the altar bench and testify to the baptism with the Holy Ghost and speak in tongues. In the children's meetings, little tots get down and seek the Lord."[173] A young girl at the Whittier, California, mission received her "Spirit baptism" during prayer time at a meeting. She also spoke and sang in an unknown language. The girl stated that she would follow the Lord wherever He led her. She said, "Her name was written in heaven and she was sealed unto the day of redemption."[174] This conversion experience gave the girl, as well as other children, much joy to know about receiving salvation. Children often had their own space reserved, and participated in meetings for young people.[175]

At the beginning of the revival, children met separately, which caused problems for the mission, because local law enforcement frequently received complaints about unsupervised children. Still, the revival organizers saw a need to coordinate meetings designed for children only, while their parents attended the adult services. This also assured that children would experience Pentecost without their parents distracting or guiding them. At the camp meeting in May 1907, children attended meetings in a separate tent and controlled their own revival. The leadership assigned some workers "to teach and help them spiritually."[176]

Often, children preached at their own services. A boy named Clayborn led many meetings. In the children's assembly, three young sisters received the Holy Spirit, and spoke many different languages. In addition, numerous children received salvation and sanctification under his leadership. In the children's meetings in Hermon, California, three children were also "baptized" with the Holy Spirit.[177]

A fourteen-year-old girl considered "saved, sanctified and baptized with the Holy Ghost" organized her own revival. One hundred and ninety people received salvation that evening.[178] One twelve-year-old girl also preached in addition to utilizing her "gift" of sign language. Another young boy approached the pulpit, began "speaking in tongues," and delivered a message.

Not just adults, but children too received "divine" healing.[179] One young girl suffered from tuberculosis and walked with crutches. While attending a meeting, she dropped them and played in the yard.[180] Another little girl who had a terrible fever was healed after a group of people "laid hands" on her and prayed. She stated, "Dear Jesus, you have heard all of these people's prayers, now heal me for Jesus' sake."[181] An infant accidentally ingested poison. His mother prayed and the baby was healed.[182] The fact that children also received "spiritual gifts" proved that God truly worked in the lives of those who participated in the revival. Members as well as observers believed that because the children were so innocent, they could not pretend to have this "power," but that God must have revealed Himself through them.[183]

The Movement's Decline

The Azusa Street Revival declined in two stages. The first includes the period ranging from 1906 through 1909, when Clara Lum and Florence Crawford broke from the mission, taking *The Apostolic Faith* with them. Robert Owens notes another period, from 1911 until 1912, as the final phase of the Azusa Street Revival, when Seymour and William S. Durham disagreed on doctrinal issues. Most scholars of Pentecostalism agree that many factors contributed to the demise of the Azusa Street Revival. Most of those reasons were social.[184]

In the beginning, the revival was interracial. It began with mostly African American women and a few Caucasian couples. Soon, people of all racial, national and ethnic backgrounds attended the Azusa Street Mission, including Latinos, Germans, Jews, Russians, Chinese, and Italians. Everyone who attended services at the mission actively participated in spreading Pentecostalism throughout the world, regardless of their heritage. As the mission's leader, William J. Seymour allowed the "Spirit to move" throughout his services, which meant that whomever God chose would deliver the sermon, sing praise and worship songs, play the piano, pray, or prophesy. People also used the mission as a prototype for establishing their own churches and missions. This zeal, however, was short-lived, and the Azusa Street Mission was in trouble by 1909.[185]

Seymour no longer allowed the Holy Spirit to take control of the services. Instead, he organized the meetings, and followed his plan precisely. He also built a throne to preside on, a total departure from the way he typically designed services. In the beginning, Seymour had usually knelt on a large shoebox in deep prayer. He rarely ever strayed from that position unless he was "moved" by the Spirit to preach, lead a corporate prayer, or to prophesy.[186]

Frank Bartleman commented that in 1909 the mission had "become more and more in bondage" and that the meetings had a prescribed order, and that there was no room for the "Spirit" to work.[187] He noted that the revival lost most of its fervor. Bartleman pointed out that the competition between local missions stifled their progress, and he attributed most of these problems to leaders taking control and rejecting the Holy Spirit. According to Bartleman, "there was considerable rejoicing, but in the 'flesh.'"[188] In addition to issues over control, some leaders abandoned Pentecostalism completely.[189]

G. B. Cashwell, one of the Azusa Street ministers, turned away from Pentecostalism and returned to his former Methodist denomination, which had never supported the revival. In fact, most Christian denominations rejected Pentecostal doctrine and the Azusa Street Revival completely. But when many abandoned their churches to join the Apostolic Faith Mission, church leaders had to accept the fact that their members had left.[190]

Some local church leaders felt relieved when people abandoned their churches to attend services at the Apostolic Faith Mission. These leaders viewed the people who participated in the revival as lowbrow, undesirable, working-class folk, and rejected Pentecostalism as a true religion. Christian leaders refused to accept the doctrine of "tongues" and described it as nonsensical. Conversely, Pentecostals considered themselves among the "spiritual elite" because of their "revelation" of "tongues" and their acceptance of the Bible in its entirety. They believed they practiced Christianity the way God intended it, rather than taking certain portions of the religion and applying them in a practical manner. Moreover, some scholars have rejected the events that occurred at the Apostolic Faith Mission as a true revival.[191]

Although he had received some theological training and ordination, illiterate and, according to scholars, nearly blind, Seymour's spiritual education was, unlike that of earlier revival leaders, limited at best. Those surrounding him also had not received formal theological training. He allowed the "Holy Spirit" to choose anyone to deliver a message to his congregation, regardless of race or religious background. The origins of each revival also indicate stark differences.

Many revivals across the country required careful preparation. In Los Angeles, in 1906, for example, many churches entered periods of revival. Meetings were scheduled, and set for specific amounts of time, and published in the local newspaper. Seymour and his followers did not intend to have a revival. While holding meetings at the Asbury home, Seymour had hoped to share his doctrine, and pray with others. The reception of his radical teaching overwhelmed him as well as those few members. They never expected the movement to grow as quickly or as much as it did. The movement lasted, at least initially, for six years without ceasing. At times services ran twenty-four hours a day, every day of the week. Most revivals, at the time lasted for a few hours over the course of a week under strict organization. Yet visitors found something special at the Apostolic Faith Mission, which encouraged them to alter their spiritual beliefs, taking new theologies with them as they traveled throughout the city and beyond. The most profound difference between these religious movements, however, was the multicultural characteristic of the Pentecostal revival.

Racial Tension and Other Social Factors

Mission observers commented on its interracial aspect. *The Apostolic Faith* even published articles discussing the mission's position on race relations. Seymour announced, "No instrument that God can use is rejected on account of color or dress or lack of education. This is why God has so built up this work."[192] This mantra Seymour repeated frequently, reminding his followers of the more important concerns and goals of the revival. This stance directly addressed the social climate of the time. Although some scholars defined the sociopolitical aspects of the First and Second Great Awakenings as revolutionary and central to revival, they have ignored the same characteristics of the Azusa Street Revival.[193]

The Pentecostal movement also contained a unique multilingual characteristic derived from the "Holy Ghost baptism" people received. Participants were equipped with the ability to communicate with members of society generally excluded in other revival movements. As the immigrant community in Los Angeles increased in vast proportions, participants of the Azusa Street Revival met and addressed immigrants in their native languages. This, in turn, influenced the overall reception of the movement. It significantly strengthened and connected relationships between those marginalized by white elites.

Scholars of the Azusa Street Revival have neglected the sociopolitical undercurrents of the time as a contributing factor in the movement's decline. Although Los Angeles today is one of the most diverse cities in the country, the multicultural aspects of the revival are reasonable at best. This, however, did not occur in a vacuum, and the initial participants of the movement lived in an interethnic community with people of other racial, cultural, and national backgrounds. Azusa Street itself was located in a multiracial, multicultural district. The leadership, very much aware of its membership, often commented on diversity. Seymour also said, "We must give God all the glory in this work. We must keep very humble at his feet. He recognizes no flesh, no color, no names. We must not glory in Azusa mission, nor in anything but the Lord Jesus Christ by whom the world is crucified unto us and we unto the world."[194] The mission's principal motivation, according to Seymour, centered on unity of all of God's people. Participants believed that God would soon return for His people, also the most common thread of all of these religious revivals.[195]

Most major revivals include some doctrinal as well as social similarities as the Pentecostal Revival. The primary connection is millennialism, or the period after the Second coming of Christ. During this time, it is believed, Satan will be imprisoned and the earth will be peaceful. After this period, Christ and Satan will battle, culminating in the end of the world. Generally, these revivals incorporated some form of eschatology, predicting the end of the world, which motivated religious involvement.[196]

While the Pentecostal movement differed in many ways from earlier revivals, it did share some race and class characteristics with them. Each movement, to some extent, included African Americans, and therefore, certain elements of West African religious practices. Black revivalists responded to the emotionalism that typified each movement. Each revival provided a doctrinal space for participants to feel great emotion through preaching styles, worship, or divine acts of grace. This element not only appealed to people of African descent, but they felt connected to these movements because they found traces of African religious practices such as trance dancing. This practice, however, manifested most prominently during the Azusa Street Revival.[197]

At the beginning of the twentieth century, African Americans continued to migrate out of the segregated South to places farther north or west. Lynching victimized many African American families. White racism heightened, and white supremacist groups organized across the country. In the North, African Americans confronted new and different forms of racism than they faced in the South. The West, especially California, was still a new territory, and considered a place of opportunity for people of all backgrounds. Los Angeles had a small but significant African American population as well as a growing international population. Though these groups may not have intermingled on a social level, they clearly integrated religiously. People from every racial and ethnic background participated in the revival, which was highly controversial.[198]

Since the mission maintained racial and cultural integration, many white Angelenos were outraged to the point that they mobilized to close it, again by calling the police and filing complaints about the activities held there. The fact that the movement's leader was African American also caused great controversy. White observers of the mission believed that it was unacceptable to have such egalitarian practices as to allow anyone to deliver messages from God. They rejected the idea of African Americans and other groups of people of color having the same authority as whites.[199]

Seymour viewed his mission as a training ground for ministry. Many participants belonged to other churches and were even ordained ministers from other Christian denominations. The majority of participants had some prior affiliation with the Holiness movement. After attending meetings at the Apostolic Faith Mission, many went back to their own churches and established new sets of doctrinal principles, which included "tongues." Some ministers also "converted" to Pentecostalism.

Charles Harrison Mason and Charles Price Jones, for example, were both Baptist ministers, and both were expelled from their church for promoting doctrine similar to Pentecostalism. Together, the two organized the Church of God in Christ (COGIC) in 1897. After meeting

Seymour in 1907, the COGIC became a Pentecostal denomination. Since Mason and Jones disagreed on certain doctrinal issues, Jones formulated his own Pentecostal denomination, the Church of Christ Holiness. Seymour maintained an African American following, while whites eventually broke away from his leadership.[200]

By 1911, the Apostolic Faith Mission had only twelve members, all of whom were African American. There were many small African American Pentecostal churches scattered throughout Los Angeles. Frank Bartleman noted that in 1909 these churches were numerous and at odds with one another. He said, "The work had gotten into a bad condition at the time we returned to Los Angeles. The missions had fought each other almost to a standstill. Little love remained."[201] Competition for members, doctrinal issues, and a breakdown of leadership plagued the Azusa Street Mission and the Pentecostal movement as a whole. Seymour tried stimulating participation by inviting another charismatic leader to the mission.[202]

William Durham traveled from Kentucky to Los Angeles to preach at the Apostolic Faith mission. Durham had visited the mission earlier, in March 1907, when he received his Spirit "baptism." Durham supported Seymour's premise that "speaking in tongues" was not the initial evidence of a Holy Spirit "baptism." Unlike Seymour, Durham rejected the doctrine of sanctification as a second work of grace, and supported the older tradition that believers received everything they needed when Jesus Christ died at Calvary. During Durham's visit to Azusa, Seymour attended preaching engagements across the country. He instructed his followers to accept Durham's preaching as "Divine revelation." Durham's teachings reinvigorated the movement and people began attending meetings again. Upon receiving word of Durham's teachings, Seymour returned to Los Angeles and locked Durham out. Many people followed Durham and abandoned Seymour once again.[203]

No single factor attributed to the demise of the Azusa Street Revival. As Frank Bartleman noted, at the beginning, the Holy Spirit controlled the revival. When people began vying for power, the movement suffered. While many scholars reject the idea of the Azusa Street Revival as the Third Great Awakening, they also fail to consider the movement's lasting effects. Most Pentecostal denominations today trace their roots to Azusa Street, and credit Seymour as instrumental in catapulting the movement. Although the modern Pentecostal movement quickly lost momentum, it is the largest and fastest growing denomination today.

The Church of God in Christ remains the largest African American Christian denomination, while the Assemblies of God outnumbers predominately white Christian denominations.[204]

If anything, the Azusa Street Revival captured the imagination of what Los Angeles was supposed to be—the multiracial and multicultural characteristics seemed to attract several local working-class African Americans while giving them hope for a better life beyond what they experienced in Los Angeles. The Revival itself served as a safe space for working-class black people who had been marginalized not only by white Angelenos, but by the upper- and middle-class black communities as well. At the same time, it gave poor black women and men the opportunity to enhance their lives in ways that the upper classes were unable. The revival embodied many of the same ideas that middle-class reformers attempted, but it was able to reach a much broader audience that was seemingly more receptive.

6
Booker T. Washington Goes West

In 1895, Booker T. Washington, the nation's foremost African American spokesman, delivered his now infamous "Atlanta Exposition" address, in which he declared, "In all things that are purely social we can be as separate as the five fingers, yet one as the hand in all things essential to mutual progress."[1] At a meeting that largely united elite farmers, black and white, as well as local and national political leaders, Washington unintentionally aided in reversing the course of post-emancipation progress for the majority of African Americans. Washington believed African Americans did not have to depend on the benevolence of whites to uplift the race onto an equal plane, but that hard work would be rewarded, thereby allowing African Americans to prove themselves to the white community. The following year, the Supreme Court's landmark *Plessy v. Ferguson* case affirmed Washington's position. Justice Brown noted, "If the two races are to meet on terms of social equality, it must be the result of natural affinities, a mutual appreciation of each other's merits and a voluntary consent of individuals."[2] These two events only fanned the flames of southern racism while ushering in the most hostile conditions for African Americans that would last well into the 1960s.

While Booker T. Washington cannot be blamed for legalized segregation in United States history, his legacy is inextricably linked to it. This is often the framework for which many students of African American history understand his complicated relationship with the African American community at the beginning of the twentieth century. Less known about Washington is the extent to which he influenced African Americans in all regions of the country. While historians of Los Angeles underscore the contribution of W. E. B. Du Bois to black Los Angeles, they overlook the influence Washington had on the community. For over a decade, he maintained relationships with some of the community leaders until he died in 1915. Although they may not have entirely agreed with Washington, the black community in Los Angeles very seriously considered his advice to accumulate wealth by owning their own property and businesses. They combined his ideas at the beginning of the twentieth century with those of other national leaders such as Du Bois and Marcus Garvey, and local leaders like Charlotta Bass, who had much stronger political aspirations for black people. This chapter examines Booker T. Washington's interactions with African Americans in the West, while highlighting the relationship he maintained with black Angelenos at the beginning of the twentieth century.

Booker T. Washington traveled to the western states at least three times at the beginning of the twentieth century. His first visit, beginning on 1 January 1903, was a tour of California that lasted two weeks. After declining invitations for almost an entire decade, Washington would return to the golden state in 1914, and visit several other states in the West, just one year before his death. Though he did not write about the 1903 trip himself, his (white) speechwriter, Max Bennett Thrasher, accompanied him, and detailed their experience. Thrasher noted that while in California Washington "made twenty-seven formal addresses, besides speaking informally a number of times at dinners, banquets, and receptions."[3] Washington spoke to approximately 24,000 people during his visit.

Washington's tour of California met several purposes. First, he raised over $8,000 for his Tuskegee Institute while promoting the school across the state. Second, he visited several prominent friends, including educators such as Leland Stanford, for whom Stanford University was named; William Thomas Reid, a former president of the University of California; and Phoebe Apperson Hearst, the first female member of the board of regents for the University of California and widow of state senator George Hearst. Washington also met with political leaders such as Governor George Pardee and his wife, Helen, and lunched with Lucretia Garfield, the widow of President James Garfield. He spent an afternoon with abolitionist John Brown's daughter, Ruth. Washington also visited with some of the most wealthy and influential black Angelenos such as Robert C. Owens (grandson of the great philanthropist Biddy Mason) and his wife, Anna. Washington toured the entire state, from San Diego to Sacramento.[4]

In addition to Stanford and Berkeley, Washington visited several educational institutions, such as Pomona College, the San Francisco State Normal School, Mrs. Mills College for Young Ladies in Oakland, the Pacific Theological Seminary, and the Belmont (preparatory) School. He visited several churches throughout the state, including the Methodist churches in Stockton, Ontario, and Pasadena, a Presbyterian church in Sacramento, Starr King Zion African Methodist Episcopal (AME) church in San Francisco, and the First Congregational churches of Los Angeles, Oakland, and San Francisco. This trip also included speeches at several clubs and organizations.[5]

Washington's first engagement in Los Angeles was at a gathering for the Friday Morning Club, one of the most influential women's clubs in the city. Over one thousand women greeted him with a standing ovation, and met him with a "Chautauqua salute of waving handkerchiefs."[6] He spoke to the State Teacher's Association later that afternoon. Thrasher estimated that between three and four thousand people crowded into Hazard's Pavilion for this event. The next day, Washington departed for Pomona and Ontario, and later returned to Los Angeles, where several wealthy black Angelenos met him. He then addressed over three thousand at the Simpson's Pavilion. Thrasher noted that although this was an event for African Americans, several white people could be seen throughout the audience.[7]

While in Los Angeles, Robert C. Owens arranged a meeting for several prominent African Americans to meet Mr. Washington and to raise money for Tuskegee Institute. According to Thrasher, "Mr. Owens, although still a young man, is the owner of much valuable property in Los Angeles, including a business block on Spring Street, the principal business street of the city, in which there are three fine stores."[8] Known as the most influential African American in Los Angeles at the time, Owens was sure to nurture his friendship with Washington for the next decade. Owens helped financially support Tuskegee Institute, and he relied on Washington to help negotiate ways to ease racial tensions in Los Angeles.[9]

In all, Washington's first visit to the West was extremely successful. Though most of his time was spent giving speeches, he was able to see most of California, and reconnect with some familiar friends. More important for him was the network he built that would extend from Tuskegee, Alabama, to the West Coast. Thrasher noted one final observation of Washington's about this visit. He said that he had felt surprise and pleasure "to find colored people of the Pacific coast, as a general thing, so prosperous, so intelligent, and so well informed not only as to matters pertaining to the race in the country as a whole, but particularly as regarding the history and work of Tuskegee."[10] While it would be another decade before Washington would visit again, he continued to communicate with African Americans from California as well as other western states until he could return to the region.

Table 6.1 The African American population in the West, 1910

State or Territory	State Total	County with the Largest Black Population	County Total	Percentage
Ariz.	2,009	Cochise	478	23.79%
Calif.	21,645	Los Angeles	9,424	43.53%
Colo.	11,453	Denver	5,426	47.37%
Idaho	651	Ada	168	25.8%
Kans.	54,030	Wyandotte	11,172	20.67%
Mont.	1,834	Lewis & Clark	430	23.44%
N.D.	617	Cass	120	19.44%
Neb.	7,689	Douglas	5,208	67.73%
N.M.	1,628	Bernalillo	311	19.1%
Nev.	513	Washoe	115	22.41%
Okla.	137,612	Muskogee	16,454	11.95%
Ore.	1,492	Multnomah	1,081	72.45%
S.D.	817	Lawrence	177	21.66%
Tex.	690,049	Harris	30,950	4.49%
Utah	1,144	Salt Lake	827	72.29%
Wash.	6,058	King	2,487	41.05%
Wyo.	2,235	Laramie	1,607	71.9%
Total	941,476		86,435	9.18%

Source: University of Virginia Geospatial and Statistical Data Center

On his second visit to the West in 1913, Washington's tour included Tacoma, Seattle, and Yakima, Washington, in addition to Montana, South Dakota, Salt Lake City, Utah, and Portland, Oregon. He did not believe there were enough black people in Helena, Montana, and North Dakota to accomplish solidarity. Table 6.1 represents counties with the largest black populations that were located in the west in 1910, just three years before, which are much smaller than those in southern and eastern cities. When he visited in March 1913, he noticed that black farmers faced competition from simple farming innovations. He wrote, "Irrigation is something strange to the colored man, and this makes me question whether colored people will ever settle in this part of the world in large numbers."[11]As opposed to farmers in the South, who relied on rain, farmers in the West relied heavily on irrigation, something Washington believed black farmers could not do. Farming was not the only occupation that presented challenges for black workers.

Washington noted that black workers were struggling for financial freedom, and that most black men worked as porters, either in banks or stores, or worked the elevators in the local hotels. Washington referred to black male workers as "the 'odd job man,' and the white people, it seems, do not expect him to occupy any other position."[12] Washington recognized the Pullman services as the most respected form of employment, and that white male workers had not broken into that position. He also noted that the trade unions excluded African Americans, thereby making it difficult for them to find work in skilled labor positions.[13] African American workers were much more economically secure in the West—something Washington had to admit was quite impressive.

African American hod carriers were paid a wage ranging from five to six dollars per day, which was much higher than a day laborer, or even a hotel worker in the South or East. Washington found this relative pay to be true of all positions, skilled and unskilled, in the West. These wages allowed many African Americans in the West to buy property, own homes, and start businesses, all of which were things encouraged by Washington. But the problem, in Helena, at least, was the small population to support such businesses. Washington noted, however, that black people were beginning to see that they needed to provide financial security to pass down to their children, and as a result, many had modest savings.[14] He identified similar circumstances in North Dakota.

To some extent, black and white children had the same educational opportunity, which led Washington to conclude that they faced very little discrimination—that is, until they reached high school. He felt that at that level black students were merely tolerated, rather than encouraged to succeed. He explained, "In a word, the Negro children have the same opportunity to get education here that the white children have, but the difficulties begin to present themselves when the Negro seeks an opportunity to use the education which the State has given him."[15] This resulted in higher dropout rates for black students, and in turn, low-wage jobs. These working-class conditions did not affect the community's moral compass.[16]

An active church life worked to keep people grounded. Washington noted that wherever an African American community of fifty to one hundred was to be found, one could locate a diverse body of small congregations. He found that the African Methodist Episcopal church was one of the largest in the area, and that the western AME church had some of the largest and most impressive buildings he had seen. But because of the small populations and memberships these churches served, it was challenging for the ministers to support themselves. Socially, church members, according to Washington, were lonely and longed for the larger congregations and camp meetings and other gatherings they had experienced in the South. Not only did the small population make religious life difficult for black westerners, they also faced discrimination in every social facet of larger cities such as restaurants, saloons, and hotels. But African Americans in the West enjoyed one major advantage that southern blacks did not—suffrage.[17]

While most African Americans in the southern states were being kept out of the voting booths, and facing horrific consequences for attempting to exercise their right to vote, African American men and women in most western states were not. As Washington noted, black westerners voted without any barriers, which "seemed to be about the only thing he can do unhindered and untrammeled."[18] Though black people could vote, Washington was skeptical about whether their political patronage could affect their circumstances. He was unconvinced that they would overcome discrimination, even with the vote. But this also made him rethink some of his hypotheses about black people in the West, namely, that the South was the best place in the country for African Americans.[19] As he continued his travels, he pondered whether this was true.

In a letter to the editor of the *New York Age*, Washington wrote, "As one travels still further in the direction of the Pacific Coast, conditions among our people change, sometimes for the better, sometimes for the worse, but on the whole, for the better."[20] In Spokane, Washington, he noted that white people respected African Americans and held them in higher regard than whites did in the South. He believed that the farther west he traveled, the more successful African Americans were. He noted more black homesteads and land ownership, black farmers cultivating soil successfully, and saw that white women's clubs often invited African American women to attend some of their events. Forty miles from North Yakima, Washington, he found an all-black colony. Washington noted that black farmers were doing well, and while they were successful economically, they did miss their churches and lodges from back home. Still, Washington could not help but acknowledge better race relations in the West.[21]

Washington noted better race relations in Seattle and Tacoma, Washington. King County, where these cities are located, had the largest black population in the state (2,487 in 1910), it was no wonder that

Washington found several "ambitious and successful" people.[22] While he noted that many African Americans in these cities became doctors, lawyers, and preachers, Washington was concerned that the community had not made more significant inroads in education. African Americans had been excluded from the trades, and from teaching in the common schools. Yet, according to Washington, southern white migrants to the region were exceedingly helpful and supportive of black migrants. He, like Du Bois, noted the fierce competition for low-level jobs from the Japanese immigrant community, whom Washington believed, dominated the hotel industry. This, in turn, created more job competition for black porters, waiters, and servants.[23]

Given the black population in these cities, Washington believed African Americans had access to good churches and black business leagues, making Seattle and Tacoma much better for technical and industrial training, should it become available. Most of this was attributed to the high degree of racial tolerance as Washington saw it. He said that Seattle, "where there is a large group of colored people, seems to harbor less prejudice than any city that I have been in," and that in Tacoma, there was "practically no racial discrimination."[24]

Washington may have been most impressed by his visit to Salt Lake City, Utah. He stayed for two days with the Mormons, and fully enjoyed this visit. He felt as though the Mormon community and culture would be helpful for African Americans, noting that "they have made the desert blossom a rose."[25] He also noted, "Wherever one finds a Mormon colony, there he finds evidence of hard work and wealth," both of which were clearly of extreme importance to Washington.[26]

It is clear that Washington identified similarities with the African American community. First, he acknowledged that Mormons endured persecution from the formation of their church. Yet he concluded that they became more determined in spite of that persecution. He also believed that Mormons had been misrepresented and therefore misunderstood, but if "outsiders" interacted with them, they could better understand and get along with them.[27]

Washington was most impressed with the Mormon schools, and was even flattered to learn that they had adopted methods from Hampton and Tuskegee. He wrote, "I was nearly taken off my feet when I went into a class in the university and the teacher showed me a large piece of pasteboard, with the pictures of our students at Tuskegee at work in the various industrial departments. They said they were taking this as their model."[28] Washington thought that African Americans could learn gymnastics from the Mormons, and encourage young people to do it. He also noted the African American community living in Salt Lake City, but was much less impressed with how organized they were.[29]

When Booker T. Washington visited Utah, the approximately one thousand African Americans in Salt Lake City made up the majority of the state's black population. While he thought they were exceptionally intelligent people (especially the women), African Americans in Salt Lake City, according to Washington, had no organizations to promote business and industry. He blamed this on their spending money on alcohol and gambling. Washington saw this as a weakness, and condemning these vices was a major part of his platform. This community, however, was not without businessmen who were successful and wealthy. They were sure to give Washington a large dose of hospitality.[30]

In addition to socializing with members of this African American community, Washington also spent time with black Mormons. They reported to him that the church treated them very well, and that they were quite content. He noted that he found no evidence of polygamy, which he had expected to see in the Mormon colony. He explained, "It seems to have been the custom in the old days that a man could not take a second or third or fourth wife without the consent of his first wife, and I was told that no colored woman in Utah would ever give consent for her husband to take a second wife."[31] Washington did not wish to focus on whether the Mormons practiced polygamy. Rather, he was interested in the ways in which Mormons, black and white, accumulated wealth.

Washington met with the leader of the black Mormons, an 82-year-old man who came to Salt Lake City in "the early days."[32] Washington referred to him as a kind of "colored Brigham Young," who had a farm worth $25,000.[33] He believed this man's success was inherent to Mormon culture and ideology. While they focused first on owning and cultivating the land, Mormons secured some wealth before extrapolating the gold, silver, and copper from it. As a result, Washington observed, Mormons were very wealthy.[34]

Washington also met one of Joseph Smith's daughters. He noted that she was one of forty-nine children. Washington was also careful in pointing out that he was not making a comment about polygamy, but simply wanted to give his impression. He was sincerely pleased about meeting a child of Smith's. He later underscored that he found no evidence of polygamy in the Mormon colony in a separate letter. After Utah, Washington returned to the Pacific Northwest.[35]

One thing that impressed Booker T. Washington about the West was the number of transplanted white southerners he met in Washington and Oregon. He referred to them as some of the most liberal white people, commenting, "Most of these people seem to have left the South because they felt that they were cramped and hampered there in too many ways in bringing up their families."[36] At the same time, according to Washington, African Americans were just as liberal. This, he determined was exhibited by their generosity. At one dinner party, for example, he collected seventy-five dollars for Tuskegee Institute.[37] But Washington was not unconvinced that the African Americans of the Pacific Northwest would have success in maintaining cohesive communities.

Washington noted that African Americans in Alabama outnumbered the entire population of black and white Oregonians. He observed a number of professional African Americans in Oregon, and that several were quite successful. He even noted a black lawyer in Portland who was a graduate of Tuskegee. But in spite of these successes, Washington believed that African Americans were not taking advantage of the educational system in the Pacific Northwest. This, he believed, was especially true in higher education.[38]

Washington noted a severely small number of black students at either agricultural or mechanical colleges, or traditional colleges and universities. He counted only nine African American graduates from the Oregon high schools, and zero black college graduates in Washington. In Utah, he said only three African Americans had graduated from secondary school, while the colleges and universities had no black graduates. While he clearly saw this as a failure of the community, he also believed it to be a place of opportunity for black people, and for Tuskegee.[39]

Without the proper education, people could not secure the kinds of labor that would allow them to take care of their own households. Washington noted a better life for skilled African American workers in Portland. Yet there was little organizational help or recognition. He said, "Here the labor union is not strong and the policy of the Chamber of Commerce and other organizations is not to recognize the unions."[40] He believed instead that African American farmers were in the best economic position, not having to rely on organized labor. To Washington, black farmers in Oregon were extremely prosperous.[41] Those who were not, he believed, were isolated and had a much harder time.

Washington could not overlook that some Oregonians were quite lonely. One woman from the town Roseburg wrote to Booker T. Washington and described how the local African American population was so small that most blacks felt uncomfortable going into the city's many public places without other African Americans. She also believed that there was an opportunity for educated African Americans in her city, but those who were uneducated typically could not make ends meet, so they either left town or engaged in some form of illegal activity, which resulted in their going to jail.[42]

Overall, Washington believed that African Americans came into contact with white people in very negative ways. He noted that black people were hired to work in the numerous social clubs to which white people belonged, therefore only interacting with them as servants and subordinates. He saw white people as being of little to no moral character, frequenting saloons and clubs. As a result, he thought that African Americans would imitate white people by engaging in drinking, smoking, and gambling. While he noted that many wealthy African Americans owned and operated saloons, he felt that it was at the expense of African American culture and character. He said, "It is unfortunate that so large a population of our people are engaged in waiting upon somebody else instead of producing something out of the natural resources of the land."[43] This was most troubling for Washington, since it ran counter to his belief that black people should focus on accumulating wealth and capital.

Booker T. Washington did not have a good impression of the Pacific Northwest. Since he had always lived in the South, he used that experience as a model for the ways in which he viewed Oregon and Washington. Southern black farmers, according to Washington, owned their land, and usually had significant acreage. To him, African Americans on the Pacific Coast were less concerned about securing land and cultivating crops, and more interested in appearing wealthy by wearing fancy clothes even though they were waiters and servants. Of his trip to Washington and Oregon, he concluded that African Americans lived better lives in the South. He stated, "I am more convinced than ever that the Negro in the South is doing better than any group of colored people that I have found in this part of the world, and I am still further convinced that the Negro in the South has a better future than in any part of the world that I have yet visited."[44] While Washington's conclusions about the West differed from those of Du Bois, he did maintain connections with those well-to-do black Angelenos, and they were staunch supporters of him in return.

Western African Americans called on Booker T. Washington to help settle racial issues in the region. In September 1914, Nettie J. Asburry, corresponding secretary of the Tacoma, Washington, NAACP, wrote to Washington, requesting that he intervene regarding the discriminatory policies at the federal building in her state. As part of a national campaign to eliminate segregation, Asburry and others sought to desegregate workers employed in the building. Asburry had noted Washington's observations about racism against the Japanese in California, and admonished him to aid the African American community. She asked, "Don't you think it is about time you lifted your voice in defense of the American Negro?"[45] She added that Tacoma's African Americans loved and supported Washington for his achievements, but stressed that they could offer more substantial respect and adoration if only he would take a more aggressive stand against racism for the black community at large.[46] But they were supportive, nonetheless. He made his second visit to Los Angeles earlier that year.

On 14 March 1914, the Los Angeles African American newspaper, the *California Eagle*, documented Washington's speech at the First Methodist Episcopal Church. The Reverend John D. Gordon, pastor of the Tabernacle Baptist Church, introduced him. The paper noted, "The educator's native wit, vibrant booming voice, and clear logic made him popular with the audiences."[47] Washington's speech addressed the state of the African American community, and cited several statistics such as population demographics, property ownership and wealth accumulation, and education. He also lectured about the treatment of black people in Brazil, likening race relations there to the treatment of Native Americans by white people in Oklahoma.[48] The society section of the paper also announced that the black women's Sojourner Truth Club hosted Washington. The paper also published a poem by Eva Carter Buckner entitled, "The Man Behind His Race." She wrote, "He must rise at early morning, sit up late at night, count and plan, save and spend to make things come out right. So we think so unselfish is deserving of this space—This brave, noble-minded leader—the man behind his race."[49] The *Eagle* celebrated Washington's visit in other ways as well.

One article in the 14 March edition of the paper touted Washington's leadership while comparing him to others. The paper said, "Within the past few months, Los Angeles has been visited by four of the greatest Afro-American scholars of this age—Du Bois, Vernon, Miller, but the greatest among them came Booker T. Washington."[50] The article described Washington as a man of integrity, and encouraged black

Angelenos to build a Tuskegee or publish their own magazine like *The Crisis*. Whatever they chose, the paper pleaded, do something to advance the race.[51] The newspaper continued its support of Washington through the end of his life.

While the majority of the coverage on Washington was positive, there were some skeptical pieces published, questioning whether his plan for African Americans would succeed. For the most part, however, the *California Eagle* supported Washington, and encouraged the community to follow suit. On 21 March 1915, an article entitled "The Man of the Hour" suggested that Washington was fulfilling "God's will" and that his life's mission was to show African Americans how they could become successful. Many city leaders also supported Washington, and treated him as royalty when he visited. Churches, for example, canceled Sunday evening services so everyone could attend one of Washington's lectures.[52] Between 1914 and 1915, the *California Eagle* printed several stories about Booker T. Washington, clearly emphasizing the paper's and the community's support. Since the *Los Angeles Times* also had a history of supporting Washington (since 1895), some prominent black Angelenos called on him to help repair the black community's image with the mainstream publication.

On 9 June 1914, attorney Hugh Ellwood Macbeth wrote to Booker T. Washington to ask for help in establishing a weekly black column in the local *Los Angeles Times*. In March, Washington met with Macbeth, Robert C. Owens, and Willis Oliver Tyler in Los Angeles, and suggested they "engage the attention of white daily newspapers"[53] in order to highlight the achievements of the black community, which would in turn, earn the respect of the larger white community. Upon Washington's departure, Macbeth began working on this endeavor through the end of May, when Harrison Gray Otis, owner and editor of the *Los Angeles Times*, granted him a meeting. While Otis was receptive to the idea, Macbeth thought it prudent for Washington to send him a letter of thanks.[54] Within a few weeks, Washington sent his first correspondence to Otis.

In a letter dated 14 July 1914, Washington emphasized the significance of highlighting black achievement in the *Los Angeles Times*, and thanked Otis for his warm reception of the idea. Speaking on behalf of the black community, Washington acknowledged, "The colored people of Los Angeles are most grateful"[55] to Otis and his newspaper. On 18 July, Otis retorted that he was "willing to print news and facts, not essays, 'preachments' or controversies, nor mere 'unconsidered trifles.'"[56] Only on these conditions, Otis underscored, would he print an African American column in his paper. As humbly as Washington and Macbeth approached Otis, his reply was nothing less than disgruntled. He warned Washington about pulling the column if he was disparaged in any way, and complained that the black community had prejudged him unfairly, and believed he was a "champion of liberty, law, and the freedom of both races."[57] In his postscript, Otis explained, "I will try the experiment because I promised to do so, but I will not be treated with suspicion, indignity, or distrust by anybody, white or black, who may seek to 'break into' the columns of the Los Angeles Times."[58] While Otis directed his frustration with the African American community at Washington, black Angelenos nevertheless agreed to the terms.

Washington relayed the Otis message to Macbeth, who was representing the black community in this transaction. After being forwarded the letter, Macbeth wrote to Washington to assure him that everyone was in agreement about the content of the new African American column in the *Times*. While Macbeth may have seen Otis's concerns as contrived, he agreed to the extent that black Angelenos would gain nothing from complaining about their hardships. This was the crux of Washington's idea to establish the column. Since several black Angelenos firmly supported Booker T. Washington, they trusted in his belief that black people must earn the respect of whites, and that they could only do so by committing to earnest, self-sufficient work. Only the endeavors of African Americans whose agendas aligned with these would be highlighted in the black column of the *Times*. Otherwise, African Americans would be referenced only in the various crime sections of the paper.[59]

Between 1881 and 1914, African Americans mostly appeared in negative stories in the *Times*, and were typically portrayed as violent, drunks, prostitutes, and gamblers. With the exception of the one hundredth anniversary of Abraham Lincoln's birth, most news coverage only disparaged the black community. Yet, on 12 February 1909, the newspaper published a series of stories about the African American community that were also written by black Angelenos. Kate Bradley-Stovall, for example, wrote an essay entitled, "The Negro Woman in Los Angeles and Vicinity—Some Notable Characters" that emphasized the important role of black women not only in their own community, but throughout the entire city of Los Angeles. Her full-page story considered the history of black women starting with Biddy Mason. She also focused on several business, church, and clubwomen who worked in various ways to uplift the race.[60]

Another section of the day's edition featured a story about black achievement and wealth accumulation in Los Angeles. This story, "Negroes Who Have Won a Place of Fortune in Los Angeles and Pasadena" emphasized the elite and middle-class lives of black business owners. This article included several pictures of the Craftsman and Victorian-style homes. The story read: "to show that the colored race has demonstrated business ability with the opportunities afforded in the Land of Sunshine, The *Times* mentions some of the negroes of Los Angeles and vicinity who have accumulated property and built up businesses."[61] The paper then listed several prominent African American business owners, beginning with a detailed account of Robert C. Owens's successful businesses. The paper referenced several other professionals including police officers, cooks, metal dealers and ironworkers, postal workers and construction contractors. While these made up the bulk of occupations for African American middle class men, a separate essay was published highlighting the group of men who were highly educated and made up the black elite.[62]

Dr. A. C. Garrott contributed a section on the educational achievements of the black community. His piece, entitled, "How the University-Trained Negro Has Advanced in the Great Professions" focused on the city's elite African American men, specifically the doctors, lawyers, dentists, and newsmen. Garrott highlighted seventeen men, all with impressive backgrounds representing a variety of university and professional education ranging from Howard University in Washington, D.C., to the University of Michigan, Harvard, Wilberforce, and the University of Southern California. There was also one veterinarian, and one pharmacist. Most impressively, Garrott noted that "there is not one drone among them, and though some of them may be classed as newcomers, the wealth of the entire lot will aggregate about $165,000."[63] His piece was placed in juxtaposition to Kate Bradley-Stovall's story about the contributions of black women to the Los Angeles community as a whole. In between the two pages was an entire page of various depictions of Abraham Lincoln.

While celebrating all of the achievements of the black Angeleno community, the paper also included a section about the black religious community as well as the Secret Orders and fraternal organizations. By the printing of this paper in 1909, the Los Angeles black community had several benevolent and fraternal organizations. S. P. Johnson contributed the piece entitled, "Secret Orders among Negroes." He noted seven prominent organizations and their auxiliaries that included the Odd

Fellows, founded in 1885; the Masons, which became the third largest in the state by 1906, merely five years after its founding; the Foresters, who began in 1897; the Knights of Pythias (1901); the Elks (1906); the United Brothers of Friendship (1888); and the True Reformers.[64] Each of these organizations aimed to help the community in different ways. The True Reformers, for example, was purposed to own and control business enterprises—something that very much was supported by Washington. The Odd Fellows purchased property at 8th and Wall streets and eventually built a two-story brick building on it. The group contracted a member to build the bricks and other members to build the building. By 1909, the property was valued at $45,000.[65]

The St. John's Lodge #5 of the Masonic lodges was the most popular among young men, according to Johnson, and the Court Solomon #8677 of the Foresters was the overall favorite. "As a beneficial organization, Court Solomon is foremost of all lodges among colored people in Los Angeles."[66] The organization offered the most benefits, at seven dollars and fifty cents per week for up to twenty-six weeks and five dollars per week thereafter. The organization provided its own doctors and medicine for the sick. It also paid a death benefit of seventy-five dollars for burial. Most of the organizations included women's branches.[67]

The majority of these organizations were open to wives, widows, sisters, mothers, and daughters of male members. The Household of Ruth, which was a female auxiliary of the Odd Fellows, was founded on 20 June 1888, and by 1909 had seventy-two members and $1,465 in cash. Household #3309 was the female branch of the Golden Rule Lodge, and was founded on 21 April 1908, and had twenty-eight members within the first year. Juanita Williamson, whose husband James was a successful grocery store owner, headed this organization. Their daughter Vassia served as the group's recorder.[68]

The Masons were not without their female branches either. In Los Angeles, there were two that black women participated in: The Electa, Chapter #5 as part of the Order of the Eastern Star was one of the first, and the Queen of Sheeba, Chapter 17 was founded on 11 June 1904. Under the Foresters was the Pride of the West Circe #207. Founded in 1900, this group was "allowed to receive in to membership all women of good character."[69] The Rose of Los Angeles Circle was founded by a group of women including Georgia-born Mary E. Bronson, whose husband was a carpenter, on 22 April 1903.[70] It was important that these organizations be noted, as later the writers' duties were to fulfill Washington's request in highlighting the positive contributions of black Angelenos. This would not be complete without noting the black religious community.

This edition of the *Times* featured two sections about religious and church life. The Reverend G. R. Bryant outlined the diverse religious background by introducing the *Times* readers to several black churches. He explained, "The Negro population of Los Angeles is largely made up of people from the South, whose ancestors were slaves."[71] Therefore, according to Rev. Bryant, the two denominations making up the largest portion of the African American community were the Methodist and the Baptist. He listed all of the churches in the two denominations before noting that the black religious community also included Episcopalians, which was a small group. Finally, Bryant noted that the Roman Catholic Church was so popular that its black membership was increasing rapidly.[72] Bryant made no mention of William J. Seymour and the Apostolic Faith Mission, which is not surprising considering that the church appealed to the working class—a group that these authors were trying to downplay in this edition of the *Times*. The Reverend J. D. Gordon contributed the section on spirituality.

John D. Gordon was the pastor of the Tabernacle Baptist Church in Los Angeles. A migrant from Georgia, the 37-year-old had a decent sized church with a membership of three hundred. He was married to Florence A. Gordon who was also from Georgia. The two owned a home, and rented a room to a 30-year-old laundress from Texas named Gertrude Holliday, and John's brother-in-law, James A. Lewis, who was a nineteen-year-old hotel porter from Georgia also lived with them.[73] Gordon noted, "The spiritual or soul life of a people will of necessity find expression, and the Godward expression of this life is its religion."[74] One of the greatest forms of expression of African Americans, according to Gordon, was song. He noted that the slave songs exemplified the will and fortitude of the African American community.

Gordon credited the religious life of the black Angeleno community as the reason they could overcome various hardships such as racism. He said, "Joseph in Egypt's jail was its deliverer, who knows but that the negro peeping from behind the iron bars of race prejudice and proscription, will prove the same to his white brother in war and in peace, all do to his spiritual nature."[75] The minister also believed that the spiritual nature of the slave was what enabled him to fight for his own emancipation, and also allowed him to firmly establish himself in the city. Lastly, Gordon paid homage to Booker T. Washington, whom he believed exemplified this, stating, "The spiritual diplomacy and tact with the race, that enabled the negro during the war to stand well with the conquering army of the North, that encamped in the house, and yet true to his hiding master under the house, finds its expression in Booker T. Washington."[76] Gordon understood that Washington had maneuvered himself in such a way as to earn respect from white people, whom he believed would eventually have to see African Americans as their equals.

Reverend Gordon's piece not only illustrates the black Angeleno community's support of Booker T. Washington, but also resonates with an article Washington contributed, entitled, "Opportunity of the Negro in America," which was included in the section about educational progress. In fact, every one of these articles echoed Washington. He wrote, "The same thing is true of the negro banker, the negro merchant, the negro real estate dealer. In almost every instance, because of the separation of the races, in their churches, in their schools . . . the white physician and the white banker have not been able to or have not cared to, perform for negroes."[77] He believed that African Americans had overcome the devastating reality of slavery and racism, and were industrious enough to build their own businesses and services that catered to their own community. Though Washington's piece mainly focused on the southern black community, it is clear that people such as the Reverends Gordon and Bryant, Kate Bradley-Stovall, Dr. A. C. Garrott, and others who contributed to the Lincoln Edition of the *Times*, agreed that it was through pure will (and most likely God's favor) that black Angelenos were able to find success in Los Angeles. Lieutenant Colonel Allen Allensworth contributed a section to the *Times* about local African Americans (including himself) who served in the military.

Allensworth argued that the black troops were the only purely American troops, as many of the white regiments included immigrants from several European countries. He wrote, "but examine the roll and you will find them mixed as the colors of Joseph's coat—Irish, German, French, Italian."[78] He linked black enlistment in the military with their spiritual life, writing, "He has heard many sermons, among them from the text, 'If any man will be My disciple, let him take up his cross and follow Me.' This appeals to the heroic. It appeals to the negro and he readily takes up his army cross daily to follow the flag."[79] He stressed that black soldiers knew they would have to work harder than white soldiers, and had no hopes as to equality or citizenship. They knew that God would recognize and reward their hard work and loyalty. He understood black participation in the military as an experiment—one that he knew would benefit African Americans in the end. He concluded that this proved "the negro can be an officer and a gentleman as well as a man and a soldier."[80] His proof was a number of soldiers serving the country in several branches of the military, including local retired soldiers in Los Angeles, much like himself. Perhaps he understood Washington's vision more than any other black Angeleno when he attempted to create a black utopian society outside of the city.

Allen Allensworth was born a slave in Kentucky in 1840. During the Civil War, he had escaped and joined the Union army. After serving for a number of years as chaplain, Allensworth settled in California—first at the Presidio of San Francisco. While Colonel Allensworth was serving in active duty during the Philippine-American War, his wife, Josephine, oversaw the paychecks of military families at the presidio, ensuring that the wives and children of soldiers received the money their husbands sent home. In 1905, Colonel Allensworth moved his family to Los Angeles, where they purchased a home not far from the Robert C. Owens family residence. The couple had two daughters: Nella, who married a building contractor named Louis Blodgett; and Eva, who married Harrie Skanks, who worked as a clerk at the post office.[81]

In Los Angeles, Allensworth, along with four other men, organized the California Colony and Home Promoting Association—a company that promoted black homeownership and self-sufficiency. Since Los Angeles already had an established African American community, Allensworth decided to look for a large portion of land for black people to establish their own separate colony, where African Americans could enjoy economic prosperity and live free of discriminatory laws. Several black towns already existed in California. In 1908 the group located a large tract in the San Joaquin Valley, just north of Bakersfield. They believed that the area was a perfect place for establishing an all-black town, much like those in Kansas and Oklahoma which had been established as early as the 1870s. They named the town Allensworth, after its most well-known founder.[82] They also planned to name the park after one of the most prominent African American leaders.

On 27 June 1908, Allensworth sent a letter from Los Angeles to Booker T. Washington. He explained that he had established his California Colony organization with the express purpose of uniting with Washington "in creating a favorable sentiment for the race."[83] The group wanted to use the town to shape public opinion about the black community, while promoting black intellect. Allensworth wanted to honor the accomplishments of African Americans throughout the city by giving streets "names of historical and educational value."[84] He wrote, "In the midst of this city we have a lake, surrounded by a park, to be named—if you have no objection—'Washington' Park, in honor of the greatest negro sentiment maker in the world."[85] Washington responded in the affirmative.

The location of the town was very important because it was perfectly situated between Los Angeles and San Francisco. But more importantly, the Santa Fe Railroad had a transfer stop for cattle farmers at Allensworth. The town opened a bakery right at the stop in order to attract business. They also built stores, a school, a library, a hotel, and a church to meet the needs of the townspeople. The location was also believed to be good farmland for sugar beets, dairy, poultry, and other goods. While the town initially had ten residents in 1912, it quickly grew to over one hundred. Colonel Allensworth divided his time between the town and Los Angeles, where he recruited families for the colony. Not only did he advertise in African American newspapers across the country, Allensworth believed that black Angelenos shared many of his ideas about the kinds of people who should live in the colony.[86]

Allensworth stressed self-sufficiency and education as two of the most important principles. He focused on recruiting families, rather than single people, men with military backgrounds, and people with strong middle-class values who were also church members. His wife, Josephine, organized the Women's Improvement Club, which established a playground for the children, and oversaw several improvement projects.[87] She also became the first president of the school board and donated the building for the town's library, while her husband gave his personal book collection. Allensworth did not tolerate drunkards, gamblers, or prostitutes. Allensworth envisioned a town that adhered to Protestant and middle class values in ways that other utopian communities were exclusive.[88]

The majority of people who lived in Allensworth were black farmers, shopkeepers, or railroad workers. Family sizes were small, averaging three or fewer people per household, and unlike Los Angeles, very few of them lived in homes with non-family members. Also, men headed the majority of the households in Allensworth. The majority of Allensworth women did not work outside of their homes, but may have helped their husbands on family farms.[89]

The Allensworth Colony Association proposed an establishment of an industrial school, Allensworth Agricultural and Manual Training

School, to be known as the Tuskegee of the West, *not* a Fisk or an Atlanta University. Residents began raising money for the school, but it never developed because many wealthy black Angelenos, especially members of the Niagara Movement and the NAACP, would not support it. Since African Americans in California had secured the right for their children to attend integrated public schools, and because black Angelenos experienced a higher degree of freedom and equality, they would not support a segregated black school.[90]

Although Allensworth attracted several families in the beginning, it simply could not sustain itself. First, water was a major problem. The utility companies that controlled the water supply were closed down due to unpaid taxes. The land had several artesian wells, and they petitioned the state for gas-powered pumps but were denied. The water supply to the town began drying up by the late 1920s. In addition, high levels of alkali were found, and everything turned to salt when the water table dropped, therefore, the water was useless. As a result, people moved out of the town to find opportunity in Los Angeles or the San Francisco Bay Area.[91]

The second major problem for Allensworth occurred in 1914 when the Santa Fe Railroad Company moved its stop to Alpaugh, seven miles away. This left the people without the ability to sell their goods and services. The railroad maintained a postal stop in Allensworth, but even that was moved to Alpaugh in 1930, thereby cutting off the few families that remained. Also, the First World War and the sudden increase in factory work called people away from the small black colony into the cities.[92]

Finally, in 1914 Colonel Allensworth was struck down by a motorcyclist and died on his way to preach at a church just outside of Los Angeles, which was a significant blow to the town's growth. Josephine Allensworth continued to visit the town, but lived with one of her daughters in Los Angeles. By 1920, Allensworth was no longer an all-black town. Forty-eight households made up the majority of the Allensworth community in 1920. Black men headed twenty-nine households, and back women, seven. There were also five white Mexican households along with six white, and included people from Germany, Switzerland, and Barbados. Between 1908 and 1920, all but one (57-year-old, Josephine Cowes) female heads of household were widows.[93]

The story of Allensworth illustrates how people were stuck between the opposing poles of national black leadership represented by Booker T. Washington and W. E. B. Du Bois (figure 6.1 is a poster that was widely circulated in Los Angeles, and exemplifies how people felt about Washington's leadership). Allen Allensworth wanted the talented tenth to live in the community, but also believed in the principles of hard work, self-sufficiency, and respectability. This, he believed, could only be achieved through living in separate communities where black children attended black schools and received an industrial and agricultural education. Even in his promotion of the town, he solicited soldiers, not scholars, and farmers rather than doctors and lawyers—many of whom drew upon agricultural skills brought with them from the South. When Booker T. Washington died one year after Allensworth, the black Angeleno community, like many black communities around the country, was deeply affected.

The *Los Angeles Times* and the *California Eagle* both printed articles announcing the death of Booker T. Washington. The *Times* published an Associated Press release on 14 November 1915 that talked about his life, and on 20 November printed the memorial service arrangements. On 20 and 27 November, the paper published a brief description of the service in its "In Memoriam" section, and on 29 November, the paper gave a tribute. Since the *Times* had supported Booker T. Washington, the paper was sure to honor his memory.[94] The *Eagle* made certain every person of color in Los Angeles celebrated Washington's life.

The 20 November 1915 edition of the paper was dedicated to Booker T. Washington. The front page announced the death, and summarized his life's work. As an illustration of how black Angelenos felt about Washington, "all race establishments" were going to close during the hours of 11:00 A.M. to 12:00 P.M. as black-owned business and schools closed across the country. The African Methodist Episcopal Zion church held a memorial service at the same time as the funeral service in Tuskegee. The service included a dramatic performance of Washington's life, and several speakers representing those prominent men and women, "in the civic, religious, commercial, and professional life of the community."[95] Owners and editors of the *California Eagle*, J. B. and Charlotta Bass, suggested a citywide memorial service, and many others paid tribute.

Mayor C. E. Sebastian and the city council held an adjourned session. He ordered all flags on public buildings to fly at half-mast. The Board of Education also ordered all public schools in the city to lower their flags to half-mast. The paper highlighted the significance in this gesture. It read, "No Negro was ever paid as distinguished an honor as the late

Figure 6.1 African American history poster. This poster shows the national black leadership (including Abraham Lincoln) with Booker T. Washington prominently displayed at the center.

Booker T. Washington."⁹⁶ In addition to the public offices, all of the black churches including Tabernacle Baptist, Westminster Presbyterian Church, First Methodist Episcopal, and Wesley Chapel, held special memorial services. The Colored YMCA held a general meeting to plan a citywide memorial service, and invited all professional men, women and "race lovers" in the area. They also requested all of the churches to announce the meeting at all of their services.⁹⁷

On 27 November 1915, the *Eagle* advertised the memorial service to be held at the Shrine Auditorium near downtown Los Angeles. A mass choir of over one hundred members was organized to pay a musical tribute, and speakers included several prominent members of the city, including the mayor. The paper noted, "All citizens are invited to attend this service in memory of one of the greatest characters for good in the history of all time."⁹⁸ There was also a commemorative Booker T. Washington souvenir button that was selling for twenty-five cents in all of the black-owned businesses. The service was held on 28 November 1915.

J. B. Bass wrote about the service in his article, "5000 People Gather at Shrine Auditorium in Memory of Dr. Washington." He paid careful attention to the tributes, noting that Booker T. Washington's close personal friend the Reverend E. W. Kinchen underscored the impact Washington had made. Kinchen said, "The world has furnished but few men who could marshal such a cosmopolitan audience as is gathered here upon this memorial occasion."⁹⁹ This was a very important point, because it not only reflected Washington's accomplishments, but it directly correlated with race relations in Los Angeles at the time. Bass stated, "The clan and clash of races become a harmonious sonnet as it meets here, and we witness the precedence of the representatives of the flowery kingdom of Japan and other races fervent in their tribute of praise and admiration as are the members of his own race."¹⁰⁰ Los Angeles certainly was no racial paradise, but through Washington's life and death, black Angelenos saw that racial cooperation could one day be achieved.

Booker T. Washington made several conclusions about the West. His initial conclusion was that African Americans fared much better in the south. First, because of the larger black population, which he believed would yield better opportunities. He also was concerned about the new irrigation systems that farmers relied on instead of rain. This required more maintenance that he felt African Americans were not equipped to handle. He also did not see African Americans physically living better in most of the western states than the South. Washington noted that

African Americans were banned from the trade unions, but that they made more money than black southerners.

Being confined to certain occupations, according to Washington, did not prohibit black people from purchasing property or accumulating wealth. The further west Washington traveled, the better the conditions for African Americans. They were more successful, had more homesteads, and more people were buying land and cultivating the soil. He noted that there was plenty of land in the West. African Americans, therefore, could farm and raise marketable crops, which was something he wanted for black southerners.

Washington noted that black westerners were not taking advantage of higher education yet, he was impressed that black students were receiving better educations and also had access to public education, especially in California. While the schools were integrated, he noticed fewer numbers of black high school and college students. Even though this was problematic, lack of education did not hinder African Americans from becoming economically successful. Nor did it prevent them from supporting his institution.

During these visits, Washington raised a great deal of money for Tuskegee, especially from California. Los Angeles had a Tuskegee Alumni Circle, which hosted some of the events, but also promoted the institute to other black Angelenos. A small number of people regularly sent money to Tuskegee, even if they did not send their children to the school. He even envisioned a Tuskegee-like institution in the West. Allensworth and other black towns were promising sites. Allen Allensworth, along with other Washington friends, almost helped him realize that dream.

Booker T. Washington had several supporters in Los Angeles and throughout the West. He was given the royal treatment when he first arrived, and maintained a relationship with black Angelenos for the last decade and a half of his life. Black Angelenos believed in his plan for black wealth accumulation through property ownership and business building. They supported the Tuskegee Institute, and they supported him. Even before he visited Los Angeles, African Americans created and maintained their own institutions and networks such as churches, clubs, newspapers, and various businesses. Washington, like Du Bois, noted a thriving black community, but was skeptical of the amount of freedom they had, suggesting that the best place in the country for African Americans was the South.

Conclusion

Most histories that have been written about black Los Angeles center on the community that developed after the Great Migration. After all, the amount of newer arrivals dwarfed the small numbers who had settled in the city before. These histories take advantage of a richer historical record than what remains of the earlier period of settlement, where migrants' experiences were virtually unknown. But that does not mean they were nonexistent. In fact, when one looks closely, one finds a small, thriving black community that worked closely with other racial and ethnic communities in order to maintain itself. This early black community, made up almost entirely of working-class people, together with a very small elite class, created black Los Angeles.

Women took the lead in community building. Sure, black men may have *physically* contributed to the construction of black Los Angeles, but black women *made* the community. They were responsible for maintaining several important religious, educational, and social institutions. In churches, women organized much of the community life by establishing tutoring and other educational programs for children, charitable events to help the poor, literary groups, and even helped organize a variety of political activities, even though California women could not vote until 1911. By 1912, however, black women (as well as men) were extremely politically active and the vast majority were registered Republicans. Charitable activity was not confined to the elite and middle classes in Los Angeles.

Since Los Angeles offered certain opportunities for African Americans, some people who would have been confined to working-class conditions in the South, Midwest, or Northeast were able to live middle-class lives in Los Angeles. It was not uncommon, therefore, for a janitor or a laundress in Los Angeles to own his or her own home, albeit a modest one. Working-class women also contributed to building networks by helping one another economically and socially. Several working-class women, for example, opened their homes and rented rooms to boarders. Several black laundresses in Los Angeles who had extra rooms often rented those rooms to other black women, who would then work with them in their homes, either also doing laundry or ironing. Although black women were given no official power in their churches, they helped to establish and maintain them by recruiting new members, organizing church functions, and holding community meetings. It was Biddy Mason who paid the majority of the taxes and fees for the First A. M. E. Church building in the 1870s, and it was black laundresses who initially attended prayer meetings and Bible studies where the Azusa Street Revival began in 1906. By the time Booker T. Washington and W. E. B. Du Bois arrived in Los Angeles, the black community had overcome several obstacles, which shaped their conclusions about race relations in the city.

Du Bois called California a "tourist's wonderland," pointing out the various forms of plant life and taking special interest in the roses, lilies, redwoods, and palms. He admired Yosemite, the San Francisco Bay, the state's mountain range, and its rivers. He also noted that the cities of California were flourishing, and more than any other, Du Bois found Los Angeles most intriguing.[1]

Du Bois noted several positive and progressive things about Los Angeles. He described the African American community as hospitable, and called them "pushing and energetic."[2] He noted their efforts in the local economy, their beautiful houses, and the ways in which they worked with other communities of color. Du Bois also believed that black Angelenos worked well with one another to create opportunities for themselves and for their community.[3]

Du Bois's observations were limited in a number of ways, especially because he focused on the small black professional class: his Los Angeles "Talented Tenth." While he did spend time with less advantaged black Angelenos, African American business owners left the strongest impression. He observed and commented on day nurseries, homes for working girls, and other organizations designed for self-help. He also toured business blocks owned and operated by local African Americans throughout the city, particularly the downtown area. Some of the businesses Du Bois found most impressive included a tailor shop, a furniture store, two real estate companies, "a contractor who was putting up some of the best buildings in the city with colored workmen,"[4] and "the largest junk dealers' business in the state."[5] He also noted several African Americans doctors, lawyers, and dentists whose offices were located in some of those "best buildings" in the city.[6]

Du Bois acknowledged the prosperity of the African American community in Los Angeles, but still found that attitudes about race and race relations were similar to those in the South and North. He also suggested that one look beyond the city's beauty in order to see that Los Angeles was not paradise. He revealed that African Americans experienced economic and social disadvantages, which sometimes hindered progress.[7]

Some black Angelenos faced discrimination in many of the city's public services. Du Bois noted that the local stores denied women service, while hotels and restaurants turned African Americans away. He concluded that whites generally discriminated against the lower classes of African Americans, but conceded that those of the professional class did work and socialize with whites. While black Angelenos faced certain kinds of discrimination, Du Bois believed they would resist this condition. "Black folk are fighters and not followers of the doctrine of surrender," he concluded.[8]

Du Bois understood that race relations in California appeared more complex for several reasons. He noted that there was no racial binary in terms of black and white. Rather, he explained that a new color distinction for race relations existed in California: "Here, I had my first sight on the Pacific and realized how California faces the newest color problem, the problem of the relation of the Orient and Occident. The colored people of California do not realize the bigness of this problem and their own logical position."[9] With a large number of immigrants from Eastern countries, and an influx of emigrants from the Western world, California became a crossroads for clashing cultures.[10] Du Bois noticed this conflict first in San Diego, then in other cities. He believed that the Japanese, in particular, further complicated race relations and he blamed them for causing competition between African Americans and other groups of people of color.[11]

African Americans in Los Angeles, according to Du Bois, experienced very different circumstances than in northern California. He described African Americans in northern California as suspicious of emigrants from eastern and southern states. The combination of new migrants and white discrimination, Du Bois believed, created a severe challenge. Rather than fighting this opposition, he worried that African Americans in northern California cities would surrender. He also noted that there was little white support to create similar opportunities he knew to be available to black Angelenos. In San Francisco, for example, Du Bois observed that African Americans recognized racism and discrimination, but had only begun challenging their circumstances. Yet, Du Bois overlooked the accomplishments of African Americans in the northern cities such as fighting for voting and testimony rights, access to public schooling, and challenging the state's laissez-faire attitude about slavery. Rather, he focused on the problems of the early twentieth century. Excluded from the labor and trades unions, African Americans were only starting to demand equality. Du Bois met with a number of white union leaders who understood that African Americans had similar labor concerns. He also won the sympathy of white social workers, but realized that they only vaguely understood the problems of local African Americans in the region.[12]

In other parts of northern California, Du Bois recognized similarities with African Americans in the eastern United States. Stockton, California, for example, had a large black population, but as in a small northeastern town, local African Americans were "shut out and almost forgotten."[13] Like African Americans in San Francisco, black people in Stockton were only beginning to understand their potential to challenge the ideology that kept them in a lower socioeconomic position than that of whites.[14]

Du Bois described his experiences in other northern California cities such as Sacramento and Shasta, but turned his discussion back to Los Angeles. He concluded that black Angelenos had made the most progress. Nowhere else in California had he seen African Americans so self-sufficient or in better relationships with whites. African Americans in Los Angeles, Du Bois concluded, challenged their oppressive circumstances and overcame adversity better than those in any other city in California.[15]

By the time Du Bois arrived in Los Angeles, the black community indeed appeared to be flourishing. By primarily observing the black elite and their accomplishments, he recognized a better standard of living than the national average, and published images of black businesses and large homes. Du Bois overlooked, however, the black non-elite, underestimating the condition of the majority of the African American community. He believed that most African Americans were able to overcome local racist attitudes because of their determination. Clearly, he believed that black accomplishments far outweighed their oppression. He was only partially correct.

During the second half of the nineteenth century, white middle-class Angelenos promoted the city as a haven in the west, where white immigrants and migrants would truly experience the myth of the "California Dream."[16] In the process, they marginalized black, Mexican, and Chinese people. Nigger Alley, as it was called, where most nonwhites lived, quickly became the bane of the city's existence. Black people sometimes managed to fare better than other people of color because their small numbers made them less of a "threat."

During the nineteenth century, the African American population in Los Angeles remained small. Many people who arrived between the 1850s and 1880s were able to etch out a nice existence. They created a community that was sustained by home ownership and a degree of economic viability, even if it was relatively disadvantaged. They also established institutions such as black-owned businesses, and formed independent churches and social organizations. They opened hotels and offered accommodations for new migrants. They purchased land, especially in the downtown section of the city. They also adhered to middle class notions of community life. When larger numbers African Americans began migrating to the region, assimilation became more difficult, opportunity began to dry up, and racist attitudes more oppressive.

Near the close of the nineteenth century, white Angelenos attached themselves to new social causes. Temperance quickly rose to the forefront of local social campaigns. The city was able to maintain its allure as the quintessential western metropolis, by publicly admonishing those whose social behavior they deemed inappropriate—drunks, petty thieves, vagrants, gamblers, and more violent types. Not surprisingly, they located most of this "anti-social" behavior in Nigger Alley. That is, they focused more of their police activity and public campaign on people of color rather than the citywide population. Because Chinese people made up the significant portion of people of color, the city targeted them first. The Chinese Exclusion Act initially aimed to halt Chinese labor, was expanded to include small business owners, students and teachers, but particularly those linked to criminal activity.

African American migrants combated this negative spotlight by joining the attempt to rid the city of its ills. Although small in numbers, some black people worked for the Los Angeles Police Department at every level of its organization. African Americans rarely appeared in early criminal records. As their community increased, however, the mainstream targeted them as a way of controlling the black population. The beginning of the twentieth century, therefore, marked a turn for African Americans. No longer the city's "model minority," they now became public enemy number one. Many forms of racial segregation, including restrictive covenants, as well as police brutality and other forms of overt racism threatened them.

Black Angelenos lived relatively better lives than black people in the South or North, especially if they were middle class. Despite the harsh circumstances of Jim Crow, black Angelenos remained unequal, but associated with other people of color to form a community that was black, but also multiracial. After World War I, many Angelenos no longer lived in predominantly integrated neighborhoods. Housing segregation in the form of racially restrictive covenants became the easiest way to get people out of middle-class neighborhoods. Racial and ethnic "minorities" established enclaves in places like Boyle Heights and South Central to the east and south of downtown. These districts housed most of the city's African American, Mexican and Mexican American, Chinese, Japanese, and ethnically defined white communities, such as Jews. At the same time, Asian and Mexican people were further racialized through immigration law that maintained white people's status at the top of the social hierarchy. People affected by these laws were overwhelmingly working class.[17]

The Pentecostal movement was, in part, a response to middle-class Angelenos' treatment of those of lower status. It happened as working-class residents erupted culturally in an outpouring that both doctrinally and practically asserted their influence apart from that of the black elite. Their goal was to reintroduce religious practices generally forbidden in mainstream Christian denominations. The Azusa Street Revival provided a space for all people, regardless of race or class, to shout, dance, sing, and cry out to God. Many of these practices resonated with black people who drew upon religious traditions that they traced back to the South as well as Africa. While the black middle class rejected the revival, people traveled from around the state and nation to Los Angeles to experience it. Participants of the movement understood that the elite faction of the city discouraged the multicultural interaction. Still, inspired revivalists embraced one another across traditional boundaries.[18]

On 29 April 2006, Pentecostals from all over the world met in Los Angeles for a centennial celebration of the Azusa Street Revival. They held meetings at the downtown Convention Center, the Noguchi Plaza in Little Tokyo, where the Apostolic Faith Mission once stood, at West Angeles Church of God in Christ in the Crenshaw district, and at 216 North Bonnie Brae Street, the home where the revival began. Although local media, such as the *Los Angeles Times* and the *Los Angeles Sentinel*, provided some coverage, the centennial celebration received little recognition. Over 40,000 people attended the conferences at their various locales. Like the original revival, people from several racial and ethnic backgrounds joined the celebration. They prayed, praised, and worshipped together. Pentecostal scholars also provided commentary about the significance of the founding revival.[19]

While local church leaders celebrated the reception of the centennial, much of its format resembled those of the last days of the revival, rather than its beginning. Over 5,000 people visited the West Angeles Cathedral to hear Bishop T. D. Jakes, founder and pastor of the 30,000-member Potter's House church in Dallas, preach the opening sermon. The church was full to capacity, and many sat in the concourse to watch on closed-circuit television. Hospitality workers reserved the front rows of the church for Hollywood's most famous, creating animosity among the laypeople. Each night, another celebrated preacher delivered the message, and gospel's premier artists provided the music. Instead of waiting for God to select a speaker, which was the founding principle of the Azusa Street Revival, every minute of every day was calculated.[20]

The impact of the Azusa Street Revival on modern Pentecostalism cannot be overlooked. As in the early twentieth century, Pentecostals came to Los Angeles, even if for only a few days to experience Pentecost. The hundred-year celebration was comprised of people representing most continents of the world, and almost all languages. African American Pentecostal leaders in Los Angeles hosted and organized the majority of the centennial events, reminiscent of the predominantly African American leadership in 1906. As such, the Centennial did encompass some characteristics of the original revival. Like at the Apostolic Faith Mission, there also was lost opportunity in the modern celebrations—opportunity to provide a lasting bridge across racial, cultural, linguistic, and class divides.[21]

Two days later, on 1 May 2006, approximately 250,000 people gathered in downtown Los Angeles and along Broadway Street to protest the impending Federal Immigration Bill. Later that afternoon, over 400,000 people filled the Wilshire Boulevard corridor for the same reason. Donned in white T-shirts, hundreds of thousands gathered in all major metropolitan areas across the country waiving American and their respective countries' flags.[22] This protest, as well as a similar demonstration that occurred a month earlier, indicated to the country that numerous people were willing to fight to protect immigrants' rights. As in the era of this study, media coverage centered on the city's desire to contain the large immigrant population of color. Several other immigrant communities, as well as most African Americans, observed rather than participated. Interracial tension among blacks and immigrant groups of color had escalated over the past few decades, with the most recent outburst in 1992.[23]

On 3 March 1991, America witnessed the horrific beating of black Los Angeles motorist Rodney King while stopped for traffic violations. Struck with batons, kicked, hit, and bound, King lay bleeding and semiconscious, as other police officers stood by and refused to intervene. The incident was captured on a camera, and played over and over again by local and national news outlets. In the fall of 1992 filmmaker Spike Lee opened his blockbuster movie *Malcolm X* with the videotape of the beating. In Simi Valley, an affluent suburb in neighboring Ventura County, a predominantly white jury decided the case of the four police offers accused of the near lynching. Two weeks after the King beating, a young African American girl was murdered in South Central Los Angeles.[24]

Latasha Harlins was only fifteen years old when she died, shot in the back of the head on 16 March after an altercation with Korean grocery store owner Soon Ja Du. An already enraged African American community followed the reports on television and in the newspaper, which provoked great anger. Yet, the community held out, hoping for justice, not only for the Harlins family and the young life that was taken, but also for Rodney King. Tempers flared when that never manifested. The following October, Soon Ja Du was convicted of voluntary manslaughter. Judge Joyce Karlin ordered a suspended sentence.[25] Appalled by this decision, the African American community waited again for justice with the verdict in the King beating case.[26]

On 29 April 1992 at approximately 3:15 P.M., the Simi Valley jury acquitted three of the police officers charged with beating King, and could not decide on the fourth. By 5:00 P.M., the black Los Angeles community had exploded in outrage. African Americans, Latinos, Koreans, and a few white people burned, looted, and destroyed property throughout the city. The "riots," in the predominantly black South Central neighborhood destroyed the community. Already a working-class neighborhood, its residents now faced larger economic and social obstacles, which in many ways seemed inevitable.

Perhaps foretelling of things to come, Du Bois made one observation about the impending problems facing the community. He stated, "To be sure, Los Angeles is no Paradise, much as the sight of its lilies and roses might lead one to believe. The color line is there and is sharply drawn."[27]

That color line was more than a simple black-white binary, as other groups of people of color and ethnically defined whites also faced hostility and discrimination in Los Angeles. When African Americans first came to the city, they had to make their own community independent of the larger Anglo population. There were both positive and negative developments that continued through the twentieth century. Clearly, there were indications of success that lasted until the 1980s such as industrialization during the first half of the twentieth century, the growing black middle class, and the election and re-election of the city's first black mayor, Tom Bradley, who served for five-terms from 1973 to 1993. At times, however, the negative experiences outweighed the good, particularly where racialized crime and violence were concerned.

Racial violence played out in very different ways, underscoring the lack of racial progress in Los Angeles, particularly for those among the working class. With the advent of immigration policies starting in the 1920s Mexicans and Latin Americans lived in fear of very public mass deportations that would last through the 1980s. The Great Depression served a severe blow to black Angelenos who had made financial gains earlier, leaving the majority of black workers in Los Angeles for the worst, lowest paying jobs. Black Angelenos and other people of color were also constant targets of white frustration, personally and legally.[28]

Japanese and Mexican Americans became the targets of obvious racial hostility during World War II. Beginning in March 1942, Japanese and Japanese Americans were forced from their homes and businesses, and placed into interment camps throughout the West. California was home to a majority of the processing centers before people were sent to the camps. One of the largest was Manzanar, located over 220 miles outside of Los Angeles. The racially charged Sleepy Lagoon murder case in 1942 and the Zoot Suit Riots in 1943 also exemplified white people's anti-Mexican and Mexican American attitudes, when young Mexican American men were violently attacked and accused of being disrespectful and unpatriotic for wearing zoot suits.[29] Even in the postwar era, black Angelenos found themselves at the center of racial violence and racialized crime.

In August 1965, the California Highway Patrol stopped and arrested 21-year-old Marquette Frye for driving under the influence in the South Central community of Watts. A scuffle, following an argument and perceived police brutality ensued, sparking six days of rioting and $40 million in damage in what had become known as the Watts Riots. The community never fully recovered, facing a series of problems. Collectively, the War on Drugs, deindustrialization, the advent of crack cocaine, the rise of street gangs, and mass incarceration have all contributed to the criminalization of racialized communities of color throughout Los Angeles, and across the country.

Perhaps Du Bois was right. California is no paradise. At times, African Americans, Asians and Asian Americans, Mexicans and Mexican Americans, and Native peoples fell victim to an imposed racial hierarchy that was constantly shifting. Other times, Los Angeles proved to be a safe haven for African Americans trying to escape horrible conditions in other parts of the country. In spite of all of this, they continued to establish social, economic, religious, and political networks, doing the necessary work of making black Los Angeles.

Notes

Introduction

1. Du Bois, "Colored California."
2. Ibid.
3. Harlan and Smock, eds., *Booker T. Washington Papers*, 7:18–25.
4. Ibid.
5. Ibid.
6. Bass, *Forty Years*; Beasley, *Negro Trailblazers of California*, 88.
7. Du Bois, *Philadelphia Negro*.
8. Ibid.; Du Bois, "Colored California."
9. For purposes of this study, anyone considered "mulatto," who is part of an African American household, will be counted as part of the black community.
10. Ruggles et al., *Integrated Public Use Microdata Series*; Haines, "Population Characteristics."
11. Haines, "Population Characteristics"; Ruggles et al., *Integrated Public Use Microdata Series*.
12. Ruggles et al., *Integrated Public Use Microdata Series*.
13. Ibid.
14. See for example, Sanchez, *Becoming Mexican American*; and Almaguer, *Racial Fault Lines*.
15. Ruggles et al., *Integrated Public Use Microdata Series*.
16. Ibid.
17. Ibid.
18. Ibid.
19. Bass, *Forty Years*, 15.

Chapter 1

1. Beebe and Senkewicz, eds., *Lands of Promise and Despair*, 11.
2. Ibid., 9.
3. Ibid., 11.
4. Ibid.
5. Ibid.
6. Beasley, *Negro Trailblazers of California*, 132.
7. De Graaf et al., eds., *Seeking El Dorado*, 73.
8. Ibid., 6.
9. Ibid. See also Forbes, "Black Pioneers."
10. De Graaf et al., eds., *Seeking El Dorado*, 6.

11. Cope, *The Limits of Racial Domination*; Bennett, *Africans in Colonial Mexico*; Bennett, *Colonial Blackness*; Martínez, *Geneological Fictions*; Kanter, *Hijos del Pueblo*.

12. Menchaca, *Recovering History, Constructing Race*.

13. Bennett, *Africans in Colonial Mexico*, 20. See also Menchaca, *Recovering History, Constructing Race*, 43.

14. Bennett, *Africans in Colonial Mexico*, 20–27; Vinson, *Bearing Arms for His Majesty*, 3.

15. Cope, *The Limits of Racial Domination*, 76.

16. Bennett, *Africans in Colonial Mexico*, and *Colonial Blackness*; Martínez, *Genealogical Fictions*; Cope, *The Limits of Domination*, 83; Menchaca, *Recovering History, Constructing Race*, 53–56; Vinson, *Bearing Arms for His Majesty*, 5, 201–2; Silva, "From Chains to Chiles." With the exception of Vinson and Cope, these scholars agree that the majority of these groups participated in endogamous marriages. Cope notes that while there was intermarriage, especially between mulattoes and other groups, they were not necessarily "social climbers" by intention, but some of those who engaged in intermarriage reaped some social benefits, 84.

17. Bennett, *Colonial Blackness*, 108; Kanter, *Hijos del Pueblo*, 28. Menchaca, *Recovering History, Constructing Race*, 62. Kanter notes that in the cases of exogamous marriages, women who married outside of their groups often resided in their husbands' villages, which had severe consequences. For example, women could be denied access to land because when their husbands died, their property rights were challenged and were often denied by his male relatives. These women bore the same financial responsibilities as men when their husbands died to take care of their families, yet they were often cheated out of their land (33–34). See also Bennett, *Africans in Colonial Mexico*, 84. This ratio, Bennett notes, resulted in a solidification of African American community formation, through marriage. The household was the basis of that community.

18. Martínez, *Genealogical Fictions*, 168; Kanter, *Hijos del Pueblo*, 27; Menchaca, *Recovering History, Constructing Race*, 57.

19. Martínez, *Genealogical Fictions*, 168.

20. Bennett, *Colonial Blackness*, 19. See also Martínez, *Genealogical Fictions*, 161. Martínez says the same thing as Bennett: that by constructing black blood as impure, Spanish men were able to maintain their status as superior.

21. Menchaca, *Recovering History, Constructing Race*, 158.

22. Martínez, *Genealogical Fictions*, 227–64. Martínez notes that the paintings have serious gender implications as well as race and class, particularly because they typically show a white man as the pinnacle of civilized society, with people of color and women in subordinate positions throughout the series of paintings. While most of the paintings are really fantasies about race, the consequences of such portrayals are produced and reproduced in Mexico's racial hierarchy. See also Katzew, *Casta Painting*.

23. Menchaca, *Recovering History, Constructing Race*, 215. Here, Menchaca defines racialization as a process that occurs when whites use the legal system to maintain racial distinctions, thereby maintaining a hierarchy placing themselves at the top

and allowing them to discriminate against people of color. See also Cope, *The Limits of Racial Domination*, 162. Cope explains the *sistema de castas* as "dual ladders" for race and class that support each other, so certain racial labels become synonymous with specific economic statuses.

24. Menchaca, *Recovering History, Constructing Race*, 221–23. Here, Menchaca refers to the California statutes of 1850 and 1851.

25. Katzew, *Casta Painting*; Lockhart and Schwartz, eds., *Early Latin America*; Almaguer, *Racial Fault Lines*, 45–74.

26. De Graaf et al., eds., *Seeking El Dorado*. See also Flamming, *Bound for Freedom*; Vivien, *The Story of the Negro in Los Angeles County*; Bass, *Forty Years*; Beasley, *Negro Trailblazers of California*; Beebe and Senkewicz, eds., *Lands of Promise and Despair*.

27. De Graaf et al., eds., *Seeking El Dorado*, 5. See also Forbes, "Black Pioneers," 234–38.

28. De Graaf et al., eds., *Seeking El Dorado*, 79. See also McCaa, "Calidad, Clase, and Marriage in Colonial Mexico."

29. Mason, *The Census of 1790*, 45.

30. De Graaf et al., eds., *Seeking El Dorado*, 79.

31. Ibid.; McCaa, "Calidad, Clase, and Marriage in Colonial Mexico."

32. De Graaf et al., eds., *Seeking El Dorado*. See also Forbes, "Black Pioneers."

33. De Graaf et al., eds., *Seeking El Dorado*, 79.

34. Menchaca, *Recovering History, Constructing Race*, 170. Alternately, Bastida is spelled Vastida.

35. De Graaf et al., eds., *Seeking El Dorado*, 83.

36. Ibid. See also Cole and Welcome, eds., *Don Pío Pico's Historical Narrative*; Rice, *Pío Pico*; "Pico Family Tree," Los Angeles: Los Angeles Public Library Collection.

37. Northrop, *Spanish-Mexican Families of Early Southern California, 1769–1850*, 1:104; De Graaf et al., eds., *Seeking El Dorado*, 83.

38. Pío Pico, "Leather Diary." Pío has very few entries in this journal, but notes on 5 May 1885 that he celebrated a birthday.

39. Northrop, *Spanish-Mexican Families*, 1:91; Cole and Welcome, eds., *Don Pío Pico's Historical Narrative*.

40. For a complete list of Spanish, Mexican, and American governors during the early period of California history, see J. M. Guinn, *A History of California and an Extended History of Los Angeles and Environs*, 1:234–35. See also De Graaf, et. al., eds., *Seeking El Dorado*, 84.

41. Northrop, *Spanish-Mexican Families*, 9.

42. "Register for the Pico House," Autry National Center.

43. Ibid.

44. Andres served as a signer of the California State Constitution in 1849, and in 1852 was appointed to the state assembly as a presidential elector.

45. Katzew, *Casta Painting*, 39–49. See also Menchaca, *Recovering History, Constructing Race*. It is difficult to determine the Picos' attitude about race. Although it is likely they considered themselves white, many of the Pico grandchildren intermarried people of various racial backgrounds. They clearly did not adhere to

notions of protecting their bloodline, or lightening their skin color. Although, according to the casta system, whether they married a person of African descent or someone white, their offspring was still considered white. Thus, one cannot tell whether the Picos truly made a conscious effort to become white, or that race simply did not matter.

46. For a discussion on interracial love relationships in the United States, see for example, Nash, *Forbidden Love*, 52–60. California adopted an extensive body of miscegenation laws between 1880 and 1948, when the state supreme court overturned them. Initially, marriages between African Americans or mulattoes and whites were banned. The statute was re-introduced in 1901, extending the prohibition to "Mongolian" and whites. The Japanese were added to the list in 1909, barring them from marrying whites, which continued in 1931 preventing Asians from marrying whites, and again in 1933 to include Malaysians. In 1945, the miscegenation laws prevented whites from marrying any African Americans, mulattoes, "Mongolians," or Malaysians. Finally, the 1947 California miscegenation law barred United States servicemen from marrying women of Japanese descent.

47. Katzew, *Casta Painting*; Nash, *Forbidden Love*. See also Hodes, ed., *Sex, Love, Race*, which includes Gary Nash's chapter "The Hidden History of Mestizo America," 10–32. Nash points out the ways in which this rule progressed from the Revolutionary period into the twentieth century. He explains that in 1785, blacks were identified as having either a parent or grandparent of African descent. If a person could prove they were less than one quarter black, they were considered white. The actual "one-drop" rule, however, was not established until quite some time after Emancipation. By 1910, anyone at least one-sixteenth black was considered "Negro," and by 1930, in Virginia the "one-drop" law applied to any person with one drop of African blood.

48. Nash, *Forbidden Love*, 51–61.

49. See, for example, Nystrom, *New Orleans After the Civil War*.

50. Cole and Welcome, eds., *Don Pío Pico's Historical Narrative*.

51. Taylor, *In Search of the Racial Frontier*; Beasley, *Negro Trailblazers of California*.

52. De Graaf et al., eds., *Seeking El Dorado*, 92n12.

53. Ibid., 80. Manuel Nieto's father was African and his mother was española. Jose Bartolome Tapia's father was mulatto and his mother was mestizo.

54. De Graaf et al., eds., *Seeking El Dorado*, 80.

55. Ibid.; see also Taylor, *In Search of the Racial Frontier*.

56. For a comprehensive study of the California Mission System and land acquisition, see Saavedra, "Competing Visions."

57. Ibid., 60–63.

58. Californians refused to take a strong position against slavery, so the original legislators left it up to interpretation. Slavery could exist within the territory only if a slaveholder could prove that he was in the state for business. If he planned a long-term stay, slaves could be freed. Otherwise, they retained their status.

59. Spanish and Mexican Land Grants Maps. For a history of the Californio society, see Gutierrez and Orsi, eds., *Contested Eden*; Blew, "Californios and

American Institutions." The term "Alcalde" is used generally for the mayor or chief magistrate of a town in a Spanish-speaking area.

60. *Beasley, Negro Trailblazers of California*, 68.

61. Ibid.

62. Ibid., 69.

63. Ibid., 72.

64. Ibid. For a discussion of the legal history of the Fugitive Slave Law, see O'Brien, *Constitutional Law and Politics*, 1275–92; and "The Constitution of the United States, with the acts of Congress, relating to slavery."

65. Bell, *Reminiscences of a Ranger*.

66. Ibid.

67. Ibid.; Chavez-Garcia, *Negotiating Conquest*, 154.

68. Los Angeles County Headline History, 1848–1865.

69. Treaty of Guadalupe Hidalgo; see also Menchaca, *Recovering History, Constructing Race*, 220–22.

70. Robinson, *Los Angeles in the Civil War Days, 1860–1865*; McNichols, and McNulty, eds., *Front Page*. See also Demaratus, *The Force of a Feather*.

71. McNichols, and McNulty, eds., *Front Page*.

72. Taylor, *In Search of the Racial Frontier*; Wheeler, *Black California*; Thurman, *The Negro in California before 1890*.

73. Historical Census Browser.

74. Jelks, *African Americans in the Furniture City*; Dabel, *A Respectable Woman*; Hine, *Hine Sight*, 59–85.

75. Lucy was in the Evertson household, and was listed as a mulatto, but when the state census was taken in 1852, she was listed as white. It is unclear whether she was part of the Evertson family, or was a servant in the household, or an orphan, or possibly an illegitimate child. The household head, John R. Evertson, was also the census taker in 1850. Because the census for that year did not record familial connections, we do not know whether she was his daughter or someone living or working in the household.

76. Ancestry.com, *1850 United States Federal Census*.

77. Ibid.

78. Ibid.

79. University of Virginia Geospatial and Statistical Data Center, *United States Historical Census Data Browser*. See also, Ancestry.com, *1860 United States Federal Census*.

80. Ancestry.com, *1860 United States Federal Census*.

81. Ancestry.com, *1860 United States Federal Census*. Initially, the U.S. Census did not count domestic service as one of the categories for occupation, stating that it wasn't a significant enough industry to count. In doing so, the census did not count hundreds of thousands of black people, especially women's work. As a result, black women in Los Angeles appear as though they have no occupation, when in fact, they may have been domestics. This will be explored further in a later chapter of this book.

82. The census only recognized white, black, and mulatto in 1850 and 1860. The enumeration instructions also included quadroons and octoroons, as well as anyone having even the slightest amount of African blood as mulatto. In 1870, Chinese and Indian categories were added to the census. In 1890, the census became more specific of people of African descent. Instructions for enumerators classified anyone containing three-fourths black blood as black, three-to-five-eighths black blood as mulatto, one-fourth black blood as quadroon, and one-eighth or any trace of black blood as octoroon. The 1900 census added Japanese to the list of racial classifications, and reverted back using black as a category for all people of African descent, and in 1910, the census created a new category of "other" for all persons not classified as white, black, Chinese, Indian, or Japanese. See Ruggles et al., *Integrated Public Use Microdata Series.*

83. University of Virginia Geospatial and Statistical Data Center, *United States Historical Census Data Browser*; California State Library California History Research Room. Initially, California aimed to take a yearly census of the state, keeping track of every person, but this goal was extremely overzealous. In addition, the first census conducted in the Los Angeles region was a county census, rather than a count of the inhabitants of the city alone. Therefore, the best information available about the population for Los Angeles during the 1850s represents a slightly larger population than if one were to focus only on the city. These numbers, however, remain useful in determining the population demographics of the region. The information also revealed places of origin for whites.

84. University of Virginia Geospatial and Statistical Data Center, *United States Historical Census Data Browser.*

85. Ibid.

86. Ibid. The census also reported that only fifteen people were born in Asian countries other than China, making up an insignificant percentage of the population.

87. Reporting that they as well as their parents were native born were 94,582 people. Of this number, 45,588 were male and 48,994 were female; 39,748 said they were native born, but that their parents were foreign born. Finally, 27,645 whites said they were foreign born, with 15,236 males and 12,409 females. The gender ratio remained equivalent for whites. A close survey of the U.S. Census shows that a significantly larger number of male Chinese than female lived in Los Angeles during this time. See also, Ancestry.com, *1900 U.S. Federal Census.* The county-level totals for these groups are taken from the Historical Census Browser, which does not include data for total Asian (Chinese and Japanese in this case) populations for 1910, rather the totals are lumped together for anyone considered a person of color who was not black. The Historical Census browser counts "Indians, Chinese, Japanese, and persons of all other races" together for a total of 11,229 for 1910 in addition to the 9,424 African Americans. See, University of Virginia Geospatial and Statistical Data Center. United States Historical Census Data Browser, http://mapserver.lib.virginia.edu/php/county.php (15 March 3006). For 1890 numbers, see, U.S. Department of the Interior, *Population of the United States at the Eleventh Census: 1890.*

88. University of Virginia Geospatial and Statistical Data Center. United States Historical Census Data Browser. See also Nash, *Forbidden Love*. For a discussion on interracial love relationships and the offspring produced from those relationships, see Cole and Welcome, eds., *Don Pío Pico's Historical Narrative*. It is important to note, however, that census takers did not always ask the people they interviewed what their racial classification was. Often, enumerators wrote in whatever category they believed a person fit, thus skewing racial classifications of not only African Americans, but other people of color.

89. Los Angeles Almanac. See also http://www.laalmanac.com/default.htm. The phrase "other people of color" will be used to refer to Mexican, Native American, and Chinese throughout this book.

90. Hine, *Hine Sight*, xxii.

Chapter 2

1. Hayes, "A Suit for Freedom" case transcripts in the *Los Angeles Star*, 2 February 1856; Demaratus, *Force of a Feather*.

2. Ancestry.com, *1850 United States Federal Census*.

3. Demaratus, *Force of a Feather*; Beasley, *Negro Trailblazers of California*; Bass, *Forty Years*.

4. Hewlett and Williams, *Negro Who's Who in California*, 6.

5. One of her northern counterparts, Mary Ellen Pleasant, played a critical role creating and maintaining an African American community in San Francisco by fighting for civil rights of blacks, and establishing self-help organizations as well. See De Graaf et al., eds., *Seeking El Dorado*, and Katz, *The Black West*. After the Civil War, many African Americans migrated out of the South and into the North and West. Much of the scholarship on black migration focuses attention on migration to northern states, painting the picture of the North being the land of promise and opportunity for free people of color. Though there is little scholarship on the migration of African Americans to the West, one can understand the migration experience for blacks during this time. See also Taylor, *In Search of the Racial Frontier*.

6. Gutierrez and Orsi, *Contested Eden*; see also, Nash, *Forbidden Love*. Tomas Almaguer discussed the ways in which whites systematically marginalized people of color. He attributes this to the establishment of white supremacy in California, which serves as the premise of his book (*Racial Fault Lines*, 6).

7. Bass, *Forty Years*, 6; and Hewlett and Williams, *Negro Who's Who in California*, 6.

8. J. M. Guinn, *A History of California and an Extended History of Los Angeles and Environs*, 1:204. At the legislatures of 1854 and 1855, Jefferson Hunt of San Bernardino introduced a bill to create a new state also known as Columbia, which would include most of the southern portion of California. This is also known as "An act to create three states out of the territory of California."

9. California Digital Library, *California State Archives and Golden State Museum*.

10. Ibid.; Eaves, *A History of California Labor Legislation*, 2:93.

11. Bancroft, *The Works of Hubert Howe Bancroft*. 23:282.

12. Ibid., 282 and 288–89. Here, Bancroft offers a complete list of names, places of origin, residences, and ages for these early delegates. Only three resided in Los Angeles, while two more resided in either Santa Barbara or San Diego. The others resided in the northern portion of the state.

13. J. M. Guinn, *A History of California*, 206. See also, C. W. A. David, "The Fugitive Slave Law of 1793 and Its Antecedents."

14. Beasley, *Negro Trailblazers of California*, 73; Eaves, *A History of California Labor Legislation*, 92–99. For a discussion of the legal history of the Fugitive Slave Law, see O'Brien, *Constitutional Law and Politics*, 1275–92; and "The Constitution of the United States, with the acts of Congress, relating to slavery, embracing, the Constitution, the Fugitive Slave Act of 1793, the Missouri Compromise Act of 1820, the Fugitive Slave Law of 1850, and the Nebraska and Kansas bill, carefully compiled"; and Bancroft, *History of California*, 339–40.

15. David M. O'Brien, *Constitutional Law and Politics*, 1293–99. Dred Scott challenged his slave status by suing for his freedom. He claimed his freedom when his owner traveled with him to Illinois, and other northern states. Using the Missouri Compromise (1820) as the legal foundation for his case, Scott believed he was free, since his owner brought him into a free state. In 1852, Scott's case went before the Missouri state Supreme Court. The state refused to uphold antislavery laws enforced by other, specifically southern states. The Missouri Court decided that Scott would retain his status as a slave, even on free soil. Scott's attorney challenged this in the Supreme Court in 1856, focusing on the fact that Scott could not enjoy the privileges of citizenship, since even free blacks were not citizens of the country. The Court sided against Scott. On March 6, 1857, Chief Justice Robert Taney delivered the opinion of the Court. He stated that Scott was not a citizen of the United States, since he was a slave who had not rights to citizenship. He stated that slaves had no rights that "the white man was bound to respect," and that slavery was beneficial to blacks. Moreover, Taney declared the antislavery portion of the Missouri Compromise unconstitutional. The decision clearly deemed slaves as chattel. This allowed slaveholders to travel throughout the country with their property regardless of whether human or not; 193–194.

16. Bucklew, "Slavery in California." *The Californian*, 15 March 1848.

17. Ibid.

18. Burnett, "State of the State Address," Sacramento, Calif., 21 March 1849, http://governors.library.ca.gov/addresses/01-Burnett.html (17 March 2015).

19. Bucklew, "Slavery in California"; Beasley, *Negro Trailblazers of California*, 72; Burnett, "Inaugural Address."

20. Burnett, "State of the State Address."

21. Ibid.

22. Ibid.

23. California Digital Library, California State Archives.

24. Beasley, *Negro Trailblazers of California*, 73, citing from the California Report, No. 2, 424. For details, see *Reports of Cases Determined in the Supreme Court of the State of California*, vol. 2.

25. California Digital Library, California State Archives and Golden State Museum.

26. Beasley, *Negro Trailblazers of California*, 70.

27. Ibid., 72.

28. Ibid.

29. *Daily Alta California*, 20 April 1853, 2.

30. Demaratus, *The Force of a Feather*. See also Beasley, *Negro Trailblazers of California*, 88–90. Beasley does not mention the gender of the person, "Brown," who attempted to recapture this particular slave. See also *Daily Placer Times and Transcript*.

31. *African-American Slavery: California Fugitive Slave Case: Stovall v. Archy*, BACM Research; Beasley, *Negro Trailblazers of California*, 80; Smith, *Freedom's Frontier*, 76–78.

32. *African-Americans Slavery: California Fugitive Slave Case: Stovall v. Archy*, BACM Research; Beasley, "Slavery in California," 43; Lapp and Moore, *Archy Lee*, 8; Beasley, *Negro Trailblazers of California*, 80.

33. *African-Americans Slavery: California Fugitive Slave Case: Stovall v. Archy*, BACM Research; Beasley, *Negro Trailblazers of California*, 80.

34. Beasley, *Negro Trailblazers of California*, 80.

35. Ibid.

36. After the Mexican-American war, whites forced Mexicans from their land. William McKendree Gwin proposed and Act to help Mexicans keep their property by having the president appoint a committee of three to preside over land claims. The California Land Claims Act, also known as the Gwin Act, backfired, since all claims were filed in both the district courts and the United States Supreme Court. Costly legal battles bankrupted many Mexican landowners, leaving them unable to afford property. In addition white squatters took possession of many Mexican-owned lands, causing even more people to lose property rights.

37. Beasley, *Negro Trailblazers*, 78–83. See also The Virtual Museum of the City of San Francisco.

38. Beasley, *Negro Trailblazers of California*, 88; *California State Constitution 1849*.

39. See, for example, Hine, *Hine Sight*; White, *Ar'n't I a Woman?*; Stevenson, *Life in Black and White*; Demaratus, *Force of a Feather*.

40. Ancestry.com, *1850 United States Federal Census*. See also Demaratus, *Force of a Feather*, 21–27; Jones, *Labor of Love, Labor of Sorrow*, 15.

41. Beasley, *Negro Trailblazers of California*, 90; Bass, *Forty Years*, 8.

42. Ancestry.com, *1850 United States Federal Census—Slave Schedules*. Original data: United States of America, Bureau of the Census. Seventh Census of the United States, 1850. NARA microfilm publication M432, 1,009 rolls; National Archives, Washington, D.C. See also Demaratus, *Force of a Feather*, 32.

43. Demaratus, *Force of A Feather*, 49. See also White, *Ar'n't I a Woman*; Stevenson, *Life in Black and White*; Jones, *Labor of Love, Labor of Sorrow*.

44. See, for example, White, *Ar'n't I a Woman*; Stevenson, *Life in Black and White*; Jones, *Labor of Love, Labor of Sorrow*; Hayes, "A Suit for Freedom"; Beasley, *Negro Trailblazers of California*, 88.

45. Beasley, *Negro Trailblazers of California*, 88; Demaratus, *Force of A Feather*, 84; Hayes, "A Suit for Freedom".

46. DeMaratus, *Force of a Feather*, 111.

47. Hayes, "A Suit for Freedom"; DeMaratus, *Force of a Feather*, 113–16.

48. Hayes, "A Suit for Freedom"; Beasley, *Negro Trailblazers of California*, 88.

49. Hayes, "A Suit for Freedom"; Beasley, *Negro Trailblazers of California*, 89.

50. Demaratus, *Force of a Feather*, 139–45.

51. Beasley, *Negro Trailblazers of California*, 89; 1850 United States Federal Census–Slave Schedules.

52. Demaratus, *Force of a Feather*, 139–45; Bass, *Forty Years*, 8.

53. Demaratus, *Force of a Feather*, 139–40; Beasley, *Negro Trailblazers of California*, 89.

54. Demaratus, *Force of a Feather*, 139–45.

55. United States Federal Census, 1860, 1870; Demaratus, *Force of a Feather*, 181.

56. Demaratus, *Force of a Feather*, 139–45; Bass, *Forty Years*, 8; Beasley, *Negro Trailblazers of California*, 109. All of these accounts state Mason's earnings as $2.50 a day, which may be unlikely. However, none of the accounts show how many days per week Mason worked, so while her earnings may seem high, it is possible she only worked a few days out of the week. Most people earned much higher wages in the West, however, which makes her earning about even with other people doing the same work, which is the equivalent to what female workers earned in a week in the South. These are the only published records of Mason's earnings for this particular job. See Jones, *Labor of Love, Labor of Sorrow*.

57. Bass, *Forty Years*, 8; Beasley, *Negro Trailblazers*, 88.

58. Beasley, *Negro Trailblazers of California*, 90; Bass, *Forty Years*, 27.

59. White, *Ar'n't I a Woman*; Stevenson, *Life in Black and White*; Jones, *Labor of Love, Labor of Sorrow*; Hine, *Hine Sight*; Hunter, *To 'Joy My Freedom*.

60. Bass, *Forty Years*, 8; De Graaf et al., eds., *Seeking El Dorado*, 19.

61. Angelenos went to great lengths to promote Los Angeles, attracting migrants from across the country to the region. In addition, the city attempted to portray a place where people could come and accumulate wealth by means of land purchases as opposed to the gold discoveries throughout the northern portion of the state. The *Los Angeles Daily Times* advertised land sales daily. In addition, the paper constantly printed stories stating that Los Angeles really was a great place to live. African Americans also promoted the city to other blacks across the country, creating a steady flow of migrants from Louisiana, Arkansas, Texas, and some northern cities as well. In addition, the land boom created many opportunities for new migrants seeking skilled work within the city.

62. Bass, *Forty Years*, 8; Demaratus, *Force of a Feather*, 178.

63. Bass, *Forty Years*, 8; De Graaf et al., eds., *Seeking El Dorado*, 13; "Documentary Explores Lives of Black Pioneers." *Los Angeles Sentinel*, Thursday, December 15, 1988, A-8. At the time, a local public channel, KCOQ, aired a documentary on four generations of the Mason-Owens family and their impact on the African American community in Los Angeles.

64. Bass, *Forty Years*, 8.

65. Ancestry.com, U.S. City Directories, 1821–1989, *Los Angeles, California City Directory*, 1893, 1900, 1910, 1913, 1920, 1921.

66. Beasley, *Negro Trailblazers of California*, 110.

67. De Graaf et al., eds., *Seeking El Dorado*, 18. See also Bass, *Forty Years*, 8–9; and Du Bois, "Colored California." For more information, see Bunch's chapter in De Graaf et al., eds., *Seeking El Dorado*, 129. Bunch notes that Robert C. Owens plays a crucial role in the makeup of the African American professional class in Los Angeles during this time, which is what Du Bois chooses to highlight in his article in this particular volume of *Crisis Magazine*. After Charles Owens died, Ellen remarried a man named G. Huddleston. Charles left her one-half of his property, and a quarter to each of his sons. See *Early California Wills Los Angeles County 1850–1890*.

68. "Biddy Mason, Landowner, 1818–1891," Los Angeles Public Library.

69. Bass, *Forty Years*, 8; Beasley, *Negro Trailblazers of California*, 88, 216; "Documentary Explores Lives of Black Pioneers."

70. Bass, *Forty Years*, 8.

71. Ibid., 7–8; De Graaf et al., eds., *Seeking El Dorado*, 19; *United States Federal Census 1860–1900*; Flamming, *Bound for Freedom*, 23; Campbell, "African American Women, Wealth Accumulation, and Social Welfare Activism in 19th-Century Los Angeles."

72. *United States Federal Census 1870–1900*; Campbell, "African American Women, Wealth Accumulation, and Social Welfare Activism in 19th-Century Los Angeles."

73. California State Library, *Great Registers, 1866–1898*; Ancestry.com, *California, Voter Registers, 1866–1898*; Campbell, "African American Women, Wealth Accumulation, and Social Welfare Activism in 19th-Century Los Angeles."

74. *1880 United States Federal Census*.

75. *1900 United States Federal Census*; Campbell, "African American Women, Wealth Accumulation, and Social Welfare Activism in 19th-Century Los Angeles."

76. Ancestry.com, *1870 United States Federal Census*.

77. Ibid.

78. Ibid. It should be noted that Biddy Mason and Winnie Owens represented the highest end of the spectrum for female estate values. In fact, their estate values were the highest of any household heads regardless of gender.

79. Ibid. It is unclear whether Sarah Jefferson was the grandmother or mother of the five children. She was sixty-two, and the children's ages ranged from five to twelve. No male adult was listed in the household, and the census did not report familial relationships the way it did in later years.

80. Ibid.

81. Occupational characteristics will be explored later. These occupations, however, made up the bulk of the jobs African American males held in 1870. See Ancestry.com, *1870 United States Federal Census*.

82. Blassingame, *The Slave Community*, 151; Stevenson, *Life in Black and White*, 160.

83. Ancestry.com, *1870 United States Federal Census*. The average age of African Americans in Los Angeles overall was just over twenty-one and a half.

84. Ibid. It is unclear whether Sarah Jefferson is the mother or grandmother of the children.

85. Ibid. While the average household membership totaled three people, none were over nine. Household with the largest membership reported heads: from Utah and Rhode Island, each with nine members, Arkansas with six, and South Carolina with five. At the other end of the spectrum, people from the West Indies and Pennsylvania made up the smallest households, with only one member. See also Jones, *Labor of Love, Labor of Sorrow*. Jones points out similar patterns in household structure in southern urban areas. After the Civil War, black families in non-rural areas became smaller in number for several reasons, including an increase in both adult and child mortality rates. Jones also notes a decline in black fertility rates by one-third between 1880 and 1910 (112–13, 123). For 1870, the University of Virginia's Geospatial and Statistical Data shows 134 people of color living in Los Angeles that year. This study accounts for 109 of them. It is important to note that the census takers calculated total numbers of "colored" people at the bottom of every census sheet. Although the numbers here differ slightly, only those taken from the actual census index are used here.

86. Ancestry.com, *1870 United States Federal Census*.

87. Ibid.

88. Beasley, *Negro Trailblazers of California*, 177. Here, she quotes Sections 56 and 57 of the Act. Section 57 states that "Children of African or Mongolian descent and Indian children not living under the care of white people shall not be admitted into public schools . . ." This Act clearly aimed to marginalize people of color further. In addition, it was an attempt to create a dependency of African Americans and other groups of people of color on whites for education, which made a significant impact on social mobility for these communities. Still, people of color in California continued to fight this discriminatory practice.

89. Ibid., 180. Beasley notes that most of those attacking the state school system migrated to the state either from the northeast or from Canada. She believed that as migrants coming from regions where they were free and took advantage of opportunities such as education, they could make a larger impact on the school board. In addition, those people of African descent who were brought to the state as slaves contributed financially to the struggle, even though they themselves were denied formal educations.

90. Ibid. Delilah Beasley pays much credit to the local ministers who organized the African American community on a larger scale. Moreover, she contends that some of those fighting for equal education typically migrated to the West and California specifically, and were educated prior to their move. When these people arrived in California, they wanted African Americans and other people of color to have the same opportunities they did. The Fourteenth Amendment dealt specifically with citizenship and the rights of due process. It states, "All persons born or naturalized in the United States, and subject to the jurisdiction thereof, are citizens of the United States and of the State wherein they reside. No State shall make or

enforce any law which shall abridge the privileges or immunities of citizens of the United States; nor shall any State deprive any person of life, liberty, or property, without due process of law; nor deny to any person within its jurisdiction the equal protection of the laws." This amendment was ratified on July 9, 1869. The Fifteenth Amendment spoke to the rights of citizens of the United States. It states, "The right of citizens of the United States to vote shall not be denied or abridged by the United States or by any State on account of race, color, or previous condition of servitude." This amendment was ratified on 13 February 1870. See Bettye Collier-Thomas, *Jesus, Jobs, and Justice*.

91. Beasley, *Negro Trailblazers of California*, 182. A *writ of mandamus* simply means that the superior court would order a lower court, public official, or body to perform a very specific duty, in this case, forcing the California Board of Education either to integrate their system or to provide better opportunities for African Americans and other children of color. See also, Broussard, *Black San Francisco*, 18–19.

92. Beasley, *Negro Trailblazers of California*, 182. At the onset of the Court's decision were the words, "separate schools for colored children." Still, they provided an outlet for people of color to send their children into predominantly white schools by stating that if colored schools could not be maintained, then the children could attend white schools. People of color took full advantage of this.

93. Ibid., 180–82.

94. Ancestry.com, *1870 United States Federal Census*. The Census Bureau reported in 1870 that in Los Angeles there were 134 African Americans, 236 Chinese, 219 Native Americans, and only 2 Japanese residents. In 1880 there were 188 African Americans, 1170 Chinese, 316 Native Americans, and only 1 Japanese resident. While these numbers continued to grow for people of color as a whole, they remained low for African Americans and Native Americans while virtually insignificant for Japanese people. During the 1880s, Chinese people became the targets of racism and discriminatory practices leading up to the 1882 Exclusion Act. These factors played a significant role in which groups of people of color gained access to education in Los Angeles. Having such small numbers per population, coupled with even lower numbers of children, and made it much easier to take advantage of the court's decision regarding admittance into public schools of African Americans and other students of color.

95. University of Virginia Geospatial and Statistical Data Center. This time, the census did not include the diverse amount of groups of people of color for this period. In fact, it was during this year that the census began to include Chinese, Japanese, and a group called "other" for the first time. Still, the numbers for people of color attending schools remained low, considering that Chinese and Hispanics were not included in this collection.

96. Ibid.

97. Ibid.

98. Ibid.

99. Ibid. The largest number of male African American students attended schools in San Francisco, totaling sixty-eight pupils, while Sacramento had the

second largest amount at thirty-four. The majority of "colored" female students in California went to school in San Francisco, with sixty-six pupils.

100. Ibid. The total population at this time for African Americans in Los Angeles sees a small increase from 134 in 1870 to 188 in 1880. While the 1890 census was destroyed, we do have numbers based on census abstracts, and according to the Historical Census Browser, the African American community in 1890 grows to ten times its size, amounting to 1,817 people, marking the beginning of the African American population boom in the city. Comparatively, the African American communities in San Francisco and Sacramento were much more consistent during these decades. In 1870, San Francisco had 1,330 African Americans, while Sacramento had 470. In 1880, these numbers changed only slightly: 1,628 for San Francisco and 560 for Sacramento. In 1890, San Francisco reported 1,847 blacks, while Sacramento reported a decrease of 47 African Americans in its community. Of the entire state of California, Los Angeles experienced the most significant increase of its African American community. Also, during the last two decades of the nineteenth century, San Francisco contained the largest Chinese population with a total of 21,745 in 1880 and 25,833 people in 1890, while Sacramento reported a total of 4,892 Chinese people in 1880, and 4,371 in 1890. Los Angeles also experienced one of the most significant increases in its Chinese population during these years, recording 1,169 in 1880 and 4,424 in 1890. Still, these numbers paled compared to white enrollment in public schools, with 9,557 males and 9,328 females. The northern California cities continued enrolling the largest amount of "colored" male and female students, totaling 220.

101. Ibid.

102. Ibid. One should note that changes were made in the census data. For the first time, the census distinguished between African Americans and other people of color. The exclusion of females for this census makes it difficult to determine all of the exact numbers. Los Angeles contained the second largest illiteracy rate for African Americans, while the highest percentage of other people of color who could neither read nor write remained in San Francisco.

103. Ibid.

104. "Los Angeles Schools Collection," Seaver Center; Beasley, *Negro Trailblazers of California*, 172–87; *United States Federal Census, 1870–1900*; Gill, *Beauty Shop Politics*, 8–18.

105. *United States Federal Census, 1870–1900*; Giddings, *When and Where I Enter*, 100–108.

Chapter 3

1. Bass, *Forty Years*. See also "Death Certificate of Charlotta Bass," L.A. Public Library. Other African American newspapers at the time included the *Liberator*, the *Enterprise*, the *Outlook*, in San Francisco, and the *Eagle*'s competitor, the *New Age*.

2. Bass, *Forty Years*, 27.

3. Ibid.

4. Ibid. The *Los Angeles Herald* became the Los Angeles Examiner in 1903, and then changed its name to the *Herald Examiner* in 1962. See also Ancestry.com, *1910 United States Federal Census*; De Graaf et al., eds., *Seeking El Dorado*, 133.

5. Bass, *Forty Years*, 16. The *California Eagle* also had an interracial readership.

6. Du Bois, "Colored California." For a brief analysis on Du Bois's visit, and African American promotion of California, see Lonnie G. Bunch III's chapter "The Greatest State for the Negro" in De Graaf et al., eds., *Seeking El Dorado*; and Flamming, *Bound for Freedom*.

7. In 1870, the African American population in the region totaled only 134 people. In 1880, the total equaled 188. By the turn of the century, the African American population jumped to 2,841, but the census also reported 6,323 *colored* people in the region, further establishing not only a significant population within the mainstream, but a strong sense of community as well. During the decades following the Reconstruction Era in the American South, African Americans began migrating west, seeking opportunity, land, and most importantly, individual wealth. See Ancestry.com, *1870 United States Federal Census*.

8. See Durant Jr. and Louden, "The Black Middle Class in America." The *californios* were descendants of the initial founding families of Los Angeles, including those of African descent. This group of people played a significant role in secularizing the California Mission system and returning the land to the Native American population. Although many *californios'* intentions did not include humanitarian efforts, many did accumulate a great deal of wealth from the secularization process. Also, see *Spanish and Mexican Land Grants*, California State Archive. Here, there are several accounts of Native Americans petitioning for large portions of land throughout Los Angeles and Southern California, specifically.

9. *1880 United States Census Index* provided by The Church of Jesus Christ of Latter-day Saints, 1999 Intellectual Reserve, Inc. (accessed 12 November 2005).

10. Ibid.

11. Ancestry.com, *1900 United States Federal Census*. It is important to note that some of the census data was unusable because certain pages were not properly preserved. For purposes of this study, most of the population is included. Every legible household including African Americans was taken from this census.

12. Ancestry.com, *1910 United States Federal Census*. These numbers are based on a count of all African American households in Los Angeles in 1910. They differ, however, from the county totals (see chapter 1), even though the majority of people in Los Angeles County lived in the city. Additionally, a small percentage of black people are unaccounted for because the quality of the documentation was not always clear, meaning that there are some census pages what are so faded, that one cannot determine who the people were. Still, 7,212 individuals were identified compared to the 9,424 people in the county, which is consistent with other counts.

13. Since the African American population in Los Angeles experienced such as tremendous increase between 1900 and 1910, a sample population of one in five people was used to conduct a survey of migration patterns for that census year. See Ancestry.com, *1910 United States Federal Census*.

14. Taylor, *In Search of the Racial Frontier*.

15. Ancestry.com, *1900 United States Federal Census*; Horton, *Free People of Color*, 112.

16. Ancestry.com, *1850–1900 United States Federal Census*; White, *Too Heavy a Load*, 30–31.

17. De Graaf et al., eds., *Seeking El Dorado*, 111, 112, 216–17. See also White, *Too Heavy a Load*, 27; Campbell, "African American Women, Wealth Accumulation, and Social Welfare in 19th-Century Los Angeles," 392–95.

18. "The Negro Women in Los Angeles and Vicinity—Some Notable Characters," *Los Angeles Times*, February 2, 1909, 4.

19. *Los Angeles Sentinel*, 15 December 1988, A-8. See also Bass, *Forty Years*, 20.

20. There is a bit of confusion about which of the two organized first. Although FAME boasts about being the oldest African American church in Los Angeles, it was not the first to get its charter. Second Baptist organized about one year later than FAME, but did not get chartered until 1885. Whether they were noticed by the city as a church or not may not be as important as knowing that African Americans organized their own worship services independently, and operated them accordingly until charters for those institutions were secured. See Bass, *Forty Years*, page 20; *Los Angeles Sentinel*, 15 December 1988, A-8; Beasley, *Negro Trailblazers of California*; Second Baptist Church, "Together We Build."

21. Campbell, " 'The Newest Religious Sect Has Started in Los Angeles,' " 6–7; Bass, *Forty Years*, 20–26.

22. Collier-Thomas, *Jesus, Jobs, and Justice*. De Graaf et al., eds., *Seeking El Dorado*, 19. Biddy Mason set the precedent for black Angelenos helping one another. Her work motivated African Americans to get involved in community service.

23. Collier-Thomas, *Jesus, Jobs, and Justice*; Higginbotham, *Righteous Discontent*, 8.

24. De Graaf et al., eds., *Seeking El Dorado*, 111; White, *Too Heavy a Load*, 39; Collier-Thomas, *Jesus, Jobs, and Justice*, xvi; Horton, *Free People of Color*, 109–12; Higginbotham, *Righteous Discontent*, 7–10, 12. Higginbotham explains that the church "housed a diversity of programs including schools, circulating libraries, concerts, restaurants, insurance companies, vocational training, athletic clubs—all catering to a population much broader than the membership of individual churches." Higginbotham notes that the church offered women "a forum through which to articulate a public discourse critical to women's subordination."

25. Higginbotham, *Righteous Discontent*, 7.

26. Ibid., 10.

27. Collier-Thomas, *Jesus Jobs and Justice*, xvi.

28. De Graaf et al., eds., *Seeking El Dorado*, 111; White, *Too Heavy a Load*, 39; Horton, *Free People of Color*, 109–12; Beasley, *Negro Trailblazers*, 226; Terborg-Penn, *African American Women in the Struggle for the Vote, 1850–1920*; Higginbotham, *Righteous Discontent*, 7–10.

29. Beasley, *Negro Trailblazers of California*, 226; Terborg-Penn, *African American Women in the Struggle for the Vote, 1850–1920*, 85–89.

30. Bradley-Stovall, "Shall Color Line Divide?" *Los Angeles Times* 6 January 1906, 11; Flamming, *Bound for Freedom*, 136.

31. Beasley, *Negro Trailblazers of California*, 193–95. Aptheker, ed., *The Correspondence of W. E. B. Du Bois*, 1, 353–354.

32. De Graaf et al., eds., *Seeking El Dorado*, 112 and 216–17.

33. Christman, *The Best Laid Plans*; De Graaf et al., eds., *Seeking El Dorado*, 112, 221–24.

34. De Graaf et al., eds., *Seeking El Dorado*, 98–125, 129–48, 210–46. These scholars all agree that the African American middle class followed similar trends as the elite white population, not only on Los Angeles, but also throughout other regions of the country. The Progressive Era proved particularly important in shaping the political attitude of the African American community, motivating them to branch off from the mainstream and focus energies on issues specific to blacks. This trend in African American political and social attitudes is no different from the ways in which blacks formed their own agenda during earlier movements such as the Abolitionist or the Reform Movements of the middle of the nineteenth century. Rather than following mainstream attitudes, African Americans chose to organize around issues concerning their community as a whole, and aimed their efforts at social, political, and economic equality.

35. Bass, *Forty Years*, 35.

36. Ibid.

37. Ibid., 36.

38. Ibid.; De Graaf et al., eds., *Seeking El Dorado*, 279–308; Freer, "L.A. Race Woman."

39. See for example, Hine, *Hine Sight*; Collier-Thomas, *Jesus, Jobs, and Justice*; Jelks, *African Americans in the Furniture City*; Hunter, *To 'Joy My Freedom*; and Gill, *Beauty Shop Politics*.

40. Ancestry.com, *1900 United States Federal Census*. Due to preservation conditions of these documents, some of the notations may have been illegible. Although some family information may be incomplete, the data remains representative.

41. Ancestry.com, *1870 United States Federal Census*.

42. Ancestry.com, *1910 United States Federal Census*.

43. Ibid.

44. Ibid.

45. *1880 United States Census Index* provided by The Church of Jesus Christ of Latter-day Saints. The average ages for women identified as non-household heads was slightly over twenty-two and a half years, and men was just over twenty-nine and a half, excluding those men listed as railroad workers and boarders in other's homes.

46. Ibid.

47. Ibid. The Ann Daniels (formerly Pepper) family is one example of how black people were listed in the census on year as black and "mulatto" in another. By 1900, they are all listed in the census as black.

48. Ibid.

49. Women made up 28 percent of the household heads for African Americans during this year, while men made up the remaining 72 percent. This represents a decrease from the previous decade, where women made up 48 percent of the household heads.

50. Ancestry.com, *1900 United States Federal Census*.

51. Ibid.

52. Ibid. Although the number for household heads born in California is small, the total number of household heads in California is a sample, and represents only 22 percent of the entire African American population.

53. Ruggles, et. al., *Integrated Public Use Microdata Series*

54. Ancestry.com, *1860 United States Federal Census*; Ancestry.com, *1870 United States Federal Census*; *1880 United States Census Index* provided by The Church of Jesus Christ of Latter-day Saints.

55. Ruggles, et. al., *Integrated Public Use Microdata Series*.

56. Ibid.

57. Foner and Lewis, eds., *The Black Worker*, 68; Ancestry.com, *1900 United States Federal Census*.

58. Tong, *Unsubmissive Women*; Kooistra, "Angels for Sale."

59. Tong, *Unsubmissive Women*; Kooistra, "Angels for Sale"; Ancestry.com, *1870 United States Federal Census*; *1880 United States Census Index*; Ancestry.com, *1900 United States Federal Census*.

60. Ancestry.com, *1870 United States Federal Census*; *1880 United States Census Index*. Foner notes that in 1890, throughout California African Americans, coupled with a small number of Chinese, worked as hairdressers and barbers, carpenters and joiners. Of the 11,322 "colored" people living in the city, the largest amount of males were employed as tailors (2,139), railroad employees (2,044), and boot and shoe makers (1,269). The majority of female workers were employed as dressmakers, milliners, and seamstresses (239). See Foner and Lewis, eds., *The Black Worker*, 4:68.

61. Ibid. This number includes six children ages four and under.

62. Ancestry.com, *1900 United States Federal Census*.

63. See, for example, Collier-Thomas, *Jesus, Jobs, and Justice*.

64. Ancestry.com, *1900 United States Federal Census*; Bass, *Forty Years*, 27; Foner and Lewis, eds., *The Black Worker*. Foner and Lewis note the significant occupations for African Americans across the country in 1900. In comparing the skilled occupations in the North and the South, Foner and Lewis show that out of 10,083 African American blacksmiths in the country, 1,140 of them worked in the North, while 8,943 worked in the South. The largest occupation for African American men was carpenters. Blacks in the North made up 1,664 and in the South, 19,403. Brick and tile labor also showed significant representation. 3,489 black Northerners and 6,442 black Southerners held this occupation. 2,531 Northern and 7,684 Southern black males worked as engineers and firefighters, while 4,452 black brick and stone masons worked in the North and 9,918 in the South. Women's work largely consisted of dressmaking—accounting for 4,235 Northern and 8,279 Southern black women—and seamstresses, of whom 1,724 were in the North, and 9,727 were in the South.

65. Ancestry.com, *1910 United States Federal Census*. See also Foner and Lewis, eds., *The Black Worker*. Foner and Lewis note that by 1910, women made up more than half of the entire African American population in the United States. Almost one-fourth of them (2,013,981) were wage earners. Laundresses were the largest

number (361,551), then cooks (205,929), dressmakers (38,148), laundry (12,196), and housekeepers (10,021). For those women who were not designated as wage earners, there is no explanation of whether they were being supported by husbands or worked sporadically when they could.

66. Ancestry.com, *1910 United States Federal Census*.

67. Ibid.

68. Ibid.; Jones, *Labor of Love, Labor of Sorrow*, 110–51.

69. See, for example, AnneMarie Kooistra, "Angels for sale: The history of prostitution in Los Angeles, 1880–1940, University of Southern California, ProQuest, UMI Dissertations Publishing, 2003. 3133298," 42–44.

70. Ancestry.com, *1850–1910 United States Federal Census*. See, Ann Butler, *Daughters of Joy, Sisters of Misery: Prostitutes in the American West, 1865–90*, Urbana: University of Illinois Press, 1985, 16; De Graaf et al., eds., Willi Coleman, "African American Women & Community Development in California" in *Seeking El Dorado*, 116; See also Tera Hunter, *To 'Joy My Freedom*; Jane Dabel, *A Respectable Woman: The Public Roles of African American Women in 19th-Century New York*, New York: NYU Press, 2008; and Darlene and Clark Hine, *Hine Sight*.

71. Bass, *Forty Years*, 43–44.

72. De Graaf, Mulroy, and Taylor et al., eds., *Seeking El Dorado*, 19; see also Bass, *Forty Years*, 14–15; Beasley, *Negro Trailblazers*, 196–200; Flamming, *Bound for Freedom*, 69.

73. Beasley, *Negro Pioneers of California*, 172–87.

74. State Normal School, Los Angeles, "10th Annual Catalogue of the State Normal School, Los Angeles for the School Year ending June 23, 1892 and Circular for 1892–93," 18.

75. Ibid., 18–19.

76. Ibid., 20.

77. Ibid., 187. See also, Du Bois, "Colored California," 194; Ancestry.com, *1920 United States Federal Census*; and Ancestry.com, *California Death Index, 1940–1997*.

78. W.E.B. Du Bois Papers (MS 312). "Complimentary Dinner to Dr. W.E. Burghardt Du Bois," May 13, 1913 event program, http://credo.library.umass.edu /view/full/mums312-b162-i248, (25 March 2015).

79. W.E.B. Du Bois Papers (MS 312). "Letter to Vada Somerville" 4 March 1925, http://credo.library.umass.edu/view/full/mums312-b031-i071, (25 March 2015); "Letter to Vada Somerville" 21 March 1925, http://credo.library.umass.edu/view /full/mums312-b031-i072, (25 March 2015); "Letter from JA Somerville to W.E.B. Du Bois," 18 November 1924, http://credo.library.umass.edu/view/full/mums312 -b026-i214, (25 March 2015); "Letter to Mrs. Mary White Ovington from the Los Angeles Branch NAACP" nominating John Somerville to the National Board, 2 May 1927, http://credo.library.umass.edu/view/full/mums312-b031-i072, (25 March 2015)

80. Flamming, *Bound for Freedom*, 24–25.

81. Bass, *Forty Years*, 9.

82. Ibid., 9, 17; Ancestry.com, *1900 United States Federal Census*. The Stricklands also participated in their local church community, and Bass noted that their

daughter Jessie was a member of Second Baptist Church, most likely, in addition to the entire family.

83. Bass, *Forty Years*, 9. Garrott represents the way in which black Angelenos interacted with whites outside of their own community. Not only did whites patronize black businesses, but also interacted with African Americans on a more social level as well. Much of this kind of interaction occurs during that second half of the nineteenth century and even the early part of the twentieth century, prior to the push toward segregation in the city. Moreover, many of the opportunities afforded to blacks in Los Angeles occur before large numbers of African Americans begin to migrate into the city at the end of the nineteenth century and into the twentieth. See, for example, Sides, *L.A. City Limits;* and Flamming, *Bound for Freedom.* For details on the kinds of middle class occupations and professions during this time period, see Bass, *Forty Years;* De Graaf et al., eds., *Seeking El Dorado;* and Beasley, *Negro Trailblazers of California.*

84. Dr. A. C. Garrott, "How the University-Trained Negro Has Advanced in the Greatest Professions," *Los Angeles Times,* 12 February 1909, III2.

85. See For a brief history of Bunche's accomplishments, see Nobel Prize.org, "Nobel Peace Prize 1950—Ralph Bunche." http://www.nobelprize.org/nobel _prizes/peace/laureates/1950/bunche-bio.html.

86. Jefferson High School was opened in 1914, only two years before Bunche came to Los Angeles. Central Avenue sat at the end of the block, perpendicular to Thirty-Seventh Street. Jefferson was within walking distance, in the same neighborhood. Both Central Avenue and Jefferson High School were to the east of the Johnson home. Second Baptist was to the west and south of the home. This neighborhood is considered South Central Los Angeles today. It soon became the home of many African Americans who, in Los Angeles, were banned from living west of Main Street. Moreover, they were pushed further and further to the southern portion of the city. The Johnson family, however, lived in the neighborhood long before whites began to migrate out, but chose to stay in their home for many years to come.

87. Conyers and Kennedy, "Negro Passing." It appears as though the Bunche family unintentionally *passed* for white, and that they clearly identified as African American. The Bunche family continued to interact with the black community socially and politically, which is another indicator that they did not intend for people to believe they were white, nor does it imply they wanted to become white.

88. Ibid.

89. Aptheker, ed., *The Correspondence of W. E. B. Du Bois,* 353–54.

90. Ibid.

91. Du Bois, "Colored California."

Chapter 4

1. *Alcalde Court Records, 1830–1860,* Seaver Center for California History; *Los Angeles Area Court Records, 1850–1910.* Huntington Library and Botanical Gardens. A survey of criminal records at both the Alcalde and the Criminal Courts in Los

Angeles reveals a pattern of violence throughout the city from the 1830s through the beginning of the twentieth century. These represent some of the most common and violent crimes people were arrested for and accused of. See also Faragher, *Eternity Street*.

2. Monkkonen, "Homicide in Los Angeles, 1827–2002."

3. This is especially true when one considers the amount of newspaper articles published in the early 1880s, when Chinese exclusion was a main political issue nationwide. Since Los Angeles and California in general had the highest number of Chinese immigrants, the local newspapers continued to publish articles about crimes committed by Chinese men. Propagandizing the situation as such made it much easier for the middle class also to focus attention on the criminal activity of men and women of other groups of color. For a discussion on discrimination in Los Angeles during the twentieth century, see Sides, *L.A. City Limits*, and Flamming, *Bound for Freedom*, both of whom explore the role of racism and its effect on the African American community. In addition, see De Graaf et al., eds., *Seeking El Dorado*; Deverell, *Whitewashed Adobe*; and Sanchez, *Becoming Mexican American*. Lastly, see Avila, *Popular Culture in the Age of White Flight*, for a discussion on race and space in Los Angeles.

4. "Calle de los Negros—A Vanished Landmark," *The Daily Mirror*, 13 October 2011. https://ladailymirror.com/2011/10/13/calle-de-los-negros-a-vanished -landmark/ (accessed 15 June 2015). Nigger Alley became a ghetto made up of various people of color and immigrants.

5. *1870–1880 U.S. Federal Census.*

6. "Calle de los Negros—A Vanished Landmark"; Los Angeles Fire Department Historical Archive. Nigger Alley became a ghetto made up of various people of color and immigrants. See Chavez-Garcia, *Negotiating Conquest*, 149.

7. California State Constitution, 1849, California State Archive.

8. Ibid., Article 1, Sections 1–7.

9. Ibid., Article 1, Sections 8–15.

10. Ibid., Article 2. This specifically refers to the Treaty of Queretaro, signed on 30 May 1848. For the language of the 1849 constitution, see http://codes.findlaw .com/ca/constitution-of-1849-the-state-of-california-with-amendments-super seded-by-constitution-of-1879/0con-sect-1-nr2.html, (accessed 15 June 2015); and *The Declaration of Independence and the Constitution of the United States*, 68–71. Most women in America did not receive the right to vote until 1920 when the Nineteenth Amendment was ratified.

11. Constitution of the State of California, Article 2. http://www.sos.ca.gov /archives/collections/constitutions/1849/full-text/ (accessed 15 June 2015).

12. These represent the premier cases regarding the status of slaves in California.

13. *Alcalde Court Records, 1830–1860.* See also Chavez-Garcia, *Negotiating Conquest*.

14. *Alcalde Court Records, 1830–1860.*

15. Ibid., 5 August 1850.

16. Ibid., 29 June 1850.

17. Ibid., 5 July 1850.

18. Ibid., 3 July 1850.

19. Ibid.

20. Ibid., 22 August 1850.

21. Ibid.

22. Ibid., 6 September 1850.

23. Ibid. For a discussion of prostitution in the American West, refer to Butler, *Daughters of Joy, Sisters of Misery*; Seagraves, *Soiled Doves*; and Hurtado, *Intimate Frontiers*.

24. *Alcalde Court Records, 1830–1860*, 14 August 1850.

25. Ibid., 2 July 1850.

26. Ibid.

27. Ibid., 3 September 1850.

28. Ibid., 10 September 1850; Faragher, *Eternity Street*, 59.

29. *Los Angeles Area Criminal Court Records Court Records, 1850–1910*.

30. *Penal Code of California*, 118–20.

31. Ibid.

32. *Alcalde Court Records, 1830–1860*, 10 September 1850.

33. "Headline History, Los Angeles County (1848–1865)," http://www.laalmanac .com/history/hi01c.htm. Approximately two decades prior, in 1835, a group of men in Texas organized, calling themselves the Texas Rangers. They became the first law enforcement agency in the region. One of the group's leaders, Stephen F. Austin, believed that the colony needed an agency for its own protection. It is unclear as to whether the Los Angeles Rangers modeled themselves after the Texas Rangers, but they certainly followed a similar format. Having a sheriff in place already, the Los Angeles Rangers organized with the express purpose of enforcing laws and seeking out criminals. This group of men initially comprised those of both Mexican and American heritages.

34. *Penal Code of California*, 436.

35. "Rain Drunks: Two Old Timers Say That the Rain Caused It," *Los Angeles Daily Times*, Wednesday, 25 January 1882.

36. "News of the Morning: The Condition of the City," *Los Angeles Daily Times*, 27 December 1881.

37. Ibid.

38. Ibid.

39. "Cold Weather the Cause," *Los Angeles Daily Times*, 12 January 1882. See also "Two Drunks," *Los Angeles Daily Times*, 12 January 1882.

40. "The Two Messages," *Los Angeles Times*, Wednesday, 19 December 1988. William H. Workman served as mayor of Los Angeles for two terms between 1886 and 1888. His opponent in 1888, John Bryson, who then served until February 1889, succeeded him.

41. "The City in Brief," *Los Angeles Times*, Wednesday, 6 February 1889. In February 1889, Judge Austin presided over a case dealing with this problem, convicting a man named Ah Hain for operating an opium house. The judge scheduled his sentencing for 6 February. Judging from the strict enforcement of the laws regarding alcohol use, and the fact that the court denied him bail, he probably

received an extremely harsh sentence. It is likely that Judge Austin used this case to set a citywide precedence against illegal drug use, because opium abuse appeared to be a growing problem.

42. Darland, "Chinese Massacre at Los Angeles in 1871"; Tong, *Unsubmissive Women*, 3–33; Hirata, "Free, Indentured, Enslaved," 3–29; Butler, *Daughters of Joy, Sisters of Misery*, 6–16; Hurtado, *Intimate Frontiers*, 90–95. It seems very likely that Ya Hit was brought to the city as a prostitute rather than a wife. While the city had only a small number of Chinese women in 1870 and 1880, most of them are represented in family units. Ya Hit, however, having been "owned" by one gang, and trying to escape with another, indicates that she most likely was not married before this event. Census takers for Los Angeles during those years did not identify women who worked as prostitutes, or men who owned brothels. San Francisco, however, was home to several brothels and prostitutes, as noted in the literature mentioned above, and also the census. This made it easier to identify prostitutes, whereas, they do not appear in the census for Los Angeles, so in Los Angeles it is very likely that most women who were prostitutes were in the shadows, and not counted into their respective communities. Additionally, there may actually have been very few African American prostitutes in Los Angeles between 1850 and 1880. There are several reasons for this. First, the populations were smaller. In terms of women of color, there were, only a few hundred women of color at the most. Most of them could be found living in familial units rather than by themselves, or in boarding houses. This is significant because in larger cities like San Francisco and Sacramento, there were more single men, which was indicative of a greater market for sex workers. Also, those places began as mining cities, where Tong, Butler, and Hurtado noted the greater likelihood of prostitutes. Lastly, African American women made up a very small percentage of prostitutes in these larger cities, whereas, Chinese women made up the largest percentages.

43. Darland, "Chinese Massacre at Los Angeles in 1871," 22.

44. Ibid., 22.

45. Ibid., 23.

46. Ibid.

47. Ibid., 23–24.

48. Ibid., 24–25.

49. Ibid., 26. Here Darland quotes "The People versus L. T. Crenshaw, et. al." from *The California Reports*, 47:66 and 532.

50. Darland, "Chinese Massacre at Los Angeles in 1871," 26.

51. Ibid.

52. "The City in Brief," *Los Angeles Times*, Wednesday, 6 February 1889.

53. "Bullets Kill and Wound . . . Italians Believed Attacked by Negro Trio," *Los Angeles Times*, 18 April 1906; "Gamblers Have the Money," *Los Angeles Times*, 17 April 1906, 16. See also Article IV, Section 72 of the Constitution of the State of California (1849), California State Archives.

54. *Penal Code of California*, 94–95.

55. The *Times* launched a significant campaign against the Chinese, raising fear and anger in its readers who, in turn, supported the Exclusion Act of 1882. Every

day, there was a story printed about the Chinese, either within the city or the state. Generally, these stories pointed out all of the cultural and religious differences between the Chinese and the Anglo community. White community members often met these differences with intolerance. See Ngai, *Impossible Subjects*, 38. The Seaver Center for Western History, Los Angeles, houses a collection of maps of the area in the 1870s. Some of those maps include Nigger Alley and Chinatown, plotting out the gambling houses and saloons in the area. These maps are part of the map collection in the Los Angeles Fire Department Historical Archive.

56. "Treaty Regulating Immigration from China" 17 November 1880, Article I http://www.pbs.org/weta/thewest/resources/archives/seven/chinxact.htm *(accessed 3 March 2015)*; in terms of racialization in Los Angeles, see also Ngai, *Impossible Subjects*, 7–8.

57. "Treaty Regulating Immigration from China" 17 November 1880, Article II http://www.pbs.org/weta/thewest/resources/archives/seven/chinxact.htm *(accessed 3 March 2015)*.

58. Ibid.

59. "Chinese Exclusion Act," 6 May 1882 http://www.pbs.org/weta/thewest /resources/archives/seven/chinxact.htm#act (accessed 3 March 2015).

60. "About Town" *Los Angeles Daily Times*, Sunday morning, 8 January 1882.

61. "Chinese Criminals," *Los Angeles Daily Times*, Thursday morning, January 26, 1882.

62. Ibid.

63. Ibid.

64. "Chinese Criminals: Chinese and Hoodlums Compared and John Ahead," *Los Angeles Daily Times*, 26 January 1882, 3.

65. Ibid.

66. *1880 United States Census Index*, Church of Jesus Christ of Latter-day Saints; University of Virginia Geospatial and Statistical Data Center, *United States Historical Census Data Browser*.

67. "Chinese Curse," *Los Angeles Daily Times*, 2 March 1882.

68. "How Atwood Thrashed a Chinaman for Insulting His Wife," *Los Angeles Daily Times*, 25 January 1882.

69. Ibid.

70. "Restriction Bill: Chinese Immigration Bill Taken up by the Senate," *Los Angeles Daily Times*, Wednesday morning, 1 March 1882.

71. Ibid.

72. Ibid.

73. Ibid.

74. "Chinatown Scorched," *Los Angeles Times*, 24 October 1886, 1.

75. "High Binders," *Los Angeles Times*, 10 October 1887, 1.

76. "Ah, Joe!" *Los Angeles Times*, 20 March 1888, 2; "Ah Joe," *Los Angeles Herald*, 20 March 1888, 3; "All Samee White Man," *Los Angeles Times*, 24 January 1897, 12; "Another Raid," *Los Angeles Times*, 18 August 1897, 9; "City Briefs," *Los Angeles Times*, 19 August 1897, 10; "Mongolian Gamblers," *Los Angeles Times*, 19 August 1897, 7; "Shot in a Chinese Gambling House," *Los Angeles Times*, 13 March 1901,

11; "Clubbing the Cribs," *Los Angeles Times*, 13 March 1901, 9; "The City in Brief," *Los Angeles Times*, 20 August 1903, 12; "Holds Chinese Boy for Trial," *Los Angeles Times*, 11 March 1906. All of these stories underscored the violent side of the city, and always was about the Chinese.

77. "Nigger Alley Again: A Suit Began 10 Years Ago Now Revived," *Los Angeles Times*, 21 September 1898, 7.

78. "Street Work: The Superintendent of Streets Will Remove Chinatown," *Los Angeles Times*, 10 January 1888, 1.

79. Ibid.

80. "San Diego," *Los Angeles Times*, November 18, 1887, 4.

81. Ibid.

82. "Nigger Alley Again."

83. "Dug Up: The First Move to Obliterate 'Nigger' Alley," *Los Angeles Times*, 14 May 1889, 3.

84. "First Street Gets Into the Federal Courts," *Los Angeles Herald*, Morning, 3 July 1889, 8.

85. *1900 United States Federal Census*.

86. "A Time Set for Hearing," *Los Angeles Times*, 14 February 14, 1900, I10.

87. "Dive of Vice Cleared Out," *Los Angeles Times*, 30 July 1905, 16.

88. "Unhappy Alley," *Los Angeles Times*, 18 October 1905.

89. This act stripped Mexican landowners of their lands, restricting their labor. Both of these laws restricted the laboring classes of these groups, leaving African Americans to replace them in both instances. Until the turn of the century, however, the African American population in California and in Los Angeles remained quite small.

90. African Americans specifically and Californians generally were increasingly literate as more people were being trained as teachers and more schools were opening. During this period, the Los Angeles Board of Education was organized, and there is much debate as to who was entitled to education in the city.

91. "How Atwood Thrashed a Chinaman for Insulting his Wife," *Los Angeles Daily Times*, 25 January 1882.

92. "Negress Bites Patrolman, Escapes," *Los Angeles Times*, 12 April 1906, 16.

93. Lonnie G. Bunch, III, "'The Greatest State for the Negro': Jefferson L. Edmonds, Black Propagandist," in De Graaf et al., eds., *Seeking El Dorado*, 133.

94. Ibid.

95. Ibid., 131.

96. Ibid., 133.

97. "Mail Box Robbers," *Los Angeles Times*, 3 January 1907, II 3. For a discussion on black women and criminal justice, see Gross, *Colored Amazons*; Leflouria, *Chained in Silence*; and Haley, "'Like I Was a Man,'" 53–77.

98. "Knocks Out Her Husband," *Los Angeles Times*, 18 January 1907, II1.

99. "Barefoot Burglar Behind Bars," *Los Angeles Times*, 1 March 1907, 17.

100. "Drink Induced Him to Talk," *Los Angeles Times*, 3 May 1907, II2.

101. "Fiend Palsied with Terror," *Los Angeles Times*, 26 June 1907, II3.

102. "Police Watch Trains for Bad Negroes," *Los Angeles Times*, 30 June 1907, II13.

103. Broome, *LAPD's Black History*, 51–52; *1910 United States Federal Census*.

104. Broome, *LAPD's Black History*, 52; *1910 United States Federal Census*. The average height for police officers was five eight, with a weight of at least 160 pounds. Most officers were between twenty-five and thirty-five years of age.

105. Broome, *LAPD's Black History*, 1–27, 51–54. For a history of the Los Angeles Police Department in general, see Woods, *The Police in Los Angeles*.

106. Broome, *LAPD's Black History*, 1–55.

Chapter 5

1. Although the revival itself lasted into the third decade of the twentieth century, the most active participation occurred during these formative years.

2. Noble, ed., *Like as of Fire*; for online copies of the newspapers, see http://www.sendrevival.com/history/azusa_street/, 15 October 2003. For other firsthand accounts of the revival, see Bartleman, *Azusa Street*. The doctrine of the Holy Ghost is called Pneumatology. The purpose of the Holy Ghost is to equip and empower "the believer, making him a more effective witness for the service in the world." In this church, salvation becomes a process. First, a person confesses to having been a sinner who now believes in Jesus. Next, the person enters sanctification, or the "continuous operation of the Holy Ghost, by which He delivers the justified sinner from the pollution of sin, renews his whole nature in the image of God and enables him to perform good works." When one receives the Baptism of the Holy Ghost, he or she will know because he or she will begin to speak in unknown tongues, just as the apostles did in the Book of Acts. The Holy Ghost baptism is not a requirement for one to receive salvation; rather, people are baptized because they are saved. Again, this occurs after one is "justified" and "sanctified." Once the baptism has occurred, the believer is generally equipped to speak in unknown tongues whenever the Spirit gives him or her utterance. More importantly, the Bible declares that one "will receive power after that the Holy Ghost has come upon you." This power is manifest in many different ways just as the apostle Paul outlined in 1 Corinthians 12:14. It includes spiritual gifts such as prophecy, speaking in tongues, healing, wisdom, knowledge, and faith.

3. Gilkes, *"If It Wasn't for the Women . . ."*, especially part 2, "Church Women and their Work," 43–117. See also Gilkes's essay "The Role of Church and Community Mothers: Ambivalent American Sexism or Fragmented African Famlyhood," in *African-American Religion*, ed. Fulop and Raboteau, 366–88.

4. Lovejoy, *Religious Enthusiasm in the New World*, 178–94; Jon Butler, "Enthusiasm Described and Decried," 324; Gaustad, *The Great Awakening in New England* and *A Religious History of America*; Stephen A. Marini, *Radical Sects of Revolutionary New England*; and Goen, *Revivalism and Separatism in New England, 1740–1800*.

5. Birdsall, "The Second Great Awakening and the New England Social Order"; and Cott, "Young Women in the Second Great Awakening in New England."

6. Range Jr., ed., *Church of God in Christ Official Manual*, 41–58; and Hayford, gen. ed., *Spirit-Filled Life Bible*; 1 Corinthians 12–14; Acts 2:4.

7. Montgomery, *Under Their Own Vine and Fig Tree*, 346.

8. Ibid., 346–47.

9. Range Jr., ed., *Church of God in Christ Official Manual*, 41–58.

10. Ibid.

11. Espinoza, *William J. Seymour and the Origins of Global Pentecostalism*; Noble, ed., *Like as of Fire*; http://www.sendrevival.com/history/azusa_street/ (15 October 2003); and Simpson, "Black Pentecostalism in the United States," 203–11.

12. Wacker, *Heaven Below*; Hollenweger, *The Pentecostals*; and Bloch-Hoell, *The Pentecostal Movement*.

13. "Heart Is Torn from Great City: San Francisco Nearly Destroyed by Earthquakes and Fire—Hundreds of Killed and Injured—Destruction of Other Coast Cities—California's Greatest Horror," *Los Angeles Times*, 19 April 1906; Bartleman, *Azusa Street*, 53–57.

14. Bartleman, *Azusa Street*, 53–57.

15. Ancestry.com, *1900 U.S. Federal Census*; Soule, "Populism and Black Lynching in Georgia, 1890–1900," 431–49; Olzak, "The Political Context of Competition," 395–421; and Stovel, "Local Sequential Patterns," 843–80.

16. Stuckey, *Slave Culture*; Raboteau, *Slave Religion*; and Genovese, *Roll, Jordan, Roll*, 209–55.

17. Bartleman, *Azusa Street*, 65–66.

18. MacRobert, "The Black Roots of Pentecostalism"; Wacker, *Heaven Below*; Anderson, *Vision of the Disinherited*; and Creech, "Visions of Glory." See also Espinoza, *William J. Seymour and the Origins of Global Pentecostalism*. Creech offers a contrary opinion on the discussion about the movement's founders. In fact, he rejects Seymour as the Movement's founder and views his role as well as the Azusa Revival as merely a component of other forms of Pentecostalism occurring around the world. Though this list is not exhaustive, these scholars are perhaps the front-runners in the debate over the leadership of the modern Pentecostal movement.

19. MacRobert, "The Black Roots of Pentecostalism."

20. Robert Mapes Anderson asserts that Ozman's "Spirit Baptism" occurred much earlier than this. He notes that in a newspaper article, Parham is quoted saying that Ozman had received her "Holy Spirit" baptism several weeks earlier. Clearly there are conflicting dates. This issue really concerns how far back to date the modern Pentecostal Movement. This study only considers the Movement as it pertains to William J. Seymour and the Los Angeles Apostolic Faith Mission. It is mentioned here only for background purposes. For further discussion, see Anderson, *Vision of the Disinherited*; and Martin. ed., *The Topeka Outpouring of 1901*.

21. Martin, ed., *The Topeka Outpouring of 1901*, 35.

22. Ancestry.com and The Church of Jesus Christ of Latter-day Saints, *1880 United States Federal Census*. Seymour, at age ten in 1880 was listed in the U.S. Census as being able to read, but not write. In 1880, Both William and Simon Jr., attended school. Simon Jr. was two years younger than William. Amos was only five, and not yet enrolled, while his baby sister, listed only as "infant," was six months at the time. Interestingly, Simon was listed in the U.S. Census as mulatto, while his wife was listed as black. All of the children were listed as mulatto.

23. *1880 United States Federal Census*; Ancestry.com, *1930 United States Federal Census* [database on-line], Provo, UT, USA: Ancestry.com Operations Inc, 2002. Original data: United States of America, Bureau of the Census, *Fifteenth Census of the United States, 1930*. Washington, D.C.: National Archives and Records Administration, 1930. T626, 2,667 rolls, *1930 United States Federal Census*. It is unclear whether Phillis and Simon had more than six children. In the 1930 census, another child, Julius was listed as one of her sons. Also, according to the 1900 census, Phillis had a 15-year-old daughter named Emma. It is unclear whether she is the same daughter listed in the 1880 census, and that there was a mistake in recording her age. All of Simon Seymour's surviving family members are also listed as black in 1900 and 1930 rather than mulatto as in the earlier census data.

24. Here there are conflicting reports of where Seymour was ordained. According to Owens (*Speak to the Rock*), Seymour was ordained at the Church of God, in Anderson, Indiana (56), but Anderson claims that Seymour was an ordained Baptist preacher of Holiness background (*Vision of the Disinherited*, 60). At any rate, both tell the same story of his sanctification process as well as his role in modern Pentecostalism. According to the 1900 U.S. Census, Seymour was still listed as a Louisiana resident, living with his mother, Phillis. There is no record of Seymour living in either Cincinnati or Indianapolis during that time (Ancestry.com, *1900 U.S. Federal Census*). The Church of God, Anderson, is a separate denomination from the Church of God.

25. Anderson, *Vision of the Disinherited*, 60; and Simpson, "Black Pentecostalism in the United States." Although Simpson spent little time giving background on the Azusa Street Revival, he clearly defined what Pentecostals believe. Most importantly, that they are fundamentalists, and that baptism by total immersion and the baptism of the "Holy Spirit" with speaking in tongues as the evidence are some of the main characteristics of the religion. Simpson noted that Pentecostals use the biblical apostolic church as their model (205). This was Seymour's vision for the movement as a whole, and he ran his church this way for the first two to four years.

26. Anderson, *Vision of the Disinherited*, 60.

27. Ibid., 61, and Owens, *Speak to the Rock*, 56–58.

28. Anderson, *Vision of the Disinherited*, 60, and Owens, *Speak to the Rock*, 57.

29. Seymour preached from Acts 2:4, which states, "And they were all filled with the Holy Spirit and began to speak in other tongues as the Spirit gave them utterance." He said that the only evidence of receiving the "Spirit Baptism" was speaking in tongues (Anderson, *Vision of the Disinherited*, 65). This is also what most Pentecostals who believe in the "gift" of tongues adhere to.

30. Lee was an Irish American who was a Holiness member (Owens, *Speak to the Rock*, 58).

31. Anderson, *Vision of the Disinherited*, 66. Lucy Farrow received her "Spirit Baptism" and could speak in tongues and received the "gift" of "laying of hands" which she used to help others to receive their own "Spirit Baptism."

32. Ibid., 65.

33. Owens, *Speak to the Rock*, 60.

34. Today the location houses the Japanese American Cultural Center.

35. Owens, *Speak to the Rock*, 62.

36. Acts 1:13–14.

37. *The Apostolic Faith*, February–March 1907, 4.

38. Owens, *Speak to the Rock*, 62. See also Engh, "'A Multiplicity and Diversity of Faiths.'"

39. Owens, *Speak to the Rock*, 62.

40. Ibid. See also "Weird Babel of Tongues: New Sect of Fanatics Is Breaking Loose. Wild Scene Last Night on Azusa Street. Gurgle of Wordless Talk by a Sister," *Los Angeles Times*, 18 April 1906, 1.

41. *The Apostolic Faith*, September 1906, 1.

42. Owens, *Speak to the Rock*, 72–73.

43. Ibid.; MacRobert, "The Black Roots of Pentecostalism"; and Bartleman, *Azusa Street*, xi–xxix.

44. *The Apostolic Faith*, May 1907, 3.

45. It is not revealed how they knew that Moore was speaking Hebrew. Generally, as the movement grew, people would come from different areas of the world, speaking other languages, and were able to interpret what was being said. It is unclear whether there were any Hebrew speakers at the initial meeting, though it is entirely possible.

46. MacRobert, "The Black Roots of Pentecostalism," 303.

47. Wacker, *Heaven Below*, 228.

48. Ibid., 230. See also Deno, "God, Authority, and the Home."

49. *The Apostolic Faith*, September 1906, 1. The "gift of laying hands" is generally when a person has some form of "divine power" in their touch, which could be used for healing or other spiritual activities. In this case, it appears as though Farrow's "gift" was used to transfer the "Holy Ghost power" into the believer's body by touching them. Evidently, when she placed her hands on a believer's body, the believer was able to receive his or her own "spirit baptism."

50. Ibid., 1.

51. *The Apostolic Faith*, December, 1906, 3.

52. Ibid.

53. *The Apostolic Faith*, October 1906, 1.

54. *The Apostolic Faith*, December 1906, 3.

55. Ibid.

56. *The Apostolic Faith*, October 1906, 1.

57. Ibid.

58. *The Apostolic Faith*, December 1906, 3.

59. Ibid.

60. *The Apostolic Faith*, December 1906. Hutchins's name and letters appeared quite frequently throughout the two years of active publication of the newspaper. She stayed in close contact with members of the Azusa Mission, who continued sharing her letters with the church.

61. *The Apostolic Faith*, October 1906, 1.

62. *The Apostolic Faith*, January, 1907, 3.

63. Crawford, *The Light of Life Brought Triumph*; Bloch-Hoell, *The Pentecostal Movement*, 48 and 63, Hacker, *Heaven Below*, 145 and 160.

64. Ibid., 163.

65. Owens, *Speak to the Rock*, 75–78; and Anderson, *Vision of the Disinherited*, 160. It is interesting to note that Owens does not explain why Crawford broke from Seymour, but that she did. Conversely, Anderson says that Crawford left because she disagreed with Seymour's doctrinal position. Regardless of her reasons, the break from Seymour dealt the Apostolic Faith Mission a major blow from which it never fully recovered.

66. For this reason, this chapter focuses on the two years of publication while under the supervision of William J. Seymour. Still, these articles have much to be explored, especially when one considers the vast information written by and about women and their role at the Azusa Street Mission and around the world.

67. Owens, *Speak to the Rock*, 75–78; and Anderson, *Vision of the Disinherited*, 160.

68. This is also characteristic of the American religious tradition, in that women have historically played a crucial role in bringing in new members, primarily family members first. Gilkes, *"If It Wasn't for the Women . . ."* 198.

69. Brenda E. Stevenson, *"'Marsa Never Sot Aunt Rebecca Down,'"* 360.

70. Collier-Thomas, *Jesus, Jobs, and Justice*, xxix.

71. Higginbotham, *Righteous Discontent*, 7; Gilkes, *"If It Wasn't for the Women . . ."* 43, 90.

72. Ibid., 81; Collier-Thomas, *Jesus, Jobs, and Justice*, xvi.

73. Seymour, *Doctrines and Discipline*, 110.

74. *The Apostolic Faith*, May 1907, 3.

75. Ibid.

76. *The Apostolic Faith*, September 1906, 1.

77. Ibid., 1 and 3.

78. *The Apostolic Faith*, September 1906, 4.

79. Ibid.

80. Ibid.

81. Ibid.

82. *The Apostolic Faith*, May 1907, 3.

83. *The Apostolic Faith*, September 1906, 3.

84. *The Apostolic Faith*, October 1906, 3

85. Ibid.

86. *The Apostolic Faith*, November 1906, 1.

87. Wacker, *Heaven Below*, 159–165.

88. *The Apostolic Faith*, November 1906, 7.

89. Ibid.; see also, Wacker, *Heaven Below*, 125–27.

90. *The Apostolic Faith*, December 1906, 2.

91. *The Apostolic Faith*, January 1907, 4.

92. William J. Seymour, *Doctrines and Discipline*, 61. Seymour cites John 3:5 and 6, Romans 8:7 and 8, Titus 3:5, and Mark 1:15 as scriptural references.

93. Many Pentecostal denominations, such as the Church of God in Christ (COGIC) and the Pentecostal Assemblies of the World (PAW) maintain that one

must be "filled" with the Holy Spirit in order to receive salvation. Moreover, they believe that speaking in "tongues" is the initial evidence of a person being "filled" with the Holy Spirit. The fact that Seymour rejected this premise, and his reaction to it, will be further explored below.

94. Seymour, *Doctrines and Discipline*, 61.

95. Ibid., 42. He cites Romans 3:25, Acts 10:42 and 43, Romans 5:1 and 10, John 3:3 and 14, and 2 Corinthians 5:17.

96. Seymour, *Doctrines and Discipline*, 42. Here he cites John 17:15 and 17 and Hebrews 13:12, 2:11, and 12:14.

97. Acts 1:8 states, "But you shall receive power when the Holy Spirit has come upon you; and you shall be witnesses to Me in Jerusalem, and in all Judea and Samaria, and to the end of the earth." Hayford, gen. ed., *Spirit-Filled Life Bible*, 1622. This is clearly the premise on which Seymour's doctrine was built. He believed that once a person received the Holy Spirit, he or she would be able to act as the disciples did following the Day of Pentecost. Seymour, *Doctrines and Discipline*, 43.

98. *The Apostolic Faith*, December 1906, 1.

99. *The Apostolic Faith*, September 1906, 1.

100. Ibid.

101. *The Apostolic Faith*, January 1907, 1.

102. *The Apostolic Faith*, November 1906, 1–2.

103. *The Apostolic Faith*, December 1906, 4.

104. *The Apostolic Faith*, October 1906, 1.

105. Ibid.

106. Ibid., 1–4.

107. *The Apostolic Faith*, October 1908, 1.

108. *The Apostolic Faith*, November 1906, 1.

109. *The Apostolic Faith*, May, 1907, 2.

110. *The Apostolic Faith*, November 1906, 1.

111. Ibid.

112. Ibid.

113. *The Apostolic Faith*, February–March 1907, 3.

114. *The Apostolic Faith*, May 1907, 4.

115. Nickel, *Azusa Street Outpouring*.

116. *The Apostolic Faith*, January 1907, 1.

117. MacRobert, "The Black Roots of Pentecostalism," 303.

118. *The Apostolic Faith*, May 1907, 3.

119. Ibid.

120. Adrienne M. Israel, "Mother's Roberson and Coffey—Pioneers of Women's Work: 1911–1964," in *Bishop C. H. Mason and the Roots of the Church of God in Christ*, ed. Clemmons, 101–21.

121. *The Apostolic Faith*, September 1906, 1.

122. *The Apostolic Faith*, November 1906, 2.

123. *The Apostolic Faith*, October 1906, 2. Dropsy is equivalent to edema, or an excessive accumulation of fluid in the body's tissues.

124. *The Apostolic Faith*, September 1906, 1.

125. Ibid.

126. Ibid.

127. *The Apostolic Faith*, February–March 1907, 4.

128. *The Apostolic Faith*, Oct, 1906, 1.

129. Ibid.

130. *The Apostolic Faith*, December 1906, 3.

131. Bloch-Hoell, *The Pentecostal Movement*; there are several references here to healing, and to women. See, for example, 27–29, 35–38, 147–51, and 175.

132. *The Apostolic Faith*, October 1906, 4.

133. *The Apostolic Faith*, November 1906, 1.

134. *The Apostolic Faith*, October 1906, 4.

135. *The Apostolic Faith*, November 1906, 3.

136. Ibid., 4.

137. Ibid.

138. *The Apostolic Faith*, May 1907, 4.

139. *The Apostolic Faith*, October 1906, 1.

140. Ibid.

141. In 1 Corinthians 12:8 and 9, Paul writes that "for to one is given the word of wisdom through the Spirit, to another the word of knowledge through the same Spirit, to another faith by the same Spirit, to other gifts of healings by the same Spirit." Hayford, gen. ed., *Spirit-Filled Life Bible*, 1736.

142. In many Pentecostal denominations, the men are given the authority to "lay hands" on everyone, regardless of gender, while women assist by praying alongside the minister, or by "laying hands" on women.

143. For more on the "gift of tongues" and on other "spiritual gifts," see 1 Corinthians 12 through 14. See also Range Jr., ed., *Church of God in Christ Official Manual*, 41–58; and Hayford, gen. ed., *Spirit-Filled Life Bible*.

144. 1 Corinthians 14:27–28 NKJV states, "If anyone speaks in a tongue, let there be two or at the most three, each in turn, and let one interpret. But if there is no interpreter, let him keep silent in church, and let him speak to himself and to God."

145. Seymour, *Doctrines and Discipline*, 82.

146. Ibid. Acts 2:4, Hayford, *Spirit-Filled Life Bible*, 1624–25.

147. *The Apostolic Faith*, Sep. 1906, 4.

148. *The Apostolic Faith*, May 1907, 3.

149. *The Apostolic Faith*, September 1906, 4.

150. Ibid.

151. *The Apostolic Faith*, October, 1906, 3.

152. Ibid., 1.

153. *The Apostolic Faith*, May 1907, 1.

154. Ibid., 2.

155. Ibid., 1.

156. *The Apostolic Faith*, October 1906, 3. This form of tongues is generally considered prophetic. Although a person may prophesy in an unknown tongue, while

another interprets, there are cases where people receive their own interpretations. Keyes is one of many examples. Moreover, Keyes's experience exemplifies the complicated characteristics of the "gift of tongues" and how one may negotiate utilization of that "gift."

157. *The Apostolic Faith*, December 1906, 3.

158. *The Apostolic Faith*, February–March 1907, 4.

159. *The Apostolic Faith*, January 1907, 1. It is important to remember that the revival was interracial, and that many of the original members were African American. It is also noteworthy that this particular case occurred in the segregated South, and the person writing the article, G. B. Cashwell, was probably Caucasian. Interestingly, he found it particularly remarkable that African Americans were also "receiving Pentecost," though it may be more interesting that African Americans and Caucasians attended these revival meetings together, defying segregation altogether.

160. *The Apostolic Faith*, May 1907, 4.

161. *The Apostolic Faith*, January 1907, 1.

162. Ibid.

163. Ibid.

164. Often, a preacher or pastor is considered a prophet, primarily due to the fact the Bible is considered prophetic. Because they use the Bible as their main instrument of information and guidance, many receive the title of "prophet." The type of prophecy mentioned here is specific to women (or people in general) who have received visions or messages from God that were supported by scriptures that are found in the Bible. This is another form of prophecy as well as a "gift" from God. 1 Corinthians 14:1–40; Hayford, gen. ed., *Spirit Filled Life Bible*, 1740–43.

165. *The Apostolic Faith*, October 1906, 2.

166. *The Apostolic Faith*, January 1907, 4.

167. *The Apostolic Faith*, September 1906, 4.

168. Seymour, *Doctrines and Discipline*, 123–24.

169. Ibid., 124.

170. Ibid.

171. Ibid., 123–24.

172. *The Apostolic Faith*, September 1906, 1.

173. *The Apostolic Faith*, November 1906, 1.

174. *The Apostolic Faith*, December 1906, 1.

175. Wacker, *Heaven Below*, 185–86.

176. *The Apostolic Faith*, May 1907, 1.

177. "Little Children Receive the Holy Ghost," *The Apostolic Faith*, October 1906, 3.

178. Ibid.

179. *The Apostolic Faith*, November 1906, 4.

180. *The Apostolic Faith*, September 1906, 1.

181. Ibid.

182. *The Apostolic Faith*, January 1907, 1.

183. *The Apostolic Faith*, December 1906, 4.

184. Clemmons, *Bishop C. H. Mason*, 46–54, MacRobert, "The Black Roots of Pentecostalism," 305; Synan, *The Holiness-Pentecostal Movement in the United States*, 52; see also Bass, *Forty Years*, 25–26.

185. Bloch-Hoell, *The Pentecostal Movement*, 30–52; and Hollenweger, *The Pentecostals*, 21–28.

186. Bartleman, *Azusa Street*, 65.

187. Ibid., 145.

188. Ibid., 144.

189. Ibid.

190. Nickel, *Azusa Street Outpouring*, 8.

191. Wacker, *Heaven Below*, 1–8; Anderson. "Writing the Pentecostal History of Africa, Asia, and Latin America"; Bloch-Hoell, *The Pentecostal Movement*, 5–17.

192. *The Apostolic Faith*, November 1906, 1.

193. Wacker, *Heaven Below*; Bloch-Hoell, *The Pentecostal Movement*; Bartleman, *Azusa Street*; Hollenweger, *The Pentecostals*; Marini, *Radical Sects*; Goen, *Revivalism and Separatism*; and Lovejoy, *Religious Enthusiasm*.

194. *The Apostolic Faith*, January 1907, 1.

195. Ibid.

196. Hayford, gen. ed., *Spirit-Filled Life Bible*; and Range Jr., *Church of God in Christ Official Manual*. The doctrine of Last Things, or eschatology, explains the ways in which the world will come to an end. This is the primary way for people to differentiate between "good" and "evil" behavior, as well as man's obligations to God. In the Book of Matthew and in Revelations, the last days are illustrated. First, if a believer dies before the "Second Coming of Christ," and is "saved," the spirit and soul of this person will be eternally with God in His Kingdom in Heaven. Should the believer live to experience the Second Coming, he or she will see Christ come from "heaven" down to Earth, and the church will be caught up to meet Him "in the air.' There will be an "anti-Christ," born of a serpent, as opposed to Jesus, who was born of a woman, who will try to deceive all people, and temp believers away from God. There also will be a "tribulation" period, where everyone left on earth after the Second Coming will be judged. This period was revealed to John the Baptist in a vision, which is published in the Book of Revelations. Next, the "Battle of Armageddon" between Christ and the anti-Christ will be fought. The "millennium," when Christ rules for one thousand years, will follow. Christ will then judge the world. During this period, evil people will receive their punishment. When Christ's reign is complete, Satan will be released from prison, and he and his followers will be "devoured," and the wicked will be "cast into a lake of fire" to spend eternity. Those who are godly will spend an eternity in heaven, a place that the church believes is where God dwells. Any church that does not support these doctrines, or modifies the biblical texts, is in opposition to the church.

197. Seeman, "'Justise Must Take Plase'; Lambert, "'I Saw the Book Talk.'"

198. Taylor, *In Search of the Racial Frontier*; Thomas Almaguer, *Racial Fault Lines*; De Graaf et al., eds., *Seeking El Dorado*; and Flamming, *Bound for Freedom*.

199. Bartleman, *Azusa Street*; see especially the introduction by Vinson Synan, xxi–xxii; and Wacker, *Heaven Below*, 144–48.

200. Clemmons, *Bishop C. H. Mason*, 1–20, and 61–71. See also Cobbins, *History of the Church of Christ (Holiness) U.S.A., 1895–1965*, 17–30; and Montgomery, *Under Their Own Vine and Fig Tree*. Montgomery notes that the Holiness movement evolved in response to the conservative directions of the First and Second Great Awakenings. As the Baptist and Methodist denominations became more conservative, they discouraged the level of emotionalism the revivals had once evoked. He defines the Holiness movement: "It incorporated a high level of emotional excitement, an ascetic doctrine that substituted the reward of spiritual salvation for material success and earthly pleasures, and a strictly literal interpretation of the Bible. Its adherents placed a great value on the sanctification, or 'holiness' in attitude and behavior, that was manifested in old-time revivalist religion" (346). Montgomery also points out that members of the Holiness movement were typically of the lower classes, shut out by their communities' elite. The movement appealed to African Americans particularly, because of its similarities to traditional religious slave practices (347). The Holiness movement, therefore, served as the social, cultural, and spiritual foundation for the Pentecostal movement.

201. Bartleman, *Azusa Street*, 144.

202. Ibid.

203. Ibid.; Wacker, *Heaven Below*, 228 and 262; Hollenweger, *The Pentecostals*, 28; and Clemmons, *Bishop C. H. Mason*, 50–51.

204. Bartleman, *Azusa Street*; Bloch-Hoell, *The Pentecostal Movement*; Wacker, *Heaven Below*, 141–76; Clemmons, *Bishop C. H. Mason*, 101–21; and Hollenweger, *The Pentecostals*, 403.

Chapter 6

1. Washington, *Up from Slavery*, 148.

2. *Plessy v. Ferguson*, 1896.

3. Max Bennett Thrasher, "An Account of Washington's California Tour," in Harlan and Smock, eds., *Booker T. Washington Papers*, 6:18.

4. Ibid., 6:18–24.

5. Ibid.

6. Ibid., 6:19.

7. Ibid., 6:18–20.

8. Ibid., 6:21.

9. Ibid., 6:21, 12:137.

10. Ibid., 6:24.

11. Ibid., 12:136.

12. Ibid., 12:137.

13. Ibid.

14. Ibid., 12:138.

15. Ibid. 12:139.

16. Ibid.

17. Ibid. 12:140.

18. Ibid.

19. Ibid.

20. Ibid. 12:141.

21. Ibid., 12:141–42.

22. Ibid., 12:142; University of Virginia Geospatial and Statistical Data Center, *United States Historical Census Data Browser.*

23. Harlan and Smock, eds., *Booker T. Washington Papers,* 12:142.

24. Ibid., 12:144.

25. Ibid., 12:149.

26. Ibid.

27. Ibid., 12:150.

28. Ibid., 12:151–52.

29. Ibid., 12:152.

30. Ibid.

31. Ibid.

32. Ibid., 12:153.

33. Ibid.

34. Ibid.

35. Ibid.

36. Ibid., 12:155.

37. Ibid.

38. Ibid.

39. Ibid.

40. Ibid., 12:156.

41. Ibid.

42. Ibid.

43. Ibid., 12:157.

44. Ibid., 12:158.

45. Nettie J. Asburry, "Letter to Booker T. Washington," in Harlan and Smock, eds., *Booker T. Washington Papers,* 12:279.

46. Ibid.

47. "Dr. Washington Makes a Great Speech," *California Eagle* 27, no. 4 (14 March 1914), 1.

48. Ibid.

49. Eva Carter Buckner, "The Man Behind His Race," in ibid., 3.

50. Ibid., 4.

51. Ibid.

52. "The Man of the Hour," *California Eagle* 27, no. 5 (14 March 1914), 1.

53. Hough Ellwood Macbeth, "Letter to Booker T. Washington," in Harlan and Smock, eds., *Booker T. Washington Papers,* 13:55–56.

54. Ibid.

55. Harlan and Smock, eds., *Booker T. Washington Papers,* 13:90.

56. Harrison Gray Otis, "Letter to Booker T. Washington," in ibid., 13:97.

57. Ibid., 98.

58. Ibid.

59. Macbeth, "Letter to Booker T. Washington," 107–8.

60. Kate Bradley-Stovall, "The Negro Woman in Los Angeles and Vicinity—Some Notable Characters," *Los Angeles Times*, 2 February 1909, 4.

61. "Negroes Who Have Won Place or Fortune in Los Angeles and Pasadena," *Los Angeles Times*, 12 February 1909, 6, http://search.proquest.com/docview /159282261?accountid=7418.

62. Ibid.

63. Dr. A. C. Garrott, "How the University-Trained Negro Has Advanced in the Great Professions," in ibid, 2.

64. S. P. Johnson, "Secret Orders among Negroes," in ibid.

65. Ibid.

66. Ibid.

67. Ibid.

68. Ibid.; Ancestry.com, *1910 United States Federal Census*.

69. Johnson, "Secret Orders among Negroes."

70. Ibid.; Ancestry.com, *1910 United States Federal Census*.

71. Reverend G. R. Bryan, "Religious Life of Los Angeles Negroes," *Los Angeles Times*, 12 February 1909, http://search.proquest.com/docview/159291892?accountid =7418.

72. Ibid.

73. Ancestry.com, *1910 United States Federal Census*.

74. Reverend J. D. Gordon, "The Spiritual and Religious Nature of the Negro," *Los Angeles Times*, 12 February1909, http://search.proquest.com/docview/15929 2077?accountid=7418.

75. Ibid.

76. Ibid.

77. Booker T. Washington "Opportunity of the Negro in America," in ibid.

78. Allen Allensworth, "The Negro, Thoroughly Tried, Proves Himself an Ideal Soldier on Every Field," in ibid.

79. Ibid.

80. Ibid.

81. Ancestry.com, *1910 United States Federal Census*.

82. Three other African American colonies existed in the area at the time—near Victorville, Abila, and Bowles.

83. Allen Allensworth, "From Allen Allensworth," in Harlan and Smock, eds., *Booker T. Washington Papers*, 13:522.

84. Ibid.

85. Ibid.; Hamilton, *Black Towns and Profit*, 142.

86. Alice C. Royal with Mickey Ellinger and Scott Barley, Allensworth, *The Freedom Colony*, 35–60; Hamilton, *Black Towns and Profit*, 145.

87. Beasley, *Negro Trailblazers of California*, 227; California State Parks, "Allensworth," 38.

88. Hamilton, *Black Towns and Profit*, 142.

89. Ancestry.com, *1920 United States Federal Census*; California Voter Registration Records, 1900–1914; 1916–1924.

90. Hamilton, *Black Towns and Profit*, 145; Harlan and Smock, eds., *Booker T. Washington Papers*, 13:523n2; Beasley, *Negro Trailblazers of California*, 185.

91. Hamilton, *Black Towns and Profit*, 145; California State Parks, "Allensworth," 38.

92. Ibid. Ancestry.com, *1920 United States Federal Census*.

93. Ibid.

94. "Booker T. Washington Is Dead at Tuskegee," *Los Angeles Times*, 15 November 1915, II; "As Memorial for Colored Leader," *Los Angeles Times*, 20 November 1915, II3; "To Eulogize Late Educator," *Los Angeles Times*, 27 November 1915, II5; "Memorial for Race's Leader," *Los Angeles Times*, 29 November 1915, II2.

95. "Great Leader Dead," *California Eagle* 28, no. 1 (20 November 1915), 1.

96. Ibid.

97. Ibid.

98. "Thousands Pay Tribute to Dr. Washington," *California Eagle* 28, no. 1 (27 November 1915), 1.

99. "5,000 People Gather at Shrine Auditorium in Memory of Dr. Booker T. Washington," *California Eagle* 28, no. 43 (4 December 1915), 1.

100. Ibid.

Conclusion

1. Du Bois, "Colored California."

2. Ibid., 193.

3. Ibid., 193–94.

4. Ibid., 193.

5. Ibid.

6. Ibid.

7. Ibid., 194.

8. Ibid.

9. Ibid.,

10. Wild, *Street Meeting*.

11. Du Bois, "Colored California," 194. Du Bois mentioned that the problem existed without going into detail about it. He referred to the Japanese as the "protagonists" in this situation, causing many problems for the African American community.

12. Ibid., 194–95.

13. Ibid., 195.

14. Ibid.

15. Ibid., 192–95.

16. For a definition of the "California Dream," see Starr, *Americans and the California Dream, 1850–1915*.

17. Ngai, *Impossible Subjects*, 9.

18. Bartleman, *Azusa Street*, 54.

19. K. Connie Kang, "Pentecostal Enthusiasm Is Spreading," *Los Angeles Times*, 28 April 2006, http://www.topix.net/content/trb/ (21 May 2006). Kang estimated over 31,000 participants, including Pentecostals and Charismatic Christians. Bishop Charles E. Blake, however, reported a count of well over 40,000 attendees (Charles E. Blake, *Mother's Day Sermon* [Los Angeles: West Angeles Church of God in Christ, 2006]. Other venues included the Angelus Temple, founded by Aimee Semple McPherson in 1923 near Bonnie Brae Street, Crenshaw Christian Center's Faithdome on South Vermont Avenue in South Los Angeles, and the Japanese American Theater, home of the original Azusa Street location. Together, all venues, excluding the Los Angeles Convention Center, held 21,180 people. Meetings began at 9:00 A.M., and ran late into the night, with the final sessions beginning at 7:00 P.M. Some participated in all-day prayer vigils for the week that took place at both the Bonnie Brae house and at the location of the original revival.

20. Speakers included a long list of mega-church Pentecostal pastors who spoke across the city. The list included, but was not limited to Bishop T. D. Jakes (Texas), Bishop Charles E. Blake (Los Angeles), Creflo Dollar (Georgia), Rod Parsley (Ohio), Bishop Noel Jones, Bishop Paul S. Morton (New Orleans), David Yonggi Cho (Korea), Paula White (Florida), Pastor Marvin Winans (Michigan), Bishop Kenneth Ulmer (Los Angeles), and Judy Jacobs (Tennessee). It is important to note that although women served as hostesses and praise leaders, and some presented scholarly papers at the centennial, only two keynote preachers, Paula White and Judy Jacobs, were female. See the Center for Spiritual Renewal, *Official Azusa Street Centennial* website, http://www.azusastreet100.net/home.cfm (24 April 2006); West Angeles Church of God in Christ, *William J. Seymour Symposium*, http://www.westa.org/azusa100.html (24 February 2006).

21. Center for Spiritual Renewal, *Official Azusa Street Centennial* website.

22. Anna Gorman, Marjorie Miller, and Mitchell Landsberg, "Immigrants Demonstrate Peaceful Power," *Los Angeles Times*, 2 May 2006, A1; and "The May Day Marches," in ibid., A9.

23. Peter Prengaman, "Thousands Again Protest Immigration Bill: Tens of Thousands Turn Out in Los Angeles for a Second Day of Protests Against Immigration Bill," 25 March 2006, http://abcnews.go.com/US/wireStory?id =1768025&page=1. Beginning on 25 March 2005, approximately 500,000 people crowded the streets of Los Angeles across the city. Students made the most significant impact in the 25 March rally, jumping over school fences and marching in the streets. ABC news reported that over 2,700 students across Los Angeles walked out of their middle and high school classrooms in order to join the marches across town. On several occasions, news media covered teenaged activists occupying major freeway commute routes, such as the 110 freeway, which runs through downtown and into South Central, stopping and aggravating Los Angeles rush hour traffic.

24. C. Randall Archibald, "Immigrants Take to US Streets in Show of Strength," *New York Times*, 2 May 2006, A1; Anna Gorman, Marjorie Miller, and Mitchell

Landsberg, "Immigrants Demonstrate Peaceful Power," *Los Angeles Times*, 2 May 2006, A1.

25. Brenda E. Stevenson, "Latasha Harlins, Soon Ja Du, and Joyce Karlin," 152–76. See also Stevenson's *The Contested Murder of Latasha Harlins*.

26. Stevenson, "Latasha Harlins, Soon Ja Du, and Joyce Karlin," 165.

27. Du Bois, "Colored California," 193–94.

28. Ngai, *Impossible Subjects*, 57; Sides, *L.A. City Limits*, 27.

29. Sanchez, *Becoming Mexican American*, 261; Ngai, *Impossible Subjects*, 174–201; Kurashige, *The Shifting Grounds of Race*, 108–31.

Bibliography

Primary Sources

Archives and Manuscript Collections

Autry National Center—Institute for the American West
  Pico, Pio. *Leather Diary*
  Pico, Pio. *Leather Notebook*
  Register for the Pico House (1870–1872)
California State Archive
  California State Constitution, 1849
  Spanish and Mexican Land Grants Maps, 1855–1875
  Supreme Court of California Records
California State Library–California History Research Room
  California Census of 1852, v. III. Copied under the direction of the Genealogical Records Committee, Daughters of the American Revolution of California, 1934.
  Court House and Church records from California, v. I. Copied under the direction of the Genealogical Records Committee, Daughters of the American Revolution of California, 1936.
  Court House and Church records from California, v. II. Los Angeles 1876–1885. California State Society, DAR. Los Angeles County Marriages 1876–1885. Compiled in 1944 by the Genealogical Records Committee, California State Society Daughters of the American Revolution. Mrs. Earl C. Frost, State Chairman.
  Court House and Church records from California, v. III. Los Angeles County Marriages to 1888. California State Society DAR. Genealogical Records Committee of the California State Society, Daughters of the American Revolution, 1946. Mrs. Earl C. Frost, State Ch.
  Early California Wills Los Angeles County 1850–1890. Daughters of the American Revolution of California. Volumes I and II with Index, 1850–1890, Los Angeles County.
  Great Registers, 1866–1898; Collection Number: 4-2A; CSL Roll Number 19; FHL Roll Number 97628.
  Index to the 1890 Los Angeles County Register State of California. Compiled by Whittier Area Genealogical Society, Whittier, Calif., 1993.
  Los Angeles County Marriages, 4 books. August 1851–May 1877. Transcribed and Indexed by Mildred Flick, Annotated by Jeanne B. Clary, the Southern California Genealogical Society, Burbank, Calif., 1985.

Wills from California Counties, volume I. California State Society Daughters
of the American Revolution. Wills and Abstracts of Wills from California
Counties Volume I. Compiled under the Direction of the Genealogical
Records Committee California State Society Daughters of the American
Revolution, 1957.

Church of Jesus Christ of Latter-day Saints

Ancestry.com. *1850 United States Federal Census* (database on-line). Provo, UT,
USA: Ancestry.com Operations, Inc., 2009. Images reproduced by
FamilySearch. Original data: *Seventh Census of the United States, 1850*;
(National Archives Microfilm Publication M432, 1009 rolls); Records of
the Bureau of the Census, Record Group 29; National Archives,
Washington, D.C.

Ancestry.com. *1850 U.S. Federal Census—Slave Schedules* (database on-line).
Provo, UT, USA: Ancestry.com Operations Inc, 2004. Original data: United
States of America, Bureau of the Census. *Seventh Census of the United States,
1850*. Washington, D.C.: National Archives and Records Administration,
1850. M432, 1,009 rolls.

Ancestry.com. *1860 U.S. Federal Census—Slave Schedules* (database on-line).
Provo, UT, USA: Ancestry.com Operations Inc, 2010. Original data: United
States of America, Bureau of the Census. *Eighth Census of the United States,
1860*. Washington, D.C.: National Archives and Records Administration,
1860. M653, 1,438 rolls.

Ancestry.com. *1870 United States Federal Census* (database on-line). Provo,
Utah: MyFamily.com, Inc., 2003. Indexed by Ancestry.com from
microfilmed schedules of the 1870 U.S. Federal Decennial Census. Original
data: Data imaged from National Archives and Records Administration.
Ninth Census of the United States, 1870. M593, 1,761 rolls. *Minnesota Census
Schedules for 1870*. T132, 13 rolls. National Archives and Records
Administration, Washington D.C.

1880 U.S. Census Index provided by The Church of Jesus Christ of Latter-
day Saints. Copyright 1999, Intellectual Reserve, Inc.

Ancestry.com. *1900 U.S. Federal Census* (database on-line). Provo, Utah:
MyFamily.com, Inc., 2004. Original data: United States. *1900 United States
Federal Census*. T623, 1854 rolls. National Archives and Records
Administration, Washington D.C.

Ancestry.com. *1910 United States Federal Census* (database on-line). Provo,
Utah: MyFamily.com, Inc., 2004. Indexed by ProQuest from microfilmed
schedules of the *1910 U.S. Federal Decennial Census*. Data imaged from
National Archives and Records Administration. *1910 Federal Population
Census*. T624, 1,784 rolls. Washington, D.C.: National Archives and Records
Administration.

City Directories

Los Angeles City Directory, 1890. Los Angeles: W. H. L. Corran, Publisher and
Printer, 1890.

Los Angeles City Directory, 1893.

Los Angeles City Directory, 1900.

Los Angeles City Directory, 1908.

Los Angeles City Directory, 1909.

Los Angeles City Directory, 1910.

Los Angeles City Directory, 1913.

Los Angeles City Directory, 1914.

Los Angeles City Directory, 1915.

Los Angeles City Directory, 1916.

Los Angeles City Directory, 1918.

Los Angeles City Directory, 1920.

Los Angeles City Directory, 1921.

Business Directory of Los Angeles, Pasadena, Long Beach, San Pedro, Santa Monica, Venice, Ocean Park, San Bernardino, Redlands, Riverside, Santa Ana, and Neighboring Towns. Los Angeles: The Foster Directory Company, 1911.

City Directory: Security and Trust Savings Bank. 1920.

Dana Burks' Directory of Householders and Street and Avenue Guide of Los Angeles. Los Angeles: Los Angeles City Directory Co., Publishers, 1906.

U.S. City Directories, 1821–1989.

The Huntington Library

Los Angeles Area Court Records, 1850–1899

The Richard Courtney Collection

Letters to Eben Hunt

Correspondence of George McKinley Murrell

Los Angeles Public Library California Regional History Collection

Ancestry.com. *1920 United States Federal Census* (database on-line). Provo, UT, USA: Ancestry.com Operations, Inc., 2010. Images reproduced by FamilySearch. Original data: *Fourteenth Census of the United States, 1920.* (NARA microfilm publication T625, 2076 rolls). Records of the Bureau of the Census, Record Group 29. National Archives, Washington, D.C. For details on the contents of the film numbers, visit the following NARA web page: http://www.archives.gov/publications/microfilm-catalogs/census /1920/part-07.html. Note: Enumeration Districts 819–839 are on roll 323 (Chicago City).

Ancestry.com. *1930 United States Federal Census* (database on-line). Provo, UT, USA: Ancestry.com Operations Inc., 2002.Original data: United States of America, Bureau of the Census. *Fifteenth Census of the United States, 1930.* Washington, D.C.: National Archives and Records Administration, 1930. T626, 2,667 rolls.

Ancestry.com. *California, Death Index, 1940–1997* (database on-line). Provo, UT, USA: Ancestry.com Operations Inc., 2000. Original data: State of California. *California Death Index, 1940–1997.* Sacramento, CA, USA: State of California Department of Health Services, Center for Health Statistics.

Los Angeles Public Library Vertical File and Biography Collection

California Biography File A—Mason, Biddy
California Biography File A—Pico, Pío
California Biography File A—Williams, Paul Revere
California Biography File—Kimbrough, Jesse L.
California Biography File—"Pío Pico"
California Biography File—Seymour, William J.
California Biography File—"Pío Pico" 1891–1904
California Eagle Photograph Collection
California Vertical File—African Americans in Los Angeles—Chronology
California Vertical File—Churches—Los Angeles
California Vertical File—Los Angeles—Central Avenue District
Los Angeles Public Library Photography Collection
Southern California Library for Social Studies and Research
Periodicals
  The Apostolic Faith, 1906–1908
  California Eagle, 1914–1915
  The Californian, 15 March 1856; 1848
  Los Angeles Daily Times, 1881–1882
  Los Angeles Herald, 1879
  Los Angeles Sentinel, 2006
  Los Angeles Star, 1856
  Los Angeles Times, 1882–1926
  Sacramento Daily Union, 1859–1860
Seaver Center
  Antonio Coronel (1817–1894) Papers, 1770–1912
  De Valle Family Papers, 1818–1920
  Jonathan D. Dunlap Papers, 1868–1890
  California Place Names Collection
  Alcalde/L.A. County Court Records, 1830–1860
  L.A. County Incorporation Records, 1854–1922
  L.A. Schools Collection
  Street and Road Maps
UCLA Special Collections
  Golden State Mutual Life Insurance Company Records
  California Ephemera Collection

Speeches/Sermons

Blake, Bishop Charles E. "Mother's Day Sermon." Los Angeles: West Angeles
  Church of God in Christ, 2006.
Rockwell, John A. *Relation to Slavery in the Territories*. Washington, D.C., United
  States House of Representatives, 17 February 1849 [published speech].
Seward, William H. *Speech of William H. Seward, on the Admission of California*.
  Washington, D.C.: United States Senate, 11 March 1850 [published speech].

Azusa Street Centennial. http://www.azusastreet100.net/home.cfm. 20 April 2006.

BACM Research and Paperless Archives.com. *African American Slavery: California Fugitive Slave Case: Stovall v Archy Legal Papers.* http://www .paperlessarchives.com/FreeTitles/StovallvArchy.pdf. 15 June 2015.

Bulletin of the Los Angeles State Normal School 1917–1918 and Announcements for 1918–1919. Sacramento, Calif.: California State Printing Office, 1918.

California Council for the Humanities. *The Otherness of the Past: Presented as Part of the Sesquicentennial Project of the California Council for the Humanities,* 1999, www.kn.pacbell.com/ wired/ca_150/mason.html. 28 May 2006.

California Digital Library. *California State Archives and Golden State Museum,* ONLINE 2000, University of California, http://www.sos.ca.gov/archives /collections. 29 May 2016.

California State Constitution 1849. California State Archives, ONLINE 2000, University of California. Available: http://www.sos.ca.gov/archives /collections/constitutions/1849/full-text/. 3 December 2003.

California State Library. *The Governors' Gallery.* http://governors.library.ca.gov /01-Burnett.html. 17 March 2015.

California State Parks. "Allensworth: A Piece of the World" A Teacher's Guide with Student Lessons and Resources. 2004.

Center for Law in the Public Interest. *Heritage Parkspace.* Los Angeles, 2000. http://www.clipi.org/ourwork/heritageparkscape.html. 28 May 2006.

Center for Spiritual Renewal. *Official Azusa Street Centennial* website. http:// www.azusastreet100.net/home.cfm. 24 April 2006

Constitution of 1849 the State of California with Amendments (Superseded by Constitution of 1879) Section 1. http://codes.findlaw.com/ca/constitution-of -1849-the-state-of-california-with-amendments-superseded-by-constitution -of-1879/ocon-sect-1-nr2.html#sthash.kXhQe9RV.dpuf.

Haines, Michael R. "Population Characteristics," in *Historical Statistics of the United States, Earliest Times to the Present: Millennial Edition,* edited by Susan B. Carter, Scott Sigmund Gartner, Michael R. Haines, Alan L. Olmstead, Richard Sutch, and Gavin Wright. New York: Cambridge University Press, 2006. http://dx.doi.org/10.1017/ISBN-9780511132971.Aa.ESS.01; 6 April 2015.

Image of Queen Calafia. Baja California, Mexico. http://www.calafiacondo.com/, 28 May 2006.

Los Angeles Fire Department Historical Archive: History of Black Firemen. http://www.lafire.com/black_ff/black.htm. 20 April 2006.

Nobel Prize.org. "Nobel Peace Prize 1950—Ralph Bunche." http://www .nobelprize.org/nobel_prizes/peace/laureates/1950/bunche-bio.html, 5 April 2005.

PBS.org. Archives of the West from 1877–1887. "Chinese Exclusion Act," 6 May 1882. http://www.pbs.org/weta/thewest/resources/archives/seven/chinxact .htm#act. 3 March 2015.

PBS.org. Archives of the West from 1877–1887. "Treaty Regulating Immigration from China," 17 November 1880, Article I. http://www.pbs.org /weta/thewest/resources/archives/seven/chinxact.htm. 3 March 2015.

PBS.org. Archives of the West from 1877–1887. "Treaty Regulating Immigration from China," 17 November 1880, Article II. http://www.pbs.org /weta/thewest/resources/archives/seven/chinxact.htm. 3 March 2015.

Report on the Debates of the Convention of California on the Formation of the State Constitution in September and October 1849. https://www.sos.ca.gov /archives/collections/1849/pdf/convention-debates-reports.pdf. 3 December 2003.

Ruggles, Steven, Matthew Sobek, Trent Alexander, Catherine A. Fitch, Ronald Goeken, Patricia Kelly Hall, Miriam King, and Chad Ronnander. *Integrated Public Use Microdata Series: Version 3.0* (Machine-readable database). Minneapolis: Minnesota Population Center, 2004, http//www.ipums.org. 26 July 2006.

San Francisco Genealogy. http://www.sfgenealogy.com/search/search.pl?Match =1&Terms=%22charles+owens%22&Realm=All. 15 April 2006.

Special Collections and University Archives, University of Massachusetts Amherst Libraries. *The W.E.B. Du Bois Papers.* http://credo.library.umass.edu /view/collection/mums312. 10 August 2015.

University of Illinois at Urbana-Champaign. *Casta Painting.* http://www.sip .uiuc.edu/melendez/BlackIdentities/CuadrodeCastas.html. 30 May 2006.

University of Virginia Geospatial and Statistical Data Center. *United States Historical Census Data Browser*, 1998. http://fisher.lib.virginia.edu/census/. 26 July 2005.

The Virtual Museum of the City of San Francisco. http://www.sfmuseum.net /hist6/blackrights.html. 26 September 2005.

W. E. B. Du Bois Papers (MS 312). Special Collections and University Archives, University of Massachusetts Amherst Libraries. http://scua.library.umass.edu /ead/mums312.html. 25 March 2015.

West Angeles Church of God in Christ. *William J. Seymour Symposium.* http:// www.westa.org/azusa100.html. 24 February 2006.

Published Primary Documents

Bancroft, Hubert Howe. *History of California.* 7 vols. San Francisco: A. L. Bancroft and Co., 1884–1890.

———. *The Works of Hubert Howe Bancroft: History of California, Vol. IV, 1840–1845.* San Francisco: A. L. Bancroft and Company, 1886.

Barnet, Miguel, ed. *The Autobiography of a Runaway Slave, Esteban Montejo.* New York: Pantheon Books, 1968.

Bartleman, Frank. *Azusa Street: The Roots of Modern-day Pentecost.* Gainesville, Fla.: Bridge-Logos Publishers, 1980.

Bass, Charlotta A. *Forty Years: Memoirs from the Pages of a Newspaper.* Los Angeles: Charlotta Bass, 1960.

Beasley, Delilah L. *The Negro Trailblazers of California.* Los Angeles, Calif., 1919. Reprint. Whitefish, Montana: Kessinger Publishing.

Bell, Horace. *Reminiscences of a Ranger; or Early Times in Southern California.* 1852. 3 vols. Norman: University of Oklahoma Press, 2000.

Brooks, Bishop P. A. *Understanding Bible Doctrine as Taught in the Church of God in Christ.* Centennial edition. Detroit, Michigan: Church of God in Christ First Jurisdiction, 2002.

Bunch, Lonnie G. *Black Angelenos: The Afro-American in Los Angeles 1850–1950.* Exhibition catalog. Los Angeles: California Afro-American Museum, 1988.

Burdette, Robert J., ed. *Greater Los Angeles and Southern California: Portraits and Personal Memoranda.* Chicago: The Lewis Publishing Co., 1910.

Bushman, Richard L., ed. *The Great Awakening: Documents on the Revival of Religion, 1740–1745.* New York: Published for the Institute of Early American History and Culture at Williamsburg, Va. [by] Atheneum, 1970 [c1969].

Charter of the City of Los Angeles. Los Angeles: Harry M. Weir & Co., Law Booksellers, 1909.

Cole, Martin, and Henry Welcome., eds. *Don Pío Pico's Historical Narrative.* Translated by Arthur P. Botello. Glendale, Calif.: The Arthur H. Clark Co., 1973.

Collier-Thomas, Bettye. *Daughters of Thunder: Black Women Preachers and Their Sermons, 1850–1979.* San Francisco: Jossey-Bass Publishers, 1998.

Conrad, Robert. *Children of God's Fire: A Documentary History of Slavery in Brazil.* University Park: Pennsylvania State University Press, 1994.

"The Constitution of the United States, with the acts of Congress, relating to slavery, embracing, the Constitution, the Fugitive Slave Act of 1793, the Missouri Compromise Act of 1820, the Fugitive Slave Law of 1850, and the Nebraska and Kansas bill, carefully compiled." Rochester, N.Y.: D. M. Dewey, 1854.

Coy, Owen C. *Guide to the County Archives of California.* Sacramento: California Historical Survey Commission, 1919.

Crawford, Raymond Robert. *The Light of Life Brought Triumph: A Brief Sketch of the Life and Labors of Florence L. [Mother] Crawford, 1872–1936, Founder of the Apostolic Faith, Headquarters, Portland, Oregon.* Jubilee edition, Portland Ore.: Apostolic Faith Publishing House, 1955.

Cunningham, Michael, and Craig Marberry. *Crowns: Portraits of Black Women in Church Hats.* New York: Doubleday, 2000.

Daily Placer Times and Transcript 4, no. 874. San Francisco: G. K. Fitch and Co., 1853.

Darland, C. P., "Chinese Massacre at Los Angeles in 1871." *Annual Publication of the Historical Society of Southern California, Los Angeles* 3, no. 2 (1894): 22–26.

The Declaration of Independence and the Constitution of the United States. New York: Bantam Books, 1998.

Department of Commerce and Labor Bureau of the Census. *Abstract of the Fourteenth Census of the United States.* Washington, D.C.: Government Printing Office, 1923.

————. *Thirteenth Census of the United States Taken in the Year 1910: Abstract of the Census; Statistics and Population, Agriculture, Manufactures, and Mining for the United States, the States, and Principal Cities with Supplement for California Containing Statistics for the State, Counties, Cities and Other Divisions.* Washington, D.C.: Government Printing Office, 1913.

Du Bois, W. E. B. "Colored California." In *The Crisis: A Record of the Darker Races.* Volumes 5–6. Reprint. New York: Arno Press, 1969. 192–96.

————. *The Philadelphia Negro: A Social Survey.* Philadelphia: University of Pennsylvania Press, 1899.

————. *The Souls of Black Folk.* In *Three Negro Classics,* 209–389. New York: Avon Books, 1965.

Duniway, Clyde Augustus. "Slavery in California after 1848." American Historical Association, 1906. 241–48.

DuPree, Sherry Sherrod. *African-American Holiness Pentecostal Movement: An Annotated Bibliography.* New York: Garland Publishing, Inc., 1996.

Ellis, J. Delano, ed. *A Brief Historical, Doctrinal and Structural Report on the Church of God in Christ.* Memphis: Church of God in Christ, 1983.

Front Page: A Collection of Historical Headlines from the Los Angeles Times. New York: Harry N. Abrams, Inc., 1987.

General Laws of California. As Amended up to the Extra Session of 1906: Containing the Laws That are in Common Use in Full, with References to Other Laws in Force, and Also to Special Laws, with Statutory History Citations up to and Including Volume 147, California Reports. Ed. John Deering. San Francisco: Bancroft Whitney Company, 1906.

Gostin, Ted. *Southern California Vital Records.* Vol. 1, Los Angeles County 1850–1859. Los Angeles: Generation Press, 2001.

Guinn, J. M. *A History of California and an Extended History of Los Angeles and Environs.* 3 vols. Los Angeles: Historic Record Company, 1915.

Hayes, Benjamin. *Pioneer Notes from the Diaries of Judge Benjamin Hayes, 1849–1875.* Los Angeles, 1929.

Hayford, Jack W., gen. ed. *Spirit-Filled Life Bible: NKJV—A Personal Study Bible Unveiling All God's Fullness in All God's Word.* Nashville: Thomas Nelson Publishers, 1991.

Hurston, Zora Neale. *The Sanctified Church: The Folklore and Writings of Zora Neale Hurston.* Berkeley, Calif.: Turtle Island Foundation, 1981.

Ibanez, Vicente Blasco. *Queen Calafia.* New York: E. P. Dutton and Co., 1924.

Lerner, Gerda, ed. *Black Women in White America: A Documentary History.* New York: Pantheon Books, 1972.

Los Angeles Almanac. Montebello, Calif.: Given Place Publishing, 2001.

Mason, Elsie W. *The Man, Charles Harrison Mason (1866–1961).* Memphis: Pioneer Series Publications, 1979.

Maxwell's Los Angeles City Directory and Gazetteer of Southern California, 1898. Los Angeles: Los Angeles Directory Company, Publishers, 1898.

McGoarty, John Steven, ed. *History of Los Angeles County.* 3 vols. Chicago: The American Historical Society, Inc., 1923.

McNichols, Dinah, and Kieran McNulty, eds. *Front Page: A Collection of Historical Headlines from the Los Angeles Times, 1881–2003.* Los Angeles: Los Angeles Times and Tribune Media Services, Inc., 2003.

Newcombe, Barbara T. *Paper Trails: A Guide to Public Records in California.* San Francisco: California Newspaper Publishers Association and the Center for Investigative Reporting, 1990.

Newmark, Maurice H., and Marco R. Newmark. *Census of the City and County of Los Angeles California for the Year 1850 Together with an Analysis and an Appendix.* Los Angeles: The Times Mirror Press, 1929.

Nickel, Thomas R. *Azusa Street Outpouring: As Told to Me by Those Who Were There.* Hanford, Calif.: Great Commission International, 1979.

Nordhoff, Charles. *California: For Health, Pleasure, and Residence: A Book for Travelers and Settlers.* New York: Harper & Brothers, 1872.

Penal Code of California, Enacted in 1872; As Amended up to and Including 1905, with Statutory History and Citation Digest up to and Including Volume 147, California Reports. Ed. John Deering. San Francisco: Bancroft-Whitney Company, 1906.

Property Book of Los Angeles City. Published by Los Angeles Map and Address Co., 1909.

Range Jr., C. F., ed. *Church of God in Christ Official Manual.* Memphis: Board of Publication of the Church of God in Christ, Inc., 1973.

Reardon, Fred L. *Catholic Directory and Census of Los Angeles City and Parish Gazetteer of the Diocese of Monterey and Los Angeles.* Los Angeles: Fred L. Reardon Inc., 1899.

Reports of Cases Determined in the Supreme Court of the State of California. 220 vols. San Francisco: Bancroft-Whitney, 1887–1934.

Second Annual Report of the Civil Service Department of Los Angeles, California with Classification and Manual. Los Angeles: Southern California Printing Co., 1904.

Second Baptist Church. "Together We Build, 1885–2000" In *Second Baptist Church 115th Anniversary Souvenir Journal.* Los Angeles: Second Baptist Church, 2000.

Sernett, Milton C. *Afro-American Religious History: A Documentary Witness.* Durham, N.C.: Duke University Press, 1985

Seymour, William J. *The Doctrine and Discipline of the Azusa Street Apostolic Faith Mission of Los Angeles, CA: With Scripture Readings.* Los Angeles: Azusa Mission, 1915.

Sterling, Dorothy. *We Are Your Sisters: Black Women in the Nineteenth Century.* New York: W. W. Norton, 1984.

Taxpayers' Association of California. *City and Count Consolidation for Los Angeles.* Los Angeles, 1917.

Tenth Annual Report of the Civil Service Department of Los Angeles, California with Classification, Charter Provision, and Rules of the Department. Los Angeles: G. E. Karstens Printer, 1912.

Turley, David, ed. *American Religion: Literary Sources and Documents.* 3 vols. East Sussex: Helm Information Ltd., 1998.

U.S. Department of the Interior, *Population of the United States at the Eleventh Census: 1890*. Part 1. Washington, D.C.: Government Printing Office, 1895.

———. *Population of the United States at the Eleventh Census: 1890*. Part 2. Washington, D.C.: Government Printing Office, 1895.

Washington, Booker T. *Up from Slavery*. In *Three Negro Classics*, 29–205. New York: Avon Books, 1965.

Wilmore, Gayraud S., and James H. Cone, eds. *Black Theology: A Documentary History, 1966–1979*. Maryknoll, N.Y.: Orbis Books, 1979.

Secondary Sources

Ahlstrom, Sydney E. *A Religious History of the American People*. New Haven, Conn.: Yale University Press, 1972.

Alexander, Leslie. *African or American? Black Identity and Political Activism in New York City, 1784–1861*. Urbana: University of Illinois Press, 2008.

Alexander, Michelle. *The New Jim Crow: Mass Incarceration in the Age of Colorblindness*. New York: The New Press, 2010.

Allmendinger, Blake. *Imagining the African American West*. Lincoln: University of Nebraska Press, 2005.

Almaguer, Tomas. *Racial Fault Lines: The Historical Origins of White Supremacy in California*. Berkeley: University of California Press, 1994.

Anderson, Allen. "Writing the Pentecostal History of Africa, Asia, and Latin America." *Journal of Beliefs and Values* 25, no. 2 (August 2004): 139–51.

Anderson, Robert Mapes. *Vision of the Disinherited: The Making of American Pentecostalism*. New York: Oxford University Press, 1979.

Andrews, George Reid. *Afro Latin America 1800–2000*. New York: Oxford University Press, 2004.

Aptheker, Herbert, ed. *The Correspondence of W. E. B. Du Bois: Volume 1, Selections, 1877–1934*. Amherst: University of Massachusetts Press, 1973.

Avila, Eric. *The Folklore of the Freeway: Race and Revolt in the Modernist City*. Minneapolis: University of Minnesota Press, 2014.

———. *Popular Culture in the Age of White Flight: Fear and Fantasy in Suburban Los Angeles*. Berkeley: University of California Press, 2004.

Baer, Hans A., and Merrill Singer. *African-American Religion in the Twentieth Century: Varieties of Protest and Accommodation*. Knoxville: University of Tennessee Press, 1992.

Baldwin, Davarian. *Chicago's New Negroes: Modernity, The Great Migration, and Black Urban Life*. Chapel Hill: University of North Carolina Press, 2007.

Barr, Juliana. *Peace Came in the Form of a Woman: Indians and Spaniards in the Texas Borderlands*. Chapel Hill: University of North Carolina Press, 2007.

Bastide, Roger. *The African Religions of Brazil: Toward a Sociology of the Interpretation of Civilizations*. Translated by Helen Sebba. Baltimore: Johns Hopkins University Press, 1978.

Beasley, Delilah. "Slavery in California." *Journal of Negro History* 3, no. 1. (January 1918): 33–44.

Beebe, Rose Marie, and Robert M. Senkewicz., eds. *Lands of Promise and Despair: Chronicles of Early California, 1535–1846.* Santa Clara, Calif.: Santa Clara University, 2001.

Bennett, Herman L. *Africans in Colonial Mexico: Absolutism, Christianity, and Afro-Creole Consciousness, 1570–1640.* Bloomington: Indiana University Press, 2003.

———. *Colonial Blackness: A History of Afro-Mexico.* Bloomington: Indiana University Press, 2009.

Berardi, Gayle K., and Thomas W. Segady. "The Development of African-American Newspapers in the American West: A Sociohistorical Perspective." *Journal of Negro History* 75, nos. 3–4 (Summer–Autumn 1990): 96–111.

Berg, Manfred. *Popular Justice: A History of Lynching in America.* Chicago: Ivan R. Dee, 2011.

Billingsley, Andrew. *Mighty Like a River: The Black Church and Social Reform.* Oxford: Oxford University Press, 1999.

Billington, Monroe L., and Roger D. Hardaway, eds. *African Americans on the Western Frontier.* Boulder: University Press of Colorado, 1998.

Blassingame, John W. *Black New Orleans 1860–1880.* Chicago: University of Chicago Press, 1973.

———. *The Slave Community: Plantation Life in the Antebellum South.* New York: Oxford University Press, 1979.

Bloch-Hoell, Nils. *The Pentecostal Movement: Its Origin, Development, and Distinctive Character.* Munksgaard, Copenhagen: Scandinavian University Books, 1964.

Blum, Edward J. *W. E. B. Du Bois: American Prophet.* Philadelphia: University of Pennsylvania Press, 2007.

Brilliant, Mark. *The Color of America Has Changed: How Racial Diversity Shaped Civil Rights in California, 1941–1978.* New York: Oxford University Press, 2010.

Brooks, Gordon. "Blacks in Los Angeles in the Twentieth Century: A Bibliography." GB–Social Science Subject Specialist, 1986.

Brooks, James F. *Captives and Cousins: Slavery, Kinship, and Community in the Southwestern Borderlands.* Chapel Hill: University of North Carolina Press, 2002.

Broome Jr., Homer F. *LAPD's Black History, 1886–1976.* Norwalk, Calif.: Stockton Trade Press, 1977.

Broussard, Albert S. *Black San Francisco: The Struggle for Racial Equality in the West, 1900–1954.* Lawrence, Kans.: The University Press of Kansas, 1993.

———. *Expectations of Equality: A History of Black Westerners.* Wheeling, Ill.: Harlan Davidson, Inc., 2012.

Brown, Diana De G. *Umbanda: Religion and Politics in Urban Brazil.* New York: Columbia University Press, 1994.

Bruce, Calvin E., and William R. Jones., eds. *Black Theology II: Essays on the Formation of Contemporary Black Theology.* Cranbury, N.J.: Associated University Presses, Inc., 1978.

Burgess, Stanley M., and Gary B. McGee., eds. *Dictionary of Pentecostal and Charismatic Movements*. Grand Rapids, Mich.: Zondervan Publishing House, 1988.

Burkett, Randall K., and Richard Newman, eds. *Black Apostles: Afro-American Clergy Confront the Twentieth Century*. Boston: G. K. Hall and Co., 1978.

Butler, Anne M. *Daughters of Joy, Sisters of Misery: Prostitutes in the American West, 1865–90*. Urbana: University of Illinois Press, 1985.

———. *Gendered Justice in the American West: Women Prisoners in Men's Penitentiaries*. Urbana: University of Illinois Press, 1997.

Butler, Jon. *Awash in a Sea of Faith: Christianizing the American People*. Cambridge, Mass.: Harvard University Press, 1990.

———. "Enthusiasm Described and Decried: The Great Awakening as Interpretive Fiction." *Journal of American History* 69, no. 2 (September 1982): 305–25.

Calavita, Kitty. "The Paradoxes of Race, Class, Identity, and 'Passing': Enforcing the Chinese Exclusion Acts, 1882–1910." *Law and Society Inquiry* 25, no. 1. (Winter 2002): 1–40.

Campbell, Marne L. "African American Women, Wealth Accumulation, and Social Welfare in 19th-Century Los Angeles." *Journal of African American History* 97, no. 4 (Fall 2012): 376–400.

———. "'The Newest Religious Sect Has Started in Los Angeles': Race, Class, and Ethnicity, and the Origins of the Pentecostal Movement, 1906–1913." *Journal of African American History* 95, no. 1 (Winter 2010): 1–25.

Canizares, Raul. *Cuban Santeria: Walking with the Night*. Rochester, Vt.: Destiny Books, 1999.

Carroll, Patrick. *Blacks in Colonial Veracruz: Race, Ethnicity, and Regional Development*. Austin: University of Texas Press, 1991.

Carwardine, Richard. "The Second Great Awakening in the Urban Centers: An Examination of Methodism and the 'New Measures.'" *Journal of American History* 59, no. 2 (September 1972): 327–40.

Cha-Jua, Sundiata. *America's First Black Town: Brooklyn, Illinois, 1830–1915*. Urbana and Chicago: University of Illinois Press, 2000.

Chapman, Mark L. *Christianity on Trial: African American Religious Thought before and after Black Power*. Maryknoll, N.Y.: Orbis Books, 1996.

Chavez-Garcia, Miroslova. *Negotiating Conquest: Gender and Power in California, 1770s–1880s*. Tucson: The University of Arizona Press. 2004.

Clemmons, Ithiel C. *Bishop C. H. Mason and the Roots of the Church of God in Christ*. Bakersfield, Calif.: Pneuma Life Publishing, 1996.

Cobbins, Otho B., ed. *History of the Church of Christ (Holiness) USA, 1895–1965*. New York: Vintage Press, 1966.

Cohen, Charles L. "The Post-Puritan Paradigm of Early American Religious History." *William and Mary Quarterly* 3rd series, 54, no. 4. (October 1997): 695–722.

Colbert, David, ed. *Eyewitness to the American West: 500 Years of Firsthand History*. New York: Penguin Books, 1998.

Collier-Thomas, Bettye. *Jesus, Jobs, and Justice: African American Women and Religion*. New York: Alfred A. Knopf, 2010.

Collins, William J. "When the Tide Turned: Immigration and the Delay of the Great Black Migration." *The Journal of Economic History* 57, no. 3 (September 1997): 607–32.

Cone, James H. "Black Theology in American Religion." *Journal of the American Academy of Religion* 53, no. 4, (December 1985): 755–71.

———. *A Black Theology of Liberation*. Philadelphia: J. B. Lippincott Company, 1970.

Conyers, James E., and T. H. Kennedy. "Negro Passing: To Pass or Not to Pass." *Phylon* 24, no. 3 (1963): 215–23.

Cope, Douglas R. *The Limits of Racial Domination: Plebeian Society in Colonial Mexico City, 1660–1720*. Madison: The University of Wisconsin Press, 1994.

Cordasco, Francesco. *Crime in America: Historical Patterns and Contemporary Realities, an Annotated Bibliography*. New York: Garland Publishing, 1985.

Cortez, Carlos E. *Mexicans in California after U.S. Conquest*. New York: Arno Press, 1976.

Creech, Joe. "Visions of Glory: The Place of the Azusa Street Revival in Pentecostal History." *Church History* 65, no. 3 (September 1996): 405–24.

Dabel, Jane E. *A Respectable Woman: The Public Roles of African American Women in 19th-Century New York*. New York: New York University Press, 2008.

David, C. W. A. "The Fugitive Slave Law of 1793 and Its Antecedents." *Journal of Negro History* 9, no. 1 (January 1924): 18–25.

Davis, Mike. *Ecology of Fear: Los Angeles and the Imagination of Disaster*. New York: Vintage Books, 1998.

Dailey, Jane. "Deference and Violence in the Postbellum Urban South: Manners and Massacres in Danville, Virginia." *Journal of Southern History* 63, no. 3 (August 1997): 553–90.

Dallam, Marie. *Daddy Grace: A Celebrity Preacher and His House of Prayer*. New York: New York University Press, 2007.

Daniels, Douglas H. *Pioneer Urbanites: A Social and Cultural History of Black San Francisco*. Berkeley: University of California Press, 1990.

De Graaf, Lawrence B., Kevin Mulroy, and Quintard Taylor, eds. *Seeking El Dorado: African Americans in California*. Los Angeles: Autry Museum of Western Heritage; Seattle: University of Washington Press, 2001.

Demaratus, DeEtta. *The Force of a Feather: The Search for a Lost Story of Slavery and Freedom*. Salt Lake City: University of Utah Press, 2002.

Deno, Vivan. "God, Authority, and the Home: Gender, Race, and U.S. Pentecostals, 1906–1926." *Journal of Women's History* 16, no. 3 (Fall 2004): 83–105.

Deverell, William. *Whitewashed Adobe: The Rise of Los Angeles and the Remaking of Its Mexican Past*. Berkeley: University of California Press, 2004.

Dieter, Melvin E. *The Holiness Revival of the Nineteenth Century*. Metuchen, N.J.: Scarecrow Press, 1980.

Dje Dje, Jaqueline Cogdell. "Gospel Music in the Los Angeles Black Community: A Historical Overview." *Black Music Research Journal* 9, no. 1 (Spring 1989): 35–79.

Dje Dje, Jaqueline Cogell, and Eddie S. Meadows, eds. *California Soul: Music of African Americans in the West.* Berkeley: University of California Press, 1998.

DuPree, Sherry Sherrod, ed. *Biographical Dictionary of African-American, Holiness-Pentecostals, 1880–1990.* Washington, D.C.: Middle Atlantic Regional Press, 1989.

Durant, Thomas J., and Joyce S. Louden. "The Black Middle Class in America: Historical and Contemporary Perspectives." *Phylon* 47, no. 4 (1986): 253–63.

Eaves, Lucille. *A History of California Labor Legislation: With an Introductory Sketch of the San Francisco Labor Movement.* University of California Publications in Economics, vol. 2. Berkeley: The University Press, August 23, 1910.

Engh, Michael E. "'A Multiplicity and Diversity of Faiths': Religion's Impact on Los Angeles and the Urban West, 1890–1940." *Western Historical Quarterly* 28, no. 4 (Winter 1997): 463–92.

Espinosa, Gastón. *William J. Seyomour and the Origins of Global Penetecostalism: A Biography & Documentary History.* Durham, N.C.: Duke University Press, 2014.

Fair, Jo Ellen. "'Black on Black': Race, Space, and News of African Americans." *Issue: A Journal of Opinion* 22, no. 1 (Winter–Spring, 1994): 35–40.

Faragher, John Mack. *Eternity Street: Violence and Justice in Frontier Los Angeles.* New York: W. W. Norton & Co., 2016.

Fernandez Olmos, Margarite, and Lizabeth Paravisini-Gebert, eds. *Sacred Possessions: Vodou, Santeria, Obeah, and the Caribbean.* New Brunswick, N.J.: Rutgers University Press, 1997.

Findlay Jr., James F. *Church People in the Struggle: The National Council of Churches and the Black Freedom Movement, 1950–1970.* New York: Oxford University Press, 1993.

Fitch, Suzanne Pullon, and Roseann M. Mandziuk. *Sojourner Truth as Orator: Wit, Story, and Song.* Westport, Conn.: Greenwood Press, 1997.

Flamming, Douglas. *African Americans in the West.* Santa Barbara, Calif.: ABC-CLIO, 2009.

Fogelson, Robert M. *The Fragmented Metropolis: Los Angeles, 1850–1930.* Cambridge, Mass.: Harvard University Press, 1967.

Foner, Phillip, and Ronald L. Lewis, eds. *The Black Worker During the Era of the American Federation of Labor and the Railroad Brotherhoods.* Vol. 4 of *The Black Worker: A Documentary History from Colonial Times to the Present.* Philadelphia: Temple University Press, 1979.

Forbes, Jack D. "Black Pioneers: The Spanish-Speaking Afroamericans of the Southwest." *Phylon* 27, no. 3 (1966): 233–46.

Frazier, E. Franklin, and C. Eric Lincoln. *The Negro Church in America/The Black Church Since Frazier.* New York: Shocken Books, 1974.

Freer, Regina. "L.A. Race Woman: Charlotta Bass and the Complexities of Black Political Development in Los Angeles." *American Quarterly* 56, no. 3 (September 2004): 607–32, http://muse.jhu.edu/journals/american_quarterly /vo56/56.3freer.html. 4 May 2006.

Frey, Sylvia, and Betty Wood. *Come Shouting to Zion: African American Protestantism in the American South and British Caribbean to 1830.* Chapel Hill: University of North Carolina Press, 1998.

Friedman, Lawrence M. *Crime and Punishment in American History.* New York: Harper Collins, 1993.

Friedricks, William B. "A Metropolitan Entrepreneur Par Excellence: Henry E. Huntington and the Growth of Southern California, 1898–1927." *Business History Review* 63, no. 2 (Summer 1989): 329–55.

Fulop, Timothy E. "'The Future Golden Day of the Race': Millennialism and Black Americans in the Nadir, 1877–1901." *Harvard Theological Review* 84, no. 1 (January 1991): 75–99.

Fulop, Timothy E., and Albert J. Raboteau, eds. *African-American Religion: Interpretive Essays in History and Culture.* New York: Routledge, 1997.

Garcia, Matt. *A World of Its Own: Race, Labor, and Citrus in the Making of Greater Los Angeles, 1900–1970.* Chapel Hill: University of North Carolina Press, 2001.

Garma, Carlos. "The Socialization of the Gifts of Tongues and Healing in Mexican Pentecostalism." *Journal of Contemporary Religion* 3, no 13 (2000): 353–63.

Garr, Daniel J. "A Rare and Desolate Land: Population and Race in Hispanic California." *Western Historical Quarterly* 6, no. 2 (April 1975): 133–48.

Gaspar, David Barry, and Darlene Clark Hine, eds. *More Than Chattel: Black Women and Slavery in the Americas.* Bloomington: Indiana University Press, 1996.

Gaustad, Edwin Scott. *The Great Awakening in New England.* Chicago: Quadrangle Books, 1957.

———. *A Religious History of America.* Revised edition. San Francisco: Harper, 1990.

Gellman, David N., and David Quigley, eds., *Jim Crow in New York: A Documentary History of Race and Citizenship, 1777–1877.* New York: New York University Press, 2003.

Genovese, Eugene D. *Roll, Jordan, Roll: The World the Slaves Made.* New York: Vintage Books, 1974.

Giddings, Paula. *Where and When I Enter: The Impact of Black Women on Race and Sex in America.* New York: Harper Collins, 1984.

Gilkes, Cheryl Townsend. *"If It Wasn't for the Women...": Black Women's Experience and Womanist Culture in Church and Community.* Maryknoll, N.Y.: Orbis Books, 2001.

Gill, Tiffany M. *Beauty Shop Politics: African American Women's Activism in the Beauty Industry.* Urbana: University of Illinois Press, 2010.

Goen, C. C. *Revivalism and Separatism in New England, 1740–1800: Strict Congregationalists and Separate Baptists in the Great Awakening.* Middletown, Conn.: Wesleyan University Press, 1987.

Goldsmith, Peter D. *When I Rise Cryin' Holy: African-American Denominationalism on the Georgia Coast.* New York: AMS Press, Inc., 1989.

Gómez, Laura E. *Manifest Destinies: The Making of the Mexican American Race.* New York: New York University Press, 2007.

Goode, Kenneth, G. *California's Black Pioneers: A Brief Historical Survey.* Santa Barbara, Calif.: McNally & Loftin, Publishers, 1974.

Gordon, Ann D., Bettye Collier-Thomas, John H. Bracey, Arlene Voski Avakian, and Joyce Avrech Berman, eds. *African American Women and the Vote, 1837–1965.* Amherst: University of Massachusetts Press, 1997.

Graham, Lawrence Otis. *Our Kind of People: Inside America's Black Upper Class.* New York: Harper Perennial, 2000.

Grant, Jacquelyn, ed. *Perspectives on Womanist Theology.* Atlanta: The ITC Press, 1995.

Gray, Dorothy. *Women of the West.* Millbrae, Calif.: Les Femmes, 1976.

Gregory, James N. *The Southern Diaspora: How the great Migrations of Black and White Southerners Transformed America.* Chapel Hill: University of North Carolina Press, 2005.

Gross, Kali. *Colored Amazons: Crime, Violence, and Black Women in the City of Brotherly Love, 1880–1910.* Durham, N.C.: Duke University Press, 2006.

Gutierrez, Ramon, and Richard J. Orsi, eds. *Contested Eden: California before the Gold Rush.* Berkeley: University of California Press, 1998.

Hagerdorn, Katherine J. *Divine Utterances: The Performance of Afro-Cuban Santeria.* Washington, D.C.: Smithsonian Institute Press, 2001.

Haley, Sarah. "'Like I Was a Man': Chain Gangs, Gender, and the Domestic Carceral Sphere in Jim Crow Georgia." *Signs,* 3, no. 1, Women, Gender, and Prison: National and Global Perspectives (Autumn 2013): 53–77.

Hall, Gwendolyn Midlo. *Blacks in Colonial Louisiana: The Development of Afro-Creole Culture in the Eighteenth Century.* Baton Rouge: Louisiana State University Press, 1992.

Hamilton, Kenneth M. *Black Towns and Profit: Promotion and Development in the Trans-Appalachian West, 1877–1915.* Urbana: University of Illinois Press, 1991.

Hamilton, Michael P., ed. *The Charismatic Movement.* Grand Rapids, Mich.: William B. Eerdmans Publishing Co., 1975.

Hammond, John L. "Revivals, Consensus, and American Political Culture." *Journal of the Academy of Religion* 46, no. 3 (September 1978): 293–314.

Harding, Rachel. *A Refuge in Thunder: Candomble and Alternative Spaces of Blackness.* Bloomington: Indiana University Press, 2000.

Harkness, Georgia. *Women in Church and Society.* Nashville: Abingdon Press, 1972.

Harlan, Louis R., and Raymond W. Smock, eds. *The Booker T. Washington Papers.* 14 vols. Urbana: University of Illinois Press, 1977–1989.

Harper, Phillip Brian. "Passing for What? Racial Masquerade and the Demands of Upward Mobility." *Callaloo* 21, no. 2, Emerging Male Writers, part 2 (Spring 1998): 381–97.

Hawkins, Homer C. "Trends in Black Migration from 1863–1960." *Phylon* 34, no. 2 (1973): 140–52.

Hayden, Delores. *The Power of Place: Urban Landscapes as Public History.* Cambridge, Mass: The MIT Press, 1997.

Hayford, Jack W. *The Charismatic Century: The Enduring Impact of the Azusa Street Revival.* New York: Warner Faith, 2006.

Heizer, Robert F., and Alan F. Almquist. *The Other Californians: Prejudice and Discrimination Under Spain, Mexico, and the United States to 1920.* Berkeley: University of California Press, 1971.

Hewlett, Rene A., and Max J. Williams. *Negro Who's Who in California.* Lithographed by W. M. Westerfield. Negro Who's Who in California Publishing Company, 1947.

———. *Negro Who's Who in California.* Lithographed by W. M. Westerfield. Negro Who's Who in California Publishing Co., 1948.

Higginbotham, Evelyn Brooks. *Righteous Discontent: The Women's Movement in the Black Baptist Church, 1880–1920.* Cambridge, Mass.: Harvard University Press, 1993.

Hine, Darlene Clark. *Hine Sight: Black Women and the Re-Construction of American History.* New York: Carlson Publishing, 1994.

Hodes, Martha, ed. *Sex, Love, Race: Crossing Boundaries in North American History.* New York: New York University Press, 1999.

Hollenweger, Walter J. *The Pentecostals; The Charismatic Movement in the Churches.* Minneapolis: Augsburg, 1972.

Horne, Gerald. *Black and Brown: African Americans and the Mexican Revolution, 1910–1920.* New York: New York University Press, 2005.

Horton, Hayward Derrick, Beverlyn Lundy Allen, Cedric Herring, and Melvin E. Thomas. "Lost in the Storm: The Sociology of the Black Working Class, 1850–1900." *American Sociological Review* 65, no. 1, Looking Forward, Looking Back: Continuity and Change at the Turn of the Millennium (February 2000): 128–37.

Horton, James Oliver. *Free People of Color: Inside the African American Community.* Washington, D.C.: Smithsonian Institution Press, 1993.

Houk, James T. *Spirits, Blood, and Drums: The Orisha Religion in Trinidad.* Philadelphia: Temple University Press, 1995.

Hudson, Lynn M. *The Making of "Mammy Pleasant": A Black Entrepreneur in Nineteenth Century San Francisco.* Urbana: University of Illinois Press, 2003.

Hunt, Darnell, and Ana-Christina Ramon. *Black Los Angeles: American Dreams and Racial Realities.* New York: New York University Press, 2010.

Hunter, Tera W. *To 'Joy My Freedom: Southern Black Women's Lives and the Labors after the Civil War.* Cambridge, Mass.: Harvard University Press: 1997.

Hurtado, Albert. *Indian Survival on the California Frontier.* New Haven, Conn.: Yale University Press, 1988.

———. *Intimate Frontiers: Sex, Gender and Culture in Old California.* Albuquerque: University of New Mexico Press, 1999.

Hustvedt, S. B. "Spanish Elements in the Style of the Los Angeles Star." *Western Folklore* 7, no. 1 (January 1948): 1–20.

Hutchinson, Janis Faye, Nestor Rodriguez, and Jacqueline Hagan. "Community Life: African Americans in Multiethnic Residential Areas." *Journal of Black Studies* 27, no. 2 (November 1996): 201–23.

Irwin, Mary Ann, and James F. Brooks, eds. *Women and Gender in the American West: Jensen-Miller Prize Essays from the Coalition for Western Women's Historians.* Albuquerque: University of New Mexico Press, 2004.

Isoardi, Steven L. *The Dark Tree: Jazz and the Community Arts in Los Angeles.* Berkeley: University of California Press, 2006.

Jameson, Elizabeth, and Susan Armitage, eds. *Writing the Range: Race, Class, and Culture in the Women's West.* Norman: University of Oklahoma Press, 1997.

Janssen, Volker. "When the 'Jungle' Met the Forest: Public Work, Civil Defense, and Prison Camps in Postwar California." *Journal of American History* 96, no. 3 (December 2009): 702–26.

Jelks, Randal M. *African Americans in the Furniture City: The Struggle for Civil Rights in Grand Rapids.* Urbana: University of Illinois Press, 2006.

Johnson, Paul E. *African-American Christianity: Essays in History.* Berkeley: University of California Press, 1994.

Johnson, Susan L. *Roaring Camp: The Social World of the California Gold Rush.* New York: W. W. Norton, 2000.

Jones, Charles Edwin. *Black Holiness: A Guide to the Study of Black Participation in Wesleyan Perfectionist and Glossolalic Pentecostal Movements.* Metuchen, N.J.: The American Theological Library and the Scarecrow Press, Inc., 1987.

Jones, Jacqueline. *Labor of Love, Labor of Sorrow: Black Women, Work, and the Family from Slavery to the Present.* New York: Random House, 1985.

Jordon, Winthrop. *White Over Black: American Attitudes Toward the Negro, 1550–1812.* Chapel Hill: University of North Carolina Press, 1968.

Juster, Susan. *Disorderly Women: Sexual Politics and Evangelicalism in Revolutionary New England.* Ithaca, N.Y.: Cornell University Press, 1994.

Kanter, Deborah E. *Hijos del Pueblo: Gender, Family, and Community in Rural Mexico, 1730–1850.* Austin: University of Texas Press, 2008.

Katz, William Loren. *Black People Who Made the Old West.* Trenton, N.J.: Africa World Press, 1992.

———. *The Black West.* New York: Doubleday and Co., Inc., 1971.

Katzew, Ilona. *Casta Painting: Images of Race in Eighteenth-century Mexico.* New Haven, Conn.: Yale University Press, 2004.

Kelley, Robin D. G. *Race Rebels: Culture, Politics, and the Black Working Class.* New York: The Free Press, 1994.

Klein, Herbert S., and Ben Vinson III. *African Slavery in Latin America and the Caribbean.* New York: Oxford University Press, 2007.

Krueger, E. T. "Negro Religious Expression." *American Journal of Sociology* 38, no. 1 (July 1932): 22–31.

Kuhn, Josh, and Laura Pulido. *Black and Brown in Los Angeles: Beyond Conflict and Coalition.* Berkeley: University of California Press, 2014.

Kurashige, Scott. *The Shifting Grounds of Race: Black and Japanese Americans in the Making of Multiethnic Los Angeles*. Princeton, N.J.: Princeton University Press, 2008.

Lambert, Frank. "'I Saw the Book Talk': Slave Readings of the First Great Awakening." *Journal of African American History* 87, The Past before Us. (Winter 2002): 12–25.

Landers, Jane G., and Barry M. Robinson, ed. *Slaves, Subjects, and Subversives: Blacks in Colonial Latin America*. Albuquerque: University of New Mexico Press, 2006.

Lapp, Rudolph M. *Archy Lee: A California Fugitive Slave Case*. Reprint. Berkeley: Heyday Books, 2008.

Laslett, Barbara, and Katherine Nash. "Family Structure in Los Angeles, California: 1850–1900." *Social Science History* 20, no. 1 (Spring 1996): 1–39.

Laslett, John M. *Sunshine Was Never Enough: Los Angeles Workers, 1880–2010*. Berkeley: University of California Press, 2012.

Layne, J. Gregg. *The Annals of Los Angeles from the Arrival of the First White Men to the Civil War, 1769–1861*. Special publication No. 9. San Francisco: California Historical Society, 1935.

Leacock, Seth, and Ruth Leacock. *Spirits of the Deep: A Study of an Afro-Brazilian Cult*. Garden City, N.Y.: Doubleday, 1972.

Leflouria, Talitha. *Chained in Silence: Black Women and Convict Labor in the New South*. Chapel Hill: University of North Carolina Press, 2015.

Lightfoot, Kent G. *Indians Missionaries, and Merchants: The Legacy of Colonial Encounters on the California Frontier*. Berkeley: University of California Press, 2005.

Lincoln, C. Eric, and Lawrence H. Maymia, eds. *The Black Church in the African American Experience*. Durham, N.C.: Duke University Press, 1990.

Lockhart, James, and Stuart B. Schwartz, eds. *Early Latin America: A History of Colonial Spanish America and Brazil*. London: Cambridge University Press, 1983.

Lovejoy, David S. "Hopkins: Religion, Slavery, and the Revolution." *New England Quarterly* 40, no. 2 (June 1967): 227–43

——. *Religious Enthusiasm in the New World: Heresy to Revolution*. Cambridge, Mass.: Harvard University Press, 1985.

MacRobert, Ian. "The Black Roots of Pentecostalism." In *African American Religion: Interpretive Essays in History and Culture*, edited by Timothy E. Fulop and Albert J. Raboteau, 295–309. New York: Routledge, 1997.

Madley, Benjamin. "California's Yuki Indians: Defining Genocide in Native American History." *Western Historical Quarterly* 39, no. 3 (Autumn 2008): 303–32.

——. "'Unholy Traffic in Human Blood and Souls': Systems of California Indian Servitude under U.S. Rule." *Pacific Historical Review* 83, no. 4 (November 2014): 626–67.

Marini, Stephen A. *Radical Sects of Revolutionary New England*. Cambridge, Mass.: Harvard University Press, 1982.

Marks, Carole. *Farewell—We're Good and Gone: The Great Black Migration.* Bloomington: Indiana University Press, 1989.

Martin, Cy. *Whiskey and Women: An Amusing Account of the Saloons and Bawds of the Old West.* New York: Hart Publishing Co., 1974.

Martin, Larry, ed. *The Topeka Outpouring of 1901: Eyewitness Accounts of the Revival that Birthed the Twentieth Century Pentecostal Movement.* Missouri: Christian Life Books, 2000.

Martínez, Maria E. "The Black Blood of New Spain: Limpieza de Sangre, Racial Violence, and Gendered Power in Early Colonial Mexico." *William and Mary Quarterly* 61 (July 2004): 479–520.

———. *Genealogical Fictions: Limpieza de Sangre, Religion, and Gender in Colonial Mexico.* Stanford, Calif.: Stanford University Press, 2008.

Mason, William Marvin. *The Census of 1790: A Demographic History of Colonial California.* Menlo Park, Calif.: Ballena Press, 1998.

Matibag, Eugenio. *Afro-Cuban Religious Experience: Cultural Reflections in Narrative.* Gainesville: University of Florida Press, 1996.

McCaa, Robert. "Calidad, Clase, and Marriage in Colonial Mexico: The Case of Parral, 1788–90." *Hispanic American Historical Review* 64, no. 3 (August 1984): 477–501.

———. "Ethnic Intermarriage and Gender in New York City." *Journal of Interdisciplinary History* 24, no. 2 (Autumn 1993): 207–31.

McGroarty, John Steven, ed. *History of Los Angeles County.* 2 vols. Chicago: The American Historical Association, 1923.

Menchaca, Martha. *Recovering History, Constructing Race: The Indian, Black, and White Roots of Mexican Americans.* Austin: University of Texas Press, 2001.

Metraux, Alfred. *Voodoo in Haiti.* New York: Shocken Books, 1972.

Miller, Ronald Dean. *Shady Ladies of the West.* Los Angeles: Westernlore Press, 1964.

Mintz, Sidney M., and Richard Price. *The Birth of Afro-American Culture: An Anthropological Perspective.* Boston: Beacon Press, 1976.

Monkkonen, Eric. "Homicide in Los Angeles, 1827–2002." *Journal of Interdisciplinary History* 36, no. 2 (Autumn 2005): 167–83.

———. "Western Homicide: The Case of Los Angeles, 1830–1870." *Pacific Historical Review* 74, no. 4 (November 2005): 603–17.

Montgomery, William E. *Under Their Own Vine and Fig Tree: The African American Church in the South, 1865–1900.* Baton Rouge: Louisiana State University Press, 1993.

Muhammad, Khalil Gibran. *The Condemnation of Blackness: Race, Crime, and the Making of Modern America.* Cambridge, Mass.: Harvard University Press, 2010.

Mumford, Kevin J. *Interzones: Black/White Sex Districts in Chicago and New York in the Early Twentieth Century.* New York: Columbia University Press, 1997.

Nash, Gary B. *Forbidden Love: The Secret History of Mixed-race Americans.* New York: Henry Holt and Co., 1999.

———. *Forging Freedom: The Formation of Philadelphia's Black Community, 1720–1840.* Cambridge, Mass.: Harvard University Press: 1988.

———. *Red, Black, and White: The Peoples of Early North America.* 1974. Reprint. Upper Saddle River, N.J.: Prentice Hall, 2000.

Ngai, Mae M. "Chinese Gold Miners and the 'Chinese Question' in Nineteenth Century California and Victoria." *Journal of American History* 101, no. 4 (March 2015): 1082–1105.

———. *Impossible Subjects: Illegal Aliens and the Making of Modern America.* Princeton, N.J.: Princeton University Press, 2004.

Noble, E. Myron, ed. *Like as of Fire: Newspapers from the Azusa Street World Wide Revival, 1906–1909.* Washington, D.C.: Middle Atlantic Regional Press, 1991.

Northrop, Marie E. *Spanish-Mexican Families of Early California: 1769–1850.* Vol. 1. New Orleans: Polyanthos, Inc., 1976.

Nystrom, Justin A. *New Orleans after the Civil War: Race, Politics, and a New Birth of Freedom.* Baltimore, Md.: Johns Hopkins Press, 2013.

O'Brien, David M. *Constitutional Law and Politics.* 6th ed. New York: W. W. Norton, 2005.

Olzak, Susan. "The Political Context of Competition: Lynching and Urban Racial Violence, 1882–1914." *Social Forces* 69, no. 2 (December 1990): 395–421.

Omi, Michael, and Howard Winant. *Racial Formation in the United States: From the 1960s to the 1990s.* New York: Routledge, 1994.

O'Toole, Rachel S. *Bound Lives: Africans, Indians, and the Making of Race in Colonial Peru.* Pittsburgh: University of Pittsburgh Press, 2012.

Outler, Albert C., ed. *John Wesley.* New York: Oxford University Press, 1964.

Overacker, Ingrid. *The African American Church Community in Rochester, New York, 1900–1940.* New York: University of Rochester Press, 1998.

Owens, Robert R. *Speak to the Rock: The Azusa Street Revival, Its Roots and Its Message.* New York: University Press of America, Inc., 1998.

Painter, Nell Irvin. *Exodusters: Black Migration to Kansas after Reconstruction, the First Major Migration to the North of Ex-Slaves.* New York: W. W. Norton, 1976.

———. *Sojourner Truth: A life, a Symbol.* New York: W. W. Norton, 1996.

Paulido, Laura. *Black, Brown, Yellow, and Left: Radical Activism in Los Angeles.* Berkeley: University of California Press, 2006.

Peffer, George Anthony. *If They Don't Bring Their Women Here: Chinese Female Immigration Before Exclusion.* Urbana: University of Illinois Press, 1999.

Peterson, Carla L. *Black Gotham: A Family History of African Americans in Nineteenth-Century New York City.* New Haven, Conn.: Yale University Press, 2011.

Pinn, Anthony B. *The Black Church in the Civil Rights Era.* Maryknoll, N.Y.: Orbis Books, 2002.

Pitts, Walter. "Keep the Fire Burnin': Language and Ritual in the Afro-Baptist Church." *Journal of the American Academy of Religion* 56, no. 1 (Spring 1988): 77–97.

Porter, Kenneth W. *The Negro on the American Frontier.* New York: Arno Press, 1971.

Raboteau, Albert J. *Slave Religion: The Invisible Institution in the Antebellum South.* Oxford: Oxford University Press, 1978.

Ramey-Berry, Daina. *Swing the Sickle for the Harvest Is Ripe: Gender and Slavery in Antebellum Georgia.* Urbana: University of Illinois Press, 2007.

Ravage, John W. *Black Pioneers: Images of the Black Experience on the North American Frontier.* Salt Lake City, Utah: The University of Utah Press, 2009.

Rice, Hallie Evelyn. *Pío Pico: The Last Mexican Governor of California.* Berkeley, Calif.: University of California, 1932.

Richards, Leonard L. *The California Gold Rush and the Coming of the Civil War.* New York: Vintage Books, 2007.

Richardson, Marilyn. *Black Women and Religion: A Bibliography.* Boston: G. K. Hall and Co., 1980.

Roberts, J. Deotis. *Roots of a Black Future: Family and Church.* Philadelphia: The Westminster Press, 1980.

Robinson, Amy. "It Takes One to Know One: Passing and Communities of Common Interest." *Critical Inquiry* 20, no. 4, Symposium on "God" (Summer 1994): 715–36.

Robinson, Beverly J. "Faith Is the Key and Prayer Unlocks the Door: Prayer in African American Life." *Journal of American Folklore* 110, no. 438 (Autumn 1997): 408–14.

Robinson, John W. *Los Angeles in Civil War Days 1860–1865.* Norman: University of Oklahoma Press, 2013.

Robinson, W. W. *Lawyers of Los Angeles: A History of the Los Angeles Bar Association and of the Bar of Los Angeles County.* Los Angeles: Los Angeles Bar Association, 1959.

———. *Los Angeles: A Profile.* Norman: University of Oklahoma Press, 1968.

Rolle, Andrew. *California: A History.* 6th ed. Wheeling, Ill.: Harlan Davidson, Inc., 2003.

Ross, German R., and Julia Mason, eds. *History and the Formative years of the Church of God in Christ.* Memphis: Church of God in Christ Publishing House, 1969.

Rossel, Robert D. "The Great Awakening: An Historical Analysis." *American Journal of Sociology* 75, no. 6 (May 1970): 907–25.

Royal, Alice C. with Mickey Ellinger and Scott Braley. *Allensworth, The Freedom Colony: A California African American Township.* Berkeley, Calif.: Heyday Books, 2008.

Ruether, Rosemary Radford, and Rosemary Skinner Keller. *Women and Religion in America.* 3 vols. San Francisco: Harper and Row, 1981.

Russell-Brown, Katheryn. *The Color of Crime.* New York: New York University Press, 2009.

Sanchez, George J., *Becoming Mexican American: Ethnicity, Culture, and Identity in Chicano Los Angeles, 1900–1945.* New York: Oxford University Press, 1993.

Sanders, J. Oswald. *The Holy Spirit and His Gifts.* 1940. Reprint. Grand Rapids, Mich.: Zondervan, 1976.

Savage, Barbara Dianne. "Du Bois and 'The Negro Church.'" *Annals of the American Academy of Political and Social Science* 568, The Study of African

American Problems: W. E. B. Du Bois's Agenda, Then and Now (March 2000): 235–49.

Savage, W. Sherman. *Blacks in the West*. Westport, Conn.: Greenwood Press, 1976.

———. "The Negro in the Westward Movement." *Journal of Negro History* 25, no. 4 (October 1940): 531–39.

Seagraves, Anne. *Soiled Doves: Prostitution in the Early West*. Hayden, Idaho: Wesanne Publications, 1994.

Seeman, Erik R. "'Justise Must Take Plase': Three African Americans Speak of Religion in Eighteenth-Century New England (in Notes and Documents)." *William and Mary Quarterly*, 3rd series, 56, no. 2, African and American Atlantic Worlds (April 1999): 393–414.

Sernett, Milton C. *Black Religion and American Evangelicalism*. Metuchen, N.J.: Scarecrow Press, 1975.

Sessoms, Nathan J., and Jennifer R. Wolch. "Measuring Concentrated Poverty in a Global Metropolis: Lessons from Los Angeles." *The Professional Geographer* 60, no. 1, (February 2008): 70–86.

Sharkey, Patrick. "Geographic Migration of Black and White Families Over Four Generations." *Demography* 52 (2015): 209–31.

Shippley, Lee. *The Los Angeles Book*. Boston: Houghton Mifflin Company, 1950.

Sides, Josh. *L.A. City Limits: African American Los Angeles from the Great Depression to the Present*. Berkeley: University of California Press, 2003.

Silva, Pablo Miguel Sierra. "From Chains to Chiles: An Elite Afro-Indigenous Couple in Colonial Mexico, 1641–1688." *Ethnohistory* 62, no. 2 (Spring 2015): 361–84.

Simpson, George Eaton. "Black Pentecostalism in the United States." *Phylon* 35, no. 2 (1974): 203–211.

Singleton, Gregory H. *Religion in the City of Angels: American Protestant Culture and Urbanization, Los Angeles, 1850–1930*. Ann Arbor: University of Michigan Research Press, 1979.

Sizer, Sandra. "Politics and Apolitical Religion: The Great Urban Revivals of the Late Nineteenth Century." *Church History* 48, no. 1 (March 1979): 81–98.

Smith, R. J. *The Great Black Way: L.A. in the 1940s and the Lost African American Renaissance*. New York: Public Affairs, 2006.

Smith, Stacey L. *Freedom's Frontier: California and the Struggle over Unfree Labor, Emancipation, and Reconstruction*. Chapel Hill: University of North Carolina Press, 2013.

Smith, Wallace Charles. *The Church in the Life of the Black Family*. Valley Forge, Penn.: Judson Press, 1958.

Sobel, Mechal. *Trabelin' On: The Slave Journey to an Afro-Baptist Faith*. Westport, Conn.: Greenwood Press, 1979.

Soule, Sarah A. "Populism and Black Lynching in Georgia, 1890–1900." *Social Forces* 71, no. 2 (December 1992): 431–49.

Spitzzeri, Paul R. "On a Case-by-Case Basis: Ethnicity and Los Angeles Courts, 1850–1875." *California History* 83, no. 2 (2005): 26–39.

Staples, Robert, ed. *The Black Family: Essays and Studies.* 5th ed. Belmont, Calif.: Wadsworth Publishing Co., 1994.

Starr, Kevin. *Americans and the California Dream, 1850–1915.* New York: Oxford University Press, 1973.

———. *The Dream Endures: California Enters the 1940s.* New York: Oxford University Press, 1997.

———. *Embattled Dreams; California in War and Peace, 1940–1950.* New York: Oxford University Press, 2002.

———. *Endangered Dreams: The Great Depression in California.* New York: Oxford University Press, 1996.

———. *Inventing the Dream: California through the Progressive Era.* New York: Oxford University Press, 1985.

———. *Material Dreams: Southern California through the 1920s.* New York: Oxford University Press, 1990.

Stern, Norton B. *The Jews of Los Angeles: Urban Pioneers.* Los Angeles: Southern California Jewish Historical Society, 1981.

Stevenson, Brenda E. *The Contested Murder of Latasha Harlins: Justice, Gender, and the Origins of the L.A. Riots.* New York: Oxford University Press, 2013.

———. "Latasha Harlins, Soon Ja Du, and Joyce Karlin: A Case Study of Multicultural Female Violence and Justice on the Urban Frontier." *Journal of African American History* 89, no. 2 (Spring 2004): 152–76.

———. *Life in Black and White: Family and Community in the Slave South.* New York: Oxford University Press, 1996.

———. "'Marsa Never Sot Aunt Rebecca Down': Enslaved Women, Religion, and Social Power in the Antebellum South." *Journal of African American History* 90, no. 4 (Fall 2005): 345–67.

Stitton, Tom, and William Deverell. *Metropolis in the Making: Los Angeles in the 1920s.* Berkeley: University of California Press, 1999.

Stovel, Katherine. "Local Sequential Patterns: The Structure of Lynching in the Deep South, 1882–1930." *Social Forces* 79, no. 3 (March 2001): 843–80.

Straus, Emily E. *Death of a Suburban Dream: Race and Schools in Compton, California.* Philadelphia: University of Pennsylvania Press, 2014.

Stuckey, Sterling. *Slave Culture: Nationalist Theory and the Foundations of Black America.* New York: Oxford University Press, 1987.

Summers Sandoval Jr., Tomás. *Latinos at the Golden Gate: Creating Community and Identity in San Francisco.* Chapel Hill: University of North Carolina Press, 2013.

Synan, H. Vinson. *The Holiness-Pentecostal Movement in the United States.* Grand Rapids, Mich.: William B. Eerdmans Publishing Co., 1971.

Taylor, Quintard. *In Search of the Racial Frontier: African Americans in the American West, 1580–1990.* New York: W. W. Norton, 1998.

Taylor, Quintard, and Shirley Ann Wilson Moore, eds. *African American Women Confront the West, 1600–2000.* Norman: University of Oklahoma Press, 2003.

Terborg-Penn, Roslyn. *African American Women in the Struggle for the Vote, 1850–1920*. Bloomington: Indiana University Press, 1998.

Terrell, JoAnne Marie. *Power in the Blood?: The Cross in the African American Experience*. Maryknoll, N.Y.: Orbis Books, 1998.

Thompson, Robert Farris. *Flash of the Spirit: African and African American Art and Philosophy*. New York: Random House, 1983.

Thurman, Odell A. *The Negro in California before 1890*. San Francisco: R and E Associates, 1973.

Tong, Benson. *Unsubmissive Women: Chinese Prostitutes in Nineteenth-Century San Francisco*. Norman: University of Oklahoma Press, 1994.

Townes, Emilie M. *In a Blaze of Glory: Womanist Spirituality as Social Witness*. Nashville: Abingdon Press, 1995.

Trotter Jr., Joe William, ed. *The Great Migration in Historical Perspective: New Dimensions of Race, Class, and Gender*. Bloomington: Indiana University Press, 1991.

Tucker, David M. *Black Pastors and Leaders: Memphis, 1819–1972*. Memphis: Memphis State University Press, 1975.

Tuttle, William M. *Race Riot: Chicago in the Red Summer of 1919*. Urbana: University of Illinois Press, 1996.

Vincent, Ted. "The Blacks Who Freed Mexico." *Journal of Negro History* 79, no. 3 (Summer 1994): 257–76.

Vinson, Ben, III. *Bearing Arms for His Majesty: The Free Colored Militia in Colonial Mexico*. Stanford, Calif.: Stanford University Press, 2001.

———. "Free Colored Voices: Issues of Representation and Racial Identity in the Colonial Mexican Militia." *Journal of Negro History* 80, no. 4 (Autumn 1995): 170–82.

Vinson, Ben, III, and Matthew Restall, eds. *Black Mexico: Race and Society from Colonial to Modern Times*. Albuquerque: University of New Mexico Press, 2009.

Vivien, Octavia. *Story of the Negro in Los Angeles County*. San Francisco: Federal Writer's Project, 1970.

Wacker, Grant. *Heaven Below: Early Pentecostals and American Culture*. Cambridge, Mass.: Harvard University Press, 2001.

Wafer, Jim. *The Taste of Blood: Spirit Possession in Brazilian Candomble*. Philadelphia: University of Pennsylvania Press, 1991.

Wagner, Tricia. *African American Women of the Old West*. Guilford, Conn.: Globe Pequot Press, 2007.

———. *Black Cowboys of the Old West: True, Sensational, and Little-Known Stories from History*. Guilford, Conn.: Globe Pequot Press, 2011.

Washington, Margaret. "African American History and the Frontier Thesis." *Journal of the Early Republic* 13, no. 2 (Summer 1993): 230–41.

Washington Jr., Joseph R. *Black Sects and Cults*. New York: University Press of America, 1984.

Weaver, John Downing. *Los Angeles: The Enormous Village, 1781–1981*. Santa Barbara, Calif.: Capra Press, 1980.

Wheeler, Gordon B. *Black California: The History of African Americans in the Golden State*. New York: Hippocrene Books, 1993.

Wheeler, Robinson, H. *The Christian Experience of the Holy Spirit*. London: Oxford University Press, 1915.

White, Deborah Gray. *Ar'n't I a Woman? Female Slaves in the Plantation South*. New York: W. W. Norton, 1985.

———. *Too Heavy a Load: Black Women in Defense of Themselves, 1894–1994*. New York: W. W. Norton, 1999.

White, Shane. *Somewhat More Independent: The End of Slavery in New York City, 1770–1810*. Athens: University of Georgia Press, 1991.

Wiese, Andre. *Places of Their Own: African American Suburbanization in the Twentieth Century*. Chicago: University of Chicago Press, 2004.

Wild, Mark. *Street Meeting: Multiethnic Neighborhoods in Early Twentieth Century Los Angeles*. Berkeley: University of California Press, 2005.

Wilkerson, Isabel. *The Warmth of Other Suns: The Epic Story of America's Great Migration*. New York: Vintage Books, 2010.

Williams, Cyril Glyndwr. *Tongues of the Spirit: A Study of Pentecostal Glossolalia and Related Phenomena*. Cardiff: University of Wales Press, 1981.

Williams, Lee E. *Post-war Riots in America, 1919 and 1946: How the Pressures of War Exacerbated American Urban Tensions to the Breaking Point*. Lewiston, N.Y.: E. Mellen Press, 1991.

Williams, Melvin D. *Community in a Black Pentecostal Church: An Anthropological Study*. Pittsburgh: University of Pittsburgh Press, 1974.

Wills, David W. and Richard Newman, Eds. *Black Apostles at Home and Abroad: Afro-Americans and the Christian Mission from the Revolution to Reconstruction*. Boston: G. K. Hall and Co., 1982.

Wilmore, Gayraud S., ed. *African American Religious Studies: An Interdisciplinary Anthology*. Durham, N.C.: Duke University Press, 1989.

———. *Black Religion and Black Radicalism: An Interpretation of the Religious History of African Americans*. 3rd edition. Maryknoll, N.Y.: Orbis Books, 1998.

Woods, Gerald. *The Police in Los Angeles: Reform and Professionalization*. New York: Garland Publishing, Inc., 1993.

Woodson, Carter G. *The History of the Negro Church*. 2nd edition. Washington, D.C.: The Associated Publishers, 1945.

Young, Henry J. *Major Black Leaders, 1755–1940*. Nashville: Abingdon, 1977.

Zetsch, Scott. *The Chinatown War: Chinese Los Angeles and the Massacre of 1871*. New York: Oxford University Press, 2012.

Dissertations

Blew, Robert. "Californios and American Institutions." Ph.D. diss., University of Southern California, 1973.

Christman, Anastasia J. "The Best Laid Plans: Women's Clubs and City Planning in Los Angeles, 1890–1930." Ph.D. diss., University of California, Los Angeles, 2000.

Kooistra, AnnMarie. "Angels for Sale: The History of Prostitution in Los Angeles, 1880–1940." Ph.D. diss., University of Southern California, 2003.

Saavedra, Yvette J. "Competing Visions: The Politics of Racial and Ethnic Identity Formation and Land Use in Pasadena, 1771–1890." Ph.D. diss., University of El Paso, 2012.

Weeks, Donald. "The History of the Church of God in Christ." Ph.D. diss., University of California, Berkeley, 1992.

Index

African Americans: appeal of revival movements, 163–64; better conditions in West for, 172; black as census racial category, 6, 7, 32, 206 (n. 82); black slavery compared to Indian, 26, 27–28; business elite, 104–6; Chinese plight as temporary relief for, 122; church's role in lives of, 79–80, 147, 216 (n. 24); in domestic and personal service, 8, 95, 97; education access, 3, 38, 63–38; endogamous marriages, 16–17, 202 (n. 16); exclusion of rights by legislature, 111–12; fraternal organizations and, 180–82; fugitive slave laws, 28, 41, 205 (n. 64), 208 (n. 14); household structure, 60–63, 86–91, 212 (n. 85); Japanese as competition, 173, 193, 238 (n. 11); literacy rates, 66–67, 81, 214 (n. 102); in local law enforcement, 130–31, 195; lower social status, 15, 17, 24; male worker as odd job man, 171; marginalized by white middle class, 194; media owned by, 69–70, 108; migrants, 56–57, 129, 131, 164, 207 (n. 5); occupational trends, 64, 94–98, 218 (n. 60); pioneers, 13; in post-Civil War era, 37–38; professional elite, 68, 104–6; property ownership, 1, 25, 57–60, 83–86; suffrage in West, 172; teachers, 68; trade union exclusion of, 171, 175, 190; verbal sharing of news, 127; ways of classifying, 36–37; women as community threat, 128–29

African Methodist Episcopal (AME) churches, 79, 171–72, 187

Africans: *bozales*, 16; *ladinos*, 16; in New Spain, 15–16

Afromestizo, 17

Ah Choy, 117, 118

Ah Hain, 222 (n. 41)

Ah Jim, 123

Ah Sam, 123

Akers, Laura, 129

Alcalde, 205 (n. 59)

Alcalde Court for the County of Los Angeles, 113–15, 220 (n. 1)

Allensworth, Allen, 104, 183–87, 190; article for the *Times*, 183–84; black utopian society formed by, 184–87; death of, 186; early life, 184; Washington Park, 184–85

Allensworth, Josephine, 184, 186

Allensworth Agricultural and Manual Training School, 185–86

Allensworth Colony Association, 184–87, 190; families recruited for, 185; industrial school, 185–86; location, 185; principles of, 185; problems with, 186; Women's Improvement Club, 185

Almaguer, Tomás, 10, 207 (n. 6)

Ambrisio, José, 113

AME churches. *See* African Methodist Episcopal (AME) churches

Amezquita, Juan Antonio, 20

Anderson, Robert Mapes, 147, 227 (n. 20)

Anderson, Tom, 153

Andrews, K. E., 149

The Apostolic Faith, 230 (n. 66); children's testimonies, 159;

Census. *See* United States Federal Census

Central Avenue corridor, 106–7

Chavez-Garcia, Miroslava, 9

Child Study Circle, 79

Chinatown, 109; attempts to close, 118, 124–26; as den of iniquity, 118; maps of, 224 (n. 55); riot and massacre in, 116–18

Chinese, 11; as bottom of racial hierarchy, 120; as census racial category, 6, 34, 213 (n. 95); community participation, 119–20; control attempts, 116–19; domestic labor, 92; education access, 63, 64, 65; exposés by the *Times*, 120, 121–22, 123, 223 (n. 55); gangs, 121, 123; as having criminal and violent tendencies, 121; immigration compared to European, 122; increasing migration to Los Angeles, 110; as largest group of people of color, 35; listed as mulatto, 33; marginalized by white middle class, 194; media attacks on, 122, 123, 223 (n. 55); occupations, 92, 110, 218 (n. 60); as other people of color, 207 (n. 89); population increase, 119; restriction of labor, 120–21; Senator Miller on, 122–23; as targets of racism, 12, 118, 119–23, 221 (n. 3); vigilantism against, 116–18

"Chinese Criminals: Chinese and Hoodlums Compared and John Ahead," 121

"Chinese Curse," 122

Chinese Exclusion Act, 119–23, 126, 195, 213 (n. 94)

Chinese Free Masons, 121–22

Ching fo-to gang, 121

Churches: as conduits to education and social welfare, 79–80; as forum for women, 80, 216 (n. 24); Holiness movement, 133–34; role in African Americans' lives, 79–80, 147, 216

(n. 24); Washington's visits to, 168–69

Church of Christ Holiness, 165

Church of God in Christ (COGIC), 164–65, 166, 230 (n. 93)

Civil Rights Movement, 2, 46, 69, 83

Class stratification, 12, 109, 138

Clifford, Harmon, 151

Club movement, 80–82

COGIC. *See* Church of God in Christ (COGIC)

Coleman, Willi, 101

College of Bethel, 139

Collier-Thomas, Bettye, 80, 147

"Colored California" (Du Bois), 1, 104–5, 211 (n. 67)

Colored Convention, 44, 45–46, 64

Colored Magazine, 53

Colored Voters League, 81

Columbia, 207 (n. 8)

Common schools act, 63–68, 212 (n. 88)

Community formation, 4, 5, 39–68; African American migrants and, 56–57; defined, 38; early land acquisition, 57–60; education access, 63–68; female-headed households and, 61; first black female network, 46–52; household structure, 60–63; occupations and, 62–63; professional elite, 68; slavery in California and, 40–46; women's role in, 39, 40, 54–56

Contreas, Merced, 114

Cook, Belt, 86–87

Cook, G. A., 151

Cota, María Isabel Ascencion, 20

Cox, Lillie May, 99

Coyotes, 19

Crawford, Florence, 146, 147–48, 150, 154, 160, 230 (n. 65)

Crime: African American women as community threat, 128–29; attention centered on people of color and, 118–19; California laws, 111–12; death penalty, 115; drunken-

Ladies' Pacific Accommodating and
  Benevolent Society, 78
Ladinos, 16
Landy, C., 119
LAPD. *See* Los Angeles Police
  Department (LAPD)
Laronde, Pierre, 124–25
Laslett, John, 9
Laying hands: Farrow's gift of, 145,
  229 (n. 49); gender differences, 232
  (n. 142); laypeople performing, 132;
  stories of, 152–54; to transfer Holy
  Ghost, 229 (n. 49)
Leatherman, Sister, 148, 156
Lee, Archy, 45–46, 113
Lee, Edward "Irish," 141, 228 (n. 30)
Lee, Spike, 198
Lee Tak, 117
Lewis, James A., 182
The Liberator, 127–28
Lilly Club, 126
Limpieza de sangre, 15, 202 (n. 20)
Literacy, 66–67, 81, 214 (n. 102)
Lobo, 16
Lockridge, Irene, 90
Lockridge, John, 90
Lopez, Chico, 113
Los Angeles, California: African
  American population, 13, 214
  (n. 100), 215 (n. 12); attitude toward
  social deviance, 115; as best location
  for Azusa Street Revival, 135–38;
  Board of Education formed, 225
  (n. 90); Central Avenue corridor,
  106–7; color line in, 198–99; crime
  rates, 109, 115; criminalization of
  racialized communities in, 200;
  Du Bois' observations on, 1, 11, 12,
  107–8, 192–94; emergent African
  American community, 31–38; first
  black female network, 46–52,
  55–56; as heaven's ghetto, 138;
  interracial bonds among nonwhites, 111; migrants' places of
  birth, 32–33, 136, 206 (n. 87);

multiracial culture of, 111, 137;
  original settlers, 15, 19; as portrayed
  in the *Times*, 116, 126; predominance
  of white residents, 36; promotion
  of, 40, 116, 210 (n. 61); small
  African American population, 195
*Los Angeles Daily Times. See Los Angeles
  Times*
Los Angeles Forum, 81
Los Angeles Herald, 215 (n. 4)
Los Angeles Police Department
  (LAPD), 130–31
Los Angeles Rangers, 115, 222 (n. 33)
Los Angeles Sentinel, 196
Los Angeles Times: African American
  women as dangerous, 128–29; Azusa
  Street Revival centennial coverage,
  196; Buckner's essays in, 81;
  campaign against lower class
  Angelenos, 109; celebrating of
  European immigration, 122;
  Chinatown as den of iniquity, 118;
  Chinese targeted by, 120, 121–22,
  123, 223 (n. 55); death of Washington, 187; dehumanizing of people of
  color, 120, 121–22, 126–30; educational achievement section, 180;
  elite readership of, 126; focus on
  black crime, 128–29, 179; fraternal
  organizations section, 180–82;
  illegal gambling investigation, 119;
  Lincoln Edition of, 179–80, 183;
  military section, 183–84; Otis'
  acquisition of, 126; portrayal of Los
  Angeles, 116, 126; positive coverage
  of African Americans in, 179–80;
  religious life sections, 182–83;
  shaping of middle class opinions,
  126; support of Washington, 178;
  wealth accumulation story, 180;
  weekly black column in, 178–79
Loving, Julius, 90
Loving, Nannie, 90
Lum, Clara, 144–45, 146, 160
Luther, Martin, 133

Macbeth, Hugh Ellwood, 178–79
Malcolm X (film), 198
"The Man Behind His Race" (Buckner), 177
"The Man of the Hour," 178
Marks, Carole, 10
Marsalles, Eloise, 99
Mason, Bridget "Biddy," 10, 33, 39, 40; belief in helping others, 52, 53, 75, 216 (n. 22); declared free, 49; defeminizing of, 56; early life, 47–48; estate value, 58, 211 (n. 78); family as influential, 52; funding help to FAME, 54, 79, 192; Judge Hayes' assistance, 49–50, 113; livestock experience, 47–48; occupations, 51, 59; Owens' guardianship of, 50; philanthropic legacy, 53–56; property ownership, 51–52, 58; purchased by Smiths, 47; ranch work responsibilities, 48; work as home nurse, 51, 210 (n. 56)
Mason, Charles Harrison, 164–65
Mason, William Marvin, 19
Masons (fraternal order). *See* Freemasonry
McClain, Sister, 149
McDuff, Littleton, 130
McKinney, Leila, 145
McPherson, Aimee Semple, 239 (n. 19)
Media: African American, 69–70, 108, 127–28, 214 (n. 1); Azusa Street Revival centennial coverage, 196; campaign against lower class, 109; Chinese attacked by, 122; coverage of intra and interracial violence, 119, 221 (n. 3); Los Angeles visit by Washington covered in, 177–78; newspaper accounts admitted as legal evidence, 112; portrayal of Native Americans in, 28; racism in "The Birth of a Nation," 82; Washington's death coverage, 187, 189

Menchaca, Martha, 18, 20
Mestizo, 16, 17, 19, 23
Mexicans: as census racial category, 7, 34, 35–36; marginalized by white middle class, 194; as other people of color, 207 (n. 89); property ownership, 29, 209 (n. 36), 225 (n. 89); racism against, 199; relations with white Angelenos, 29–30; targeted by whites, 12
Middle class, 12; common school rules as upholding values of, 68; foundation provided by black community, 71; occupations and professions, 220 (n. 83); overemphasis on accomplishments, 5; political and social trends similar to elite whites, 217 (n. 34)
Migration patterns, 12, 71–75, 76–77, 215 (n. 7)
Millennialism, 163
Miller, John Frank, 122–23
Miscegenation, 16–17, 18, 204 (n. 46)
Missouri Compromise, 41
Monkkonen, Eric, 109
Montalvo, Garci Rodriguez De, 14
Montgomery, John, 27
Montgomery, William E., 134
Moore, Shirley Ann Wilson, 10
Mormons, 173–75
Mount Zion Missionary Baptist Church, 79
"Mrs. Daisy Bateman's Testimony," 150
Mulatto, 6, 7, 40; as census racial category, 32–33, 206 (n. 82); Chinese listed as, 33; defined for study, 201 (n. 9); disallowance of native heritage, 22–23; in early Los Angeles, 19; marrying *mestizo*, 19; in New Spain, 16

NAACP. *See* National Association for the Advancement of Colored People (NAACP)

ington's visits, 54, 168; as wealthiest African American in West, 53

Owens, Winnie, 52; boarding house, 62; estate value, 58, 211 (n. 78); mutual aid tradition of, 75; occupation, 59

Ozman, Agnes N., 139, 227 (n. 20)

Painter, Nell Irvin, 10

Palmer, George, 83

Pardee, George, 168

Pardo, 16

Parham, Charles Fox, 11, 138–39; Divine healing, 152; early life, 139; Holiness theology, 139; Seymour's enrollment in school of, 140; Spirit Baptism, 139; *vs.* Seymour as Pentecostal movement founder, 138, 227 (n. 18)

Parham, Sarah Thistlewaite, 139

Parker, Harriet, 86

The Passadena Searchlight, 127

PAW. *See* Pentecostal Assemblies of the World (PAW)

Pentecostal Assemblies of the World (PAW), 230 (n. 93)

Pentecostalism, 11, 196–97; children and, 159–60; class stratification and, 138; defined, 134–36; differences from other religious movements, 162; divine healing, 152–55; full immersion baptism, 135; gift of Holy Spirit, 134; Holiness movement as foundation for, 134; laying hands, 132, 152, 154, 229 (n. 49), 232 (n. 142); in Los Angeles, 136–38; multilingual characteristic, 163; pneumatology, 134; problems plaguing, 165; prophecy, 158–59; proponents as spiritual elite, 161–62; rejection by Christian denominations, 161; roots in Azusa Street Revival, 165, 228 (n. 25); salvation experiences, 150–52, 230 (n. 93); similarities to other revival

movements, 163–64; speaking in tongues, 134, 135, 141, 155–58, 228 (n. 29), 232 (n. 156); *vs.* Holiness churches, 133–34. *See also* Azusa Street Revival; Holiness movement

Pepper, Ann. *See* Daniels, Ann Pepper

Pepper, Manuel, Jr., 84, 93

Pepper, Manuel, Sr., 50, 55, 84

Perkins, Mary, 149

Perry, Birdie, 85

Perry, Charles, 85

The Philadelphia Negro (Du Bois), 3

Pico, Andrés, 20, 21–22, 26, 203 (n. 44)

Pico, Estefana Pico Carillo, 20

Pico, Francisco, 21

Pico, Jacinta de la Bastida, 20

Pico, Jacinta Pico Carillo, 20

Pico, José Antonio, 20

Pico, José Dolores, 20

Pico, José María, 20

Pico, María Concepción Pico Carillo, 20

Pico, María Estaquia Gutiérrez, 20

Pico, María Gertrudis Amezquita, 20

Pico, María Ignacio Alvarado, 21

Pico, Pío, 20–21, 26, 27, 203 (n. 38)

Pico, Santiago de la Cruz, 20

Pico family, 19–26; assimilation into Los Angeles society, 26; attitude about race, 203 (n. 45); leadership roles, 20–22; marriage patterns, 20–21, 203 (n. 45); as model for opportunity, 25; racial heritage, 20, 21–25; use of whiteness, 24–25

Pico House, 21, 24–25

Pleasant, Mary Ellen, 207 (n. 5)

Plessy v. Ferguson, 3, 167

Pneumatology, 135, 226 (n. 2)

Political institutions, 81–83

Potter's House Church, 197

Practice School, 104

Price, Viola, 159

Primoneas, Feliciano, 113

"A Proclamation to the Inhabitants of California" (Montgomery), 27

Property ownership: African Americans, 1, 25, 57–60, 83–86; gender and, 83–86; increase in, 84–85; Mexicans, 29, 209 (n. 36), 225 (n. 89); Native Americans, 26–27; as sign of accomplishment, 57; women, 53–54, 56, 85–86

Prophecy, 158–60, 233 (n. 164)

Prostitution, 92, 101, 114, 222 (n. 23), 223 (n. 42)

Purity of the blood, 15, 17, 202 (n. 20)

Quadroon, 6, 40, 206 (n. 82)

Race relations: as better in West, 172–73; Du Bois's studies of, 3–4; Los Angeles culture as shaping, 111; under Mexican rule, 14–15; under Spanish colonial rule, 14–15; under United States rule, 29–30

Racial categories: black, 6, 7, 32, 206 (n. 82); Chinese, 6, 34, 213 (n. 95); Indians, 34–35; Japanese, 6, 7, 206 (n. 82), 213 (n. 95); Mexican, 7, 34, 35–36; mulatto, 32–33, 206 (n. 82); negro, 32

Racial formation, 14–38; California mission system and, 26–28; census racial categories, 32–33; emergent African American community, 31–38; endogamous marriage, 16–17, 202 (n. 16); increased migration, 30–31; intermarriage, 16, 22, 202 (n. 16), 203 (n. 45); migrants' places of birth, 32–33, 136, 206 (n. 87); new political ideologies, 25–26; new racial identities, 19; Pico family, 20–25; post-Civil War era, 37–38; relations of whites and Mexicans, 29–30

Racial hierarchy, 4–5, 202 (n. 23); California laws as creators of, 111–13; Chinese as bottom of, 120; in colonial Mexico, 15–19, 202 (n. 22); establishment in California,

10; in Los Angeles, 108; violent characteristic of, 113–15

Racial minorities database, 8–9

Racial uplift, 5, 78, 80–82

Racism: Chinese as targets of, 12, 118, 119–23, 221 (n. 3); increase in, 164; against Japanese, 177, 199; in media, 28, 82; against Mexicans, 199; in North, 164; in "The Birth of a Nation," 82; toward migrants, 102–3

Ramón, Ana-Christina, 9

Rape, 114–15

Raymond, Henry, 116

Red Summer, 11

Reed, Florence, 99

Reid, William Thomas, 168

Religious institutions, 79–80, 97, 216 (n. 24)

Restrictive covenants: African Americans forced out by, 12, 105; after World War I, 53, 196; declared unconstitutional, 103. *See also* Segregation

Reyes, Francisco, 25

Reyes, María del Carmen Domínguez, 25

Riley, J. T., 116

Ring shout, 137

Robbins, Joseph, 154

Robinson, Georgia, 2, 130

Rose of the Los Angeles Circle, 181

Rowan, Charles, 57, 58, 59

Rowan, Elizabeth, 57

Ruiz, 29

Russell, Lindsay, 130

Sales, Francisco, 27

Salvation, 149–52; as defined by Seymour, 149; distances traveled for, 150; experiences, 150–52; ministers seeking, 151; substance abuse and, 151

Sam Yeun, 117

Sanchez, George, 10

Sanchez, William, 113

Sanctification: concept of entire, 140; as defined by Seymour, 146, 149; described, 135, 226 (n. 2); as second act of grace, 140; value to Holiness movement, 134, 235 (n. 200)

Sanford, Frank W., 139

San Francisco: African American population, 36, 214 (n. 100); crime in, 109; education access, 64; literacy rate, 67; 1906 earthquake, 136; prostitution in, 101

Scott, R. J., 258

Sebastian, C. E., 187

Second Baptist Church, 79, 216 (n. 20)

"Secret Orders among Negroes" (Johnson), 180–81

Seeley, Sister, 154

Segregation: campaign to eliminate, 177; in early twentieth century, 81, 195; in education, 63–65; housing, 196; legalization of, 3. *See also* Restrictive covenants

Self-help organizations, 70–71, 81–82

Separate but Equal clause, 3

Sepúlveda, Charles, 21

"A Sermon from a Dress" (Wiley), 148

Sex workers, 92, 101, 222 (n. 23), 223 (n. 42)

Seymour, Jennie Evans Moore, 143–44, 146, 148, 229 (n. 45)

Seymour, Phillis, 139–40, 228 (n. 23)

Seymour, Simon, 139, 227 (n. 22), 228 (n. 23)

Seymour, William J., 2, 11; assisting Los Angeles Holiness missions, 140–41; basis of doctrine, 231 (n. 97); changes to Azusa Street Revival meetings, 160–61; differences with Hutchins, 141; divine healing, 152; doctrinal disagreement with Durham, 160, 165; on duty of children, 159; early life, 139–40, 227 (n. 22); Farrow sent to assist, 141; Holiness church attendance, 140;

justification defined by, 149; love triangle, 144–45; mission as ministry training ground, 164; ordination, 228 (n. 24); original vision of, 135; in Parham's school, 140; prayer meetings in Los Angeles, 141; purchase of Azusa Street building, 141–42; reliance on women's help, 143, 144–45; salvation views, 149; sanctification defined by, 149; Spirit Baptism, 141; spiritual education as limited, 162; union with Moore disapproved of, 144, 146; vision for Pentecostal movement, 159; *vs.* Parham as Pentecostal movement founder, 138, 227 (n. 18); wife's role at mission, 144; on women in ministry, 147–48

Shelly v. Kramer, 103

Shepherd, Arthur B., 142

Sides, Josh, 9

Simpson, George, 135, 228 (n. 25)

Sinaloa, Mexico, 15, 19

Sistema de castas, 15, 17, 202 (n. 22), 203 (n. 23)

Slavery: Bucklew on, 42; Burnett on, 42; in California, 8, 40–46, 204 (n. 58), 208 (n. 12); effect on community formation, 40–46; *Fugitive Slave Law*, 28, 41, 205 (n. 64), 208 (n. 14); impact on free African Americans, 41; Indian compared to black, 26, 27–28; Missouri Compromise, 41; pre-1850 experiences in California, 43–44; protection for slaveholders, 43–45; slave population lists, 8

Sleepy Lagoon murder, 199

Smart, Sarah, 87

Smith, Rebecca Dorn, 39, 47

Smith, R. J., 9

Smith, Robert Mays, 39, 47–51; attempted kidnapping charges, 50–51; in Los Angeles, 48–49; move to California, 48; purchase of Biddy

Westminster Presbyterian Church, 79, 189
Wheaton, "Mother," 149
"Whisperings of the Comforter" (Perkins), 149
White, Deborah Gray, 60
White, Frank, 130
White Angelenos: attack on black Angelenos' reputation, 126; attempts to close Azusa Street Revival, 164; competition with Chinese for jobs, 120; ethnically white immigrants welcomed by, 122; interaction with blacks, 220 (n. 83); marginalization of people of color, 29–30, 109, 131, 207 (n. 6); predominance of, 36; promotion of city, 116, 210 (n. 61); relations with Mexicans, 29–30
Whitefield, George, 133
Whiteness, 19, 20, 24–25
White people: Pacific Northwest as most liberal, 175; passing for, 107, 220 (n. 87); racial heritage qualifying as, 21–24; reform programs used to control people of color, 111; as responsible for civilizing Native Americans, 28; as top of social hierarchy, 196
White supremacy, 82, 102, 164, 207 (n. 6)
Wild, Mark, 9
Wildberger, Catherine, 85–86
Wiley, Orphelia, 148
Wilkerson, Isabel, 10
Williams, Max J., 40
Williams, Paul Revere, 104
Williamson, Juanita, 181
Williamson, Vassia, 181
Winans, Joseph W., 45
Women, 4, 5; African American as community threat, 128–29; Azusa Street Revival and, 68, 143–46, 147–49, 192, 230 (n. 66); as

boardinghouse owners, 75, 76; census recognition of work, 8; charitable activities, 78–79; church as forum for, 80, 216 (n. 24); club movement, 80–82; community building, 54–56, 191; in domestic service, 8, 92, 99; education as priority, 64; exogamous marriage, 202 (n. 17); first black female network, 46–52, 55–56; fraternal organizations and, 181–82; heads of household, 87, 217 (n. 49); influence, 12; as institution organizers, 39, 192; labor information lack, 91–92; as ministers, 147–48; in personal service jobs, 8, 68; property ownership, 53–54, 56, 85–86; real and personal estate values, 58–59; salvation experiences and, 150–52; as teachers, 68; uplift organizations, 78, 80–82; as violent crime targets, 114–15
Women's Day Nursery Association, 78–79
Women's Improvement Club, 185
Women's Progressive Club, 80–81
Wong Sin, 119
Working class, 2, 4; Azusa Street Revival as safe space for, 166; barriers, 108; interracial cooperation, 5, 12, 111; neighborhoods as multiracial, 137; Nigger Alley as home to, 108; opportunities in Los Angeles for, 191–92. See also Underclass
Workman, William H., 116, 222 (n. 40)
Writ of mandamus, 65, 213 (n. 91)

Ya Hit, 116–17, 223 (n. 42)
YMCA. See Young Men's Christian Association (YMCA)
Yo Hing, 117, 118
Young, Elizabeth, 2

Young, Joseph, 2
Young Men's Christian Association (YMCA), 2
Young Women's Christian Association (YWCA), 81

Young Women's Dramatic Club, 81
Young Women's Married Thimble Club, 81

Zoot Suit Riots, 199